Mother-tongue and fatherland

dedicated to my mother
and to the memory of my father

Mother-tongue and fatherland

Language and politics in German

Michael Townson

Manchester University Press
Manchester and New York

distributed in the USA and Canada by St. Martin's Press, New York

Copyright © Michael Townson 1992

Published by Manchester University Press
Oxford Road, Manchester M13 9PL, UK
and Room 400, 175 Fifth Avenue, New York, NY 10010, USA

Distributed exclusively in the USA and Canada
by St. Martin's Press, Inc.,
175 Fifth Avenue, New York, NY 10010, USA

British Library Cataloguing-in-Publication Data
A catalogue record for this book is available from the British Library

Library of Congress Cataloging-in-Publication Data
Townson, Michael.
   Mother-tongue and fatherland : language and politics in German /
     Michael Townson.
       p. cm.
   Includes bibliographical references and index.
   ISBN 0-7190-3439-6
     1. German language—Political aspects. 2. German language—Social
aspects. 3. Sociolinguistics—Germany—History—19th century.
4. Sociolinguistics—Germany—History—20th century.
5. Nationalism—Germany—History. I. Title.
PF3074.73.T68   1992
306.4'4'0943—dc20   91-43429

ISBN 0 7190 3439 6 *hardback*

Typeset in Stone Serif and Sans Serif
by Koinonia Limited, Manchester

Printed in Great Britain
by Biddles Ltd, Guildford & King's Lynn

PF
3074.73
T68
1992

Contents

Tables and figure

Preface and acknowledgements

The work on which this book is based goes back some eight years, when my interest in the political aspects of language was first aroused by attempts to formulate a linguistic contribution to the work of the peace movement.

Since then, the scope of my work has widened considerably, but the basic objective of aiding a process of political emancipation has remained.

It is a truism from many prefatory texts that, the author's name on the cover notwithstanding, a book is seldom the work of one person alone. This book is no exception, having benefited from material, intellectual and idealistic support from many quarters over and above those acknowledged in the text.

Professor Martin Durrell, now Henry Simon Professor of German at the University of Manchester, first planted the idea of writing the book in my mind and then, several years later, introduced me to the Manchester University Press.

Charles Russ from the University of York and John West from the University of Newcastle have given me opportunities to try out some of my ideas at symposia and conferences, and my Aston colleagues Eva Kolinsky (now Professor of German at the University of Keele), Roger Woods and John Gaffney have invited me to publish papers, which then formed the basis for three chapters of the present book.

Among my German colleagues and benefactors, I must above all acknowledge my huge debt to the Directors and staff of the Institut für Deutsche Sprache in Mannheim, where most of the work for the book was done. Professor Gerhard Stickel (who first introduced me to the Institute) and Professor Rainer Wimmer have been unstinting in their support and encouragement, allowing me to make extensive use of the Institute's facilities and sharing their ideas with me. Special thanks go to Eva Teubert and her colleagues in the Library, who ensured a steady supply not only of books, references and photocopies, but also of coffee and sympathy. Wolfgang Teubert and Ulrike Hass have shared valuable insights with me, and the original plan for the book was much enhanced by Wolfgang's critical comments.

During visits to Leipzig and the Academy of Arts and Sciences of the German Democratic Republic in Berlin, I had the pleasure and privilege of conversing with Professors Wolfgang Fleischer, Joachim Schildt and Werner Neumann, and spent many instructive hours with Rainer Hopfer.

Armin Burkhardt (now at the University of Braunschweig) has not only involved me in a German network of politico-linguists but also, together with Professor Rudo Hoberg (University of Darmstadt), invited me to take part in a Darmstadt symposium which gave me a chance to meet other key German colleagues.

Professors Dennis Ager, Frank Knowles and Nigel Reeves as successive Heads of the Aston University Modern Languages Department have not only been unswerving in their support and encouragement, but have also released scarce departmental funds which have made visits to Mannheim possible. I am particularly grateful to Nigel Reeves for taking the time and trouble to read draft chapters during his extremely busy first year in post at Aston.

My special thanks go to Andreas Musolff of the Aston University Modern Languages Department, in whom I have discovered not only an expert and conscientious colleague but above all a kindred spirit and friend. His close reading of my drafts has proved to be of inestimable value.

At this point, convention requires that I accept the ultimate responsibility for the book's shortcomings.

Financial support for work on this book has come from the Economic and Social Research Council, the British Council and the British Academy under the auspices of their various exchange programmes with West and East Germany.

In the private sphere, my thanks go to my consort for her support and her tolerance of my many absences, and to my family and friends for their interest and encouragement.

Introduction

The actual writing of this book started against the background of rapid change and development in Central and Eastern Europe, with attention focused on the imminent accession of what was then still the German Democratic Republic to the Federal Republic of Germany. This accession has marked the sudden end of the policies of rapprochement and demarcation pursued by the two German states towards each other, but at the same time heralds a new political era in Europe, in which questions of German power and Germany's role will play a significant role.

Germany's unification (or 'reunification', depending on one's political point of view) again raises the question of German nationhood and nationality, coupled with the perennial problem of Germany's borders.

For much of German history, the question of what constitutes the German nation has been closely – though not exclusively – linked with the German language: it is significant that in discussions of German nationhood a distinction is made between the nation as an ethnic, political and linguistic entity – *Volk, Staatsnation* and *Sprachnation,* with varying degrees of overlap between them.

The equation of language and nation, which holds for a large number of polities, is of particular relevance for a Germany which has been divided and fragmented for much of its history, with little or no tradition of territorial coherence or unified central government. The 'reality' of Germany was for centuries a cultural and psychological reality rather than a political one, and in the constitution of that reality the German language played a central role. In the seventeenth century, Leibniz equated the status of a nation with the status of its language, complaining that in Germany too much emphasis was placed on Latin and art, and not enough on nature and the mother-tongue.[1] For Jacob Grimm, in

the nineteenth century, the German language and German literature were the sole unifying band of the German nation,[2] and for
the social psychologist Peter Brückner just over a hundred years
later, the question of the identity of Germany was reduced to one
of nomenclature.[3]

These three examples are significant not only for an understanding of the concept of 'German nationhood', but also for the
way in which they point to two important political functions of
language: language as a symbol and instrument of solidarity, and
language as a creator of political realities, which are to form two of
the main themes of the present book.

The work is designed both as a theoretical consideration of the
role and function of language in the political process and as a
contribution to the socio-cultural history of the German language,
with case studies from the history of German serving to illustrate
the political roles and functions of language.

The consideration of basic theoretical issues in Chapter 1 addresses itself first to the question of whether there is such a thing
as 'the language of politics' as a special–purposes language in the
same way that there is 'a language of chemistry' or 'a language of
aviation', i.e., a particular register characterised by a specialist
vocabulary and particular syntactic frequency patterns. It will
examine the lexical approaches explored in Germany by linguists
such as Klein and Strauß before proceeding to attempt a categorisation of 'language in politics' by text-types and text-functions.
'Political' texts will be viewed as manifestations of general text
functions of the types suggested by Leech and Grünert (following
Halliday), and from these will be derived three main operational
categories which will serve as a basis for the further argument, in
which the twin themes of solidarity and power will be treated.

The second fundamental question to be approached is that of
the role of language in the political process and of the relationship
between language and politics. Here, the discussion will pick up
the twin themes of solidarity and power, and will complement
these with a consideration of the mutual influence of linguistic
change and socio-economic change.

It is the relationship between language change and socio-
economic change which forms the theme of the second chapter,
which will examine the ways in which the Industrial Revolution

in Germany created new communicative needs which had to be met for the process of industrialisation to proceed. The effects of the Industrial Revolution on the German language and the role played by the German language in the development of the Industrial Revolution support a materialist view of language, which sees languages as the products and constituents of human societies and postulates cross-fertilisation between language change and social practice.

Materialist theories of language can be contrasted with 'idealistic' views, which regard languages as possessing an inherent force peculiar to a particular people or nation, and in which language is perceived as incorporating the 'spirit' or 'genius' of a nation.

The idealistic view of language was particularly prevalent in the nineteenth century when, following the classical Cartesian dichotomy of 'body' and 'spirit', a nation was seen as the 'body' and the language as the manifestation of the nation's spirit, and Chapter 3 will examine the role played by idealistic views of language in views of nationhood and in the process of German unification in the nineteenth century. In this process, in which language became a metaphor of nation, the integrity and 'purity' of the language became inextricably linked with the integrity of the German nation. Moving forward into the twentieth century, we shall observe how language as the symbol of national unity gradually became recast as an instrument of nationalist expansionism, until, in the discourse of German fascism, idealist views of language were extended to the point where the German language was viewed not just as incorporating the spirit of the German people, but was materialised as an instrument of war and domination.

If Chapter 3 can be subsumed under the heading of 'solidarity', Chapter 4, which deals with the discourse of German Fascism from 1933-1945, takes up the theme of 'power' by illustrating the way in which a totalitarian regime attempts to impose a uniformity of discourse in the furtherance of its ends.

The period of fascist domination in Germany (usually known by its self-appointed title of 'National Socialism') from 1933-45 is often viewed as a unique phenomenon, and 'Nazi propaganda' seen as a special case of the 'abuse' of language. In the present analysis, however, it will be argued that the linguistic and discursive phenomena observed under German fascism can be treated within the general theoretical framework set up, and that although there may have been quantitative excesses, these phenomena do not differ qualitatively from those which can be observed elsewhere.

Interesting though a study of fascist discourse undoubtedly is, the reception accorded to it is perhaps even more interesting, and it is this which provides the material for the first part of Chapter 5, which, together with Chapter 6, treats aspects of politico-linguistic developments in Germany after 1945. In these final chapters, the twin themes of solidarity and power will again provide the basic framework, but underlying the argument will be the thesis that the issues of what is known as *Sprachkritik* – the criticism of language use – reflect general political issues and concerns, which themselves are seen as having specific linguistic dimensions.

The arrangement of Chapter 5 will be largely chronological; it will be shown how the initial attempts to come to terms with fascist discourse were soon superseded by the perceived need to deal with the linguistic consequences of the 'division of Germany', in the same way that the political processes of denazification and initial *Vergangenheitsbewältigung* were soon overtaken by the concerns of the Cold War.

For the first twenty years of its history, the new West German state was concerned to establish its legitimation by setting itself off from the pre-1945 fascist state (on the temporal and ideological dimension) and the post-1949 'real socialist' state to the East (on the spatial and ideological dimension). However, with the demise of the CDU as the leading party of government and the establishment of an SPD-led government after the interregnum of the 'Grand Coalition', demarcation turned from being primarily an external affair to an internal one, with 'competing' agendas and discourses 'vying for supremacy'. The most apparent manifestation of this was the *semantische Kämpfe* initiated by the CDU in the 1970s in an attempt to counter the intellectual supremacy established by the SPD and to regain the ideological initiative.

Finally, Chapter 6 will use three case studies from the 1970s and 1980s to demonstrate how language is used to 'construct realities' in the exercise and pursuit of political power. Using the examples of two major debates – the nuclear arms debate and the aggregated issues of the environment and civil rights – we shall observe ways in which attempts were made to establish the dominance of certain discourses and thus to impose particular perceptions of 'reality'. The discussion of these attempts to establish the dominance of a particular discourse then leads on to a consideration of ways in which the German women's movement – in common with its sisters in other countries – have sought to create a discourse which would 'make women visible' in order to help counter the discrimination and disadvantagement to which they see themselves subjected.

Notes

1 'In Teutschland aber hat man annoch dem latein und der kunst zuviel, der Muttersprach aber und der Natur zu wenig zugeschrieben.' G.W. Leibniz, 'Ermahnung an die Teutsche, ihren verstand und sprache besser zu üben, sammt beygefügten vorschlag einer Teutsch gesinten Gesellschaft' (ca. 1630) reprinted in *Wissenschaftliche Beihefte zur Zeitschrift des allgemeinen deutschen Sprachvereins*, 4, 29, 1907, p. 302

2 'was haben wir dann gemeinsames als unsere sprache und literatur?' J. Grimm, 'Vorrede' to J. & W. Grimm, *Deutsches Wörterbuch*, Bd. 1, Leipzig, 1854, p. III

3 'Die Frage, "Was ist des Deutschen Vaterland?" lautet heute: wie *heißt* es?' P. Brückner, *Versuch, uns und anderen die Bundesrepublik zu erklären*, Berlin, 1978, p. 7

1 Some theoretical preliminaries

The relationship of language and politics

Introduction

In this introductory chapter we shall set up a framework and establish some working definitions for the ensuing discussion on language and politics in German, drawing in the main on German work in the field.

A survey of the field of language and politics reveals a range of terminology; some talk of 'the language of politics', others of 'political language', still others prefer 'language in politics' or 'language and politics' – and this is without considering other variants such as the 'politics of language'. Working from the premiss that a difference in terminology can indicate a difference in approach, we shall start by examining the assumptions behind some of these terms in an attempt to understand the role of language in the political process.

Is there a 'language of politics'?

Some underlying assumptions

The term 'the language of politics' is based on two underlying assumptions. The first suggests the existence of a specialist language or register analogous to that of 'the language of chemistry' or 'the language of seafaring', i.e., postulates that there is a defined subject area 'politics', and a 'language' which is used in the description or practice of that subject area.

The second assumption is that, if there is a 'language of politics' as a specialist language, then this must stand in some kind of definable relationship to 'the common-core language'. Let us start by examining these assumptions.

The dualism of content and expression – what is politics?

The 'language of x' presupposes the existence of a field or subject area x for the description or practice of which there is a specialist language or register, in other words the 'language of x' is predicated on a dualism of content and expression. We must assume, therefore, that these conditions also apply to the 'language of politics', which means that we can define 'politics' and can identify its particular language or register (as a system of lexis, syntax and communicative conventions).

The problems which confront such an undertaking are three-fold:

firstly, to provide a satisfactory definition of 'politics', which involves distinguishing it from other subject areas;

secondly, to identify its register(s) and distinguish them from other specialist registers;

thirdly, to preserve the dualism of content and expression by separating 'politics' from its 'language'.

Unless we are to restrict our understanding of 'politics' to that of politics as an academic discipline (i.e., political science) we are faced here with almost insuperable difficulties. It might be possible to reduce the scope of 'politics' to that of the interaction of the state with other states and with its own citizens, though even this would be difficult enough, given the all-pervading presence of the state in citizens' everyday lives. Such a reduction, however, would then exclude whole areas of 'party politics', including the involvement of citizens in the process of forming and formulating opinion and policy within party fora, so that it would be necessary to extend the definition to include perhaps constitutionalised activity directed towards influencing the interaction of the state with other states and with its own citizens. Here, however, we would be excluding the activities of non-party pressure-groups and formers of public opinion – for example Greenpeace, the *Deutscher Gewerkschaftsbund* and the *Verband der chemischen Industrie*. Thus it would be necessary to extend the definition still further to include all forms of institutionalised activity directed towards influencing the interaction of the state with other states and with its own citizens. Then, however, we would still be excluding non-institutionalised forms of activity, such as those undertaken by individual public figures (e.g., Günter Grass, Wolf Biermann) or by single-issue citizens' movements or by loose groupings, such as the feminist movement.

If all these elements were to be included in the definition of 'politics', as they would have to be to make the definition comprehensive, we would end up with a definition which encompassed virtually the whole of public life, as we are dealing not only with the interaction of the state with other states and with its own citizens and with activity directed towards the state with the intention of influencing its interaction with other states and with its own citizens, but also with actions directed towards other citizens with the intention of creating a climate which will influence the state's interaction with other states and with its own citizens.

Is there a specialist 'language of politics'? – problems of the relationship between 'common-core' and 'specialist' language

A discussion of 'specialist' languages must consider the relationship of the specialist language to the 'common-core', and here three models suggest themselves.

The first assumes the existence of a 'language' (say, German), which is made up of a set of sub-languages (e.g., 'language of poetry', 'language of physics'), one of which is the 'common' or 'everyday' language, which thus is accorded the same status as the other sub-languages.

The second postulates a virtual identity of the 'language' and the 'common language', which is then seen as the sum of a series of sub-languages.

The third model is a variation on the second, and sees the 'common language' at the centre of the language, with the various sub-languages arranged around its periphery and partially overlapping both with it and with each other.

For our present purposes it is not necessary to enter into the merits or otherwise of the models indicated above. The important point is that, given the range of areas covered by modern politics, and the extent of its linguistic manifestations, it is difficult to see how a category 'language of politics' could be made to fit into any of them. The best that one could hope to do would be to subdivide politics into a number of specialist areas (e.g., law, government, public administration) which undoubtedly do have interlinked 'specialist languages' and, using the third model, consign the rest of the 'language of politics' (which would probably be the major part) to the common-core.

Such a procedure would be in line with the nature of 'specialist languages', as expressed for example by Wilhelm Schmidt, who defined them as :

an optimum means of communication among experts in a specialist field. They are characterised by a specific specialist vocabulary and special norms for the selection, use and frequency of common-core and grammatical items.

They do not exist as an independent manifestation of language, but are realised in specialist texts which always contain common-core elements in addition to the specialist layer.[1]

The important part of this definition is not so much what it says about lexis and syntax, but the conditions it identifies for the use of a *Fachsprache* 'an optimum means of communication among experts in a specialist field', and it is this that brings us to a discussion of levels of specialist language and its communicative conditions.

In the introduction to the section on 'Politik und Ideologie' in their monographic dictionary *Brisante Wörter*,[2] Strauß, Haß and Harras distinguish three main areas of political communication, which they label as 'internal political communication within institutions', 'external communication from institutions' and 'public political communication', this last being seen as the most important functional area.[3]

Of the three areas, it is essentially only the first which qualifies as a specialist language as defined by Schmidt: texts are generated principally for internal use among experts and their lexis is marked by a high incidence of technical terms. Although the texts will affect the lives of 'ordinary' citizens, these are excluded from the communicative process or, at best, are admitted as spectators.

In those texts emanating from the bureaucracy and directed towards the citizens, some of the technical terms and the structures found in the first area will also occur (often giving rise to the charge of 'incomprehensibility' levelled against such texts).[4]

Texts generated for 'external institutional communication' are, however, also marked by 'ideological elements, e.g., with formulations such as … "social market economy" or "citizens in uniform". Such expressions are coined primarily for public consumption, and thus belong rather to public language'.[5]

The third area is defined as follows:

'The area of public political communication … is characterised by subjective or ideological usage and the whole range of ideological vocabulary. This language conveys specific interpretations of reality which are often ideologically motivated'.[6]

Obviously, the three functional areas identified by Strauß, Haß and Harras are not in hermetically sealed compartments, and the second area in particular is marked by a mixture of areas 1 and 3, the 'mix' depending to a large extent on the purpose which the text is serving. Strauß, Haß and Harras define two main purposes of political communication – the formulation of political objectives and the exercise of power – and it is suggested here that in the second of their functional areas, the particular mix of 'bureaucratic' and 'opinion-forming' language will be determined by the purpose for which a particular text is produced; the exercise of power presupposes the legitimation of the powerful and the threat of sanctions in the event of non-compliance, and in a society in which one of the values is the 'rule of law', legitimation comes from reference to the law – as with the reference to 'gem. § 47 Abs. 4 i.V.m. §60 des 1. Buches SGB' in the example quoted in footnote 4. The attempt to form or influence public opinion, however, though still requiring legitimation, cannot threaten direct sanctions in the event of non-compliance, but has to have recourse to allegedly shared values, which will be expressed through ideologically determined language.

The question of functional areas and the addresseeship and purpose of 'political texts' is one to which we shall return later, after considering further aspects of the language used in political texts.

The 'vocabulary of politics' – lexical approaches, e.g., Klein, Strauß/Haß/Harras

Although Strauß, Haß and Harras take account of the functionality of the texts in their corpus, their approach is essentially a lexical one, and one which they share with a number of other studies of 'political language', for example with Josef Klein,[7] who justifies his word-based approach by claiming that as the whole field of politics is linguistically constituted and political argument is conducted in language and about language, the question of the political vocabulary is of central importance.[8]

Although the first and second premises can be regarded as either controversial or trivial, the attempt to categorise 'political vocabulary' requires closer examination.

Klein distinguishes four main areas of political vocabulary, 'institutional vocabulary', 'vocabulary of specialist fields', 'general interactional vocabulary' and 'ideological vocabulary'.[9] As he himself states, his categorisation is based on one put forward by Dieckmann, who distinguished the three categories of 'ideological language', 'institutional language' and 'specialist language of administrative areas',[10] and which Klein has now extended to include the category of general interactional vocabulary.

Klein agrees that the language of politics cannot be regarded as a specialist language but shares the opinion that 'specialist features are most likely to be found in the vocabulary of political institutions',[11] which he then divides into the four sub-categories of

'– Items referring state organisations, political institutions and their sub-divisions, ... items referring roles in the state and politics, ...Terms for codes covering institutional activity (e.g. United Nations Charter), ...Terms for political actions, processes and conditions, ...'[12]

'Specialist elements' are also to be found in Klein's second category, 'the vocabulary of specialist fields', but here the specialist terms are not those of 'politics', but of the areas which fall within the ambit of political administration – what Dieckmann calls the 'specialist language of administrative areas'.[13]

The level of specialisation varies, however, according to situation and context, depending on whether one is dealing with 'internal' or 'external' communication, so the distinction which

Klein makes cuts across the distinction by functional areas made by Strauß, Haß and Harras.

Klein's third category of political vocabulary – general interactional vocabulary – is, he claims, justified by the fact that 'language in politics is pervaded by common-core terms for human interaction and its various aspects ... this includes a comprehensive range of vocabulary covering linguistic action.'[14]

The fact, however, that certain subsets of the lexis are found in political texts does not necessarily mean that they have to be ascribed to 'political vocabulary'; their presence could just as well be explained using the third model of the relationship between specialist languages and the common-core, unless it can be shown that their frequency in political texts differs greatly from that in texts from any other area, or that there is a particular pattern of action and interaction in the political sphere. Klein does not, however, attempt to justify his inclusion of this category with these or similar arguments, but contents himself with the observation that political texts contain areas of vocabulary which do not fall under any of his other categories.

Klein's fourth category – ideological vocabulary – also poses a number of theoretical difficulties. He defines it as 'the words with which political groups formulate their interpretation and evaluation of the political and social world, together with their principles and priorities.'[15]

Within this category he then further subdivides between lexemes articulating basic patterns of social relationships and structures, those referencing preferred patterns of political organisation, and those expressing basic values and ethical principles.

The theoretical difficulties caused by this category are threefold. Firstly, the postulation of this category suggests that the other categories, particularly 'institutional vocabulary ', are in some way ideologically neutral, which is not necessarily the case, as can be seen by examples such as 'Ministry of Defence'.[16] Secondly, there is nothing inherent in the reference of these lexemes – e.g. *Familie, Gesellschaft, Fleiß* –which identifies them as belonging to this category rather than to another. The third difficulty is caused by Klein's further definition of the category, which he sees as a subset of a 'language of political opinion' (which up to this point has not featured in his categorisation).[17]

If this is indeed the case – and here Klein finds himself at variance with Strauß, Haß and Harras, who equate 'the language of ideology' with 'the language of opinion'[18] – one feels justified in asking why Klein includes as a category of political vocabulary a sub-category of another category, and why he does not either follow Strauß, Haß and Harras or include the full category of 'the language of opinion', for which there would be just as much justification as there is for including 'general interactional vocabulary' as a category. The failure to include a category of 'the language of opinion' is all the more surprising as Klein devotes the rest of his paper to the Conflict about words', which he perceives as a 'Conflict of opinions'.[19]

Critique of purely lexical approach

There appear to be two fundamental problems with the approach which Klein takes: the first is that the categories which he sets up are defined partly by reference ('institutional vocabulary', 'vocabulary of specialist fields', and, to a lesser extent, 'general interactional vocabulary') and partly by function ('ideological vocabulary') without having a more general notion of 'political language' from which to work, and the second is that he tends to identify 'language' with 'vocabulary'.

This is not to deny the linguistic usefulness of a lexical approach, and some of the analyses of 'Disputed words' (*'Kampfwörter'*) and dominant word fields which Klein and others have undertaken afford valuable insights to which we shall return later; what is being criticised here is the absence of a general notion of 'political language' and the identification of 'language' with 'vocabulary', together with the methodological reductionism inherent in the approach.

At this point, it is useful to return to Klein's opening statements that 'the whole field of politics is constituted in words' and 'that political conflict is conducted in words',[20] and to examine their implications in more detail.

When, in Act 2 Scene 2 of Shakespeare's *Hamlet*, Polonius asks Hamlet 'What do you read, my lord?', the reply he receives is 'Words, words, words'. It is perhaps significant that when Hamlet gives this answer, he is either mad or feigning madness, for the reply is not normally what one would expect. To derive any sense or benefit, we do not just read 'words', we read texts, and an analysis of political language which starts from the concept of 'text' is more likely to be useful than one which starts from the lexis.

Categorisation by text-types and text-functions

It is argued that a text-based approach will not only afford greater insights into the role of language in political processes, but that shifting the emphasis from language (as a system) to text (its realisation) will also help to counter some of the theoretical and methodological problems inherent in an analysis of political language. An example of the type of criticism raised against attempts to define 'political language' as reported by Wülfing is that the whole field of 'language and politics' lacks specifically linguistic criteria for its definition, i.e. that there is no distinctive feature by which the language of politics can be distinguished from other 'languages'.[21]

This objection can be countered by taking a functional rather than a strictly language-immanent systemic approach and by regarding 'political' texts as a set of texts which serve as exemplars of certain more general language functions.

Strauß *et al.* demonstrate for example that, although their main concern is – quite legitimately – with a section of the lexicon, this must be viewed in the context of a larger text-based functional approach, as political action and discourse is conducted within the context of language games which are task-oriented and often strategic in nature, and these language games cannot be accessed by assuming the existence of a specialist vocabulary of politics but only by examining the types of communicative situation or the types of text in the various functional areas.[22]

Within the present context, we shall concentrate on those aspects of text which appear to be of particular significance for the present analysis, while disregarding those (such as 'coherence' and 'cohesion') which are only of tangential interest.

The first point to be made is that a text, as an actual realisation of language, is generated in a particular context or situation as a form of social interaction with an intention or purpose, all of which help determine the form or style of the text. As Grünert puts it: 'We do not grasp the "reality" of a text by seeing it simply as an ordered and structured sequence of linguistic signs. Each text is "realised" in a complex context of sense and action.'[23]

Figure 1. Conduit model of communication

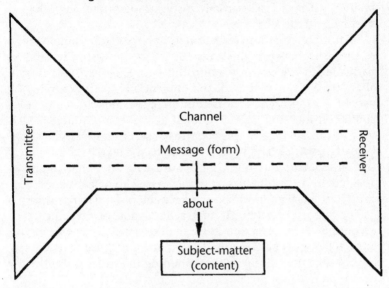

Source: G. Leech, *Semantics*, Harmondsworth, 1974

If we are regarding 'political texts' as realisations of more general text functions, then we must start from a more general model of the role of language in social interaction. Here we shall take as our starting point the discussion of language functions presented by Leech.[24] In a chapter entitled 'Semantics and Society', he works from a conventional 'conduit' model of communication, to which he then relates five different language functions, each of which is oriented towards one of the factors in the model:

FUNCTION	ORIENTATION TOWARDS
informational:	subject-matter
expressive:	speaker/writer
directive:	listener/reader
phatic:	channel of communication
aesthetic:	message.[25]

As Leech himself admits, this classification is not perfect,[26] and for our present purposes it will be necessary to elaborate on various aspects of the situation and to propose a further differentiation in some of the categories (particularly the directive and the phatic), while at least partially disregarding others (e.g., the expressive and the aesthetic).

Within the situation, attention must be paid for example to the relationship between the participants in the discourse, and in particular to the power-relationship between them, as this will affect the form and style of the interaction. As an example of a very broad approach to the definition of situation and context we could continue the passage quoted above from Grünert : 'Each text is 'realised' in a complex context of sense and action. By that, I mean the whole field which conditions the text, its communicative antecedents and intention, those acting through it and those affected by it, individual and social psychological conditions, situation, social environment and general power relationships.'[27]

The suggestion, then, is that a discussion of text must take account of all these factors; as we shall see later, the consideration of such factors is particularly important for political texts in view of their role in creating and maintaining the social reality which they represent.

Such an approach transcends the limitations of a strictly systemic one, and to pre-empt the possible charge that we are employing a 'bootstrap' approach,[28] we can quote a comment by Palmer on the proper concern of semantics: 'semantics is not a clearly defined level of linguistics ... Rather it is a set of studies of the use of language in relation to many different aspects of experience, to linguistic and non-linguistic context, to participants in discourse, to their knowledge and experience, to the conditions under which a particular bit of language is appropriate'.[29]

Grünert sees texts as elements within a wider pattern of interaction; using a term borrowed from Wittgenstein, he labels them 'language games', which can be taken as the totality of the interaction. Within the political domain, he identifies four main types of 'game', the 'regulative', the 'instrumental or petitioning', the 'integrative' and the 'informative-persuasive'.[30]

Grünert's four categories are mirrored almost exactly by the four categories established four years later by Bochmann et al., who wrote that: 'Political texts can be divided into four categories, which have gradually developed in a mutual relationship with types of political action: regulative-stabilising, prospective-changing, integrative and publicistic-persuasive',[31] the functions of which can be glossed as follows:

Regulative-stabilising: the maintenance of power;

Prospective-changing: the expression of the desires and aspirations of the political subjects;

Integrative: the stabilisation and/or the demarcation of political groupings;

 Publicistic-persuasive: motivation, preparation and coordination of political action within the political grouping and beyond its boundaries.[32]

If we relate the four categories established by Grünert and by Bochmann *et al.* to the functions proposed by Leech, it would appear that the regulative and prospective categories are realisations of the directive function (in each case the text is focused on the listener), the difference being in the direction of the gradient of power, which in the first case is from author down to recipient and in the second from recipient down to author: from the power gradient can be derived a further distinction, which is that directive texts are backed up by sanctions, whereas prospective texts can at best be backed up by threats of action which lacks inherent institutionalised legitimacy (e.g., withdrawal of labour, non-payment of taxes). The integrative category can be seen as a realisation of the phatic function, with the focus being on maintaining a bond between author and recipients, while the persuasive category represents a complex function composed of the directive and the phatic, with the phatic emphasis being on creating a bond rather than maintaining an existing one.

As an illustration, it might be useful to indicate some of the texts which fall into the four categories:

Regulative: laws, edicts, regulations, proclamations, commands, summonses;

Prospective: petitions, motions, (open) letters;

Integrative: manifestos, national anthems, campaign songs;

Persuasive: election posters, party political broadcasts, advertisements.

Separation of content and expression

At the beginning of this chapter, it was suggested that terms such as 'the language of politics' presuppose a dualism of content and expression, i.e., that there is a domain labelled 'politics' and a particular linguistic system or subsystem used to reflect it.

So far, we have looked at the difficulties of defining the domain and identifying the language. It is now time to go one step further, and examine the presupposed underlying dualism; this will be done in two ways, firstly by suggesting that political action is in the main linguistic action, and secondly by considering the nature of political realities. The hypothesis which is being advanced is that the implied dualism is untenable for our present purposes; a corollary is that this dualism is also open to question in other areas of language use.

Text as an element of political action – the role of language in political action

Although Klein was criticised above for his contention that 'the whole field of politics is constituted in words,' the criticism was directed towards his use of the term 'words' and his implicit acceptance of the content/expression dualism, and was not intended to deny the importance of language in the political process, an importance which is underlined, for example by Greiffenhagen, who sees language not just as a political instrument but as the element within which the politician operates; for him, politics is a linguistic activity.[33]

For Greiffenhagen, language is the 'element' in which the politician operates and the instrument with which he operates; Grünert defines a language game as 'a context of sense and action', Bochmann et al. classify political discourse under four 'action types ...', which have gradually developed in a mutual relationship with types of political action': and in the labels used by Grünert, by Bochmann et al. and indeed by Leech (e.g. 'directive', 'persuasive') one sees evidence of a speech-act approach to the analysis of political discourse. Putting it simply, the view which will be propounded here is that political action is essentially linguistic action. As Strauß et al. express it, proposing a view of politics which differs quite radically from the state-oriented approach taken by Grünert, politics is a sophisticated area of communication, in which matters of public interest are negotiated, opinions are formed and binding or controversial social decisions are prepared and effected. For them, political action is essentially linguistic or communicative action, or at least requires linguistic mediation.[34] A good example of the significance of linguistic action as political action was given in the columns of *The Guardian* on 26 August 1991 in the aftermath of the thwarted coup in the Soviet Union when Jonathan Steele wrote:

After all the dramas of the preceding days – the tanks in the streets, the barricades, the liberated President, the euphoria, the funeral, the triumph of Boris Yeltsin – could a man in a grey suit on a television programme reading a piece of text on a desk in front of him really change the world?
He could, and he did.[35]

Thus, politics is essentially defined in terms of communicative function. This view regards politics as one manifestation of more general patterns of social and personal interaction, and fits in with Greiffenhagen's proposition that 'Language makes it possible for humans to live in groups'.[36] In other words, it is being suggested that the major part of human social and personal interaction is linguistic. In extension it could be argued that non-linguistic interaction only comes in when linguistic interaction has failed, and that even then the non-linguistic action has to be prepared and possibly justified linguistically, and usually has some form of linguistic epilogue, for example with the purpose of reconciliation or retribution.

The main outlines of the position that is being advanced here should by now be becoming clear. In particular, a view of politics is being proposed which sees politics as a form of action and interaction which is not only mediated linguistically, but is essentially grounded in communicative acts which are realised through language. The dualism of content and expression which is inherent in some treatments of 'political language' cannot be sustained where political action is concerned, indeed, it might be argued that the only area in which the dualism could have any validity is that of reflective discourse about politics – e.g. in academic writing – but discourse *about* politics must not be confused with the discourse *of* politics.

The nature of political reality

In his consideration of the role of language in politics, Greiffenhagen identifies four ways in which language makes human social life possible:

as intellectual experiencing of reality;
as an institution which relieves individuals of the excessive need for making decisions;
as a vehicle of social norms;
as an instrument of social control.[37]

The third and fourth of these were implicit in the discussion in the previous section, but the first and second require elaboration, as they are central to the relationship between 'language' and 'reality' in the sphere of politics.

It has been suggested so far that in relation to political activity, the dualism of 'language' and 'politics' is difficult to maintain, as political action is in the main linguistic action. An important political activity lies in the establishment of definitions and the creation of political realities; definitions are established and realities created by linguistic means, and subsequent (non-linguistic) actions are in the main directed towards maintaining (or combating) the linguistic realities which have been created. A bald statement such as this obviously requires further elaboration, impinging as it does on the whole discussion of the relationship between 'language' and 'reality'.

The position which it is proposed to advance here is essentially that put forward by Shapiro, for example, who wrote:

The position to be presented and elaborated throughout this analysis is that language is not *about* objects and experience; it is *constitutive* of objects and experience. This is not the subjectivist position that there is nothing (no thing) in the world until we cognize it or speak of it. Rather, it is the position that the world of 'things' has no meaningful structure except in connection with the standards we employ to ascribe qualities to it.[38]

and in this he accords with the thesis advanced by Rubinstein, among others, that 'language does not just serve to express thoughts ... We formulate thoughts in language, and by formulating them we also form them. Language is more than the external instrument of thoughts. As form, it is part of the process of thinking, and is linked with its contents.'[39]

Thus the position taken up here is opposed to that of the positivists, who 'viewed the world of experience as possessing a coherent structure unimposed by the perceiver'[40] and believed that 'we can speak *correctly* about objects and situations'[41] which for Shapiro is 'predicated on an indefensible theory of meaning and is a misleading way to represent the relationship between speech and phenomena'.[42]

The positivist approach also seems to be implicit in Greiffenhagen's view that one of the social functions of language is 'the intellectual experience of reality', whereas what is being suggested here is that one of the functions of language is to *create* realities.

The present discussion is not only of interest in itself, but is part of a wider one, that of whether the nature of political meaning which is being propagated here is illustrative of more general relations between 'language' and 'reality', or whether political language represents a special case from which it is not necessarily possible to generalise about such relations.

The positivist view of meaning that there is an 'objective reality' which can be mirrored in language is based on a dualism of mind and matter, which can be traced back to Descartes, and which together with Newtonian mechanical determinism has dominated scientific enquiry for over two centuries and has generally been taken to represent the epitome of 'scientific method'.

As the natural sciences have often provided a role-model for other disciplines – not least for linguistics – which were concerned to show that they were just as 'exact' in their methods and findings as the natural sciences, it is perhaps instructive to glance at the way the 'received' scientific method has developed in the twentieth century. For this, we shall consider briefly an important change occasioned by the 'new physics' represented by relativity theory and quantum mechanics.

In one of the seminal works of the 'alternative movement', the Austro-Californian physicist Fritjof Capra writes:

The crucial feature of quantum theory is that the observer is not only necessary to observe the properties of an atomic phenomenon, but is necessary even to bring about these properties. My conscious decision about how to observe, say, an electron will determine the electron's properties to some extent. ... The electron does not *have* objective properties independent of my mind. In atomic physics the sharp Cartesian division between mind and matter, between the observer and the observed, can no longer be maintained. We can never speak about nature without, at the same time, speaking about ourselves.[43]

While not wishing to elevate Capra to the status of holy writ, he does seem to provide some support for the approach being taken here, which is that the dualism of mind and matter which lies behind one view of the relationship between 'language' and 'reality' is radically open to question.

The postulation of a 'creative' function of language in the realm of politics goes further than this, however. If we question the existence of an 'objective reality' independent of observation and consciousness and replace it with the notion of 'ideated reality', we are raising all kinds of questions about the nature of 'truth', and are throwing open the gates to a multiplicity of 'realities' or 'truths'. These would engender individualistic systems of beliefs and values which would apparently be at odds with the notion put forward by Greiffenhagen that part of the social function of language lies in a (common) 'intellectual experience of reality'. How is it possible, given the notion of reality being proposed here, for this social function to be maintained? If in a society there are divergent systems of belief and conflicting perceptions of 'reality', how can social cohesion be brought about?

Basically, the answer appears to be that conflicts are 'resolved' by certain constructs of reality with their attendant systems of beliefs and values achieving dominance and establishing dominant discourses. In this process of domination, two complementary mechanisms can be observed: on the one hand, the attempt to portray one's own perception as incorporating some notion of 'absolute truth' or 'objective reality', and on the other the disqualification of opposing views as 'untrue' (or 'heretical') or 'unrealistic' (or 'insane').

The identification of such 'mechanisms' does not, however, explain *why* it is that certain perceptions and discourses achieve dominance, and this is a question which must be addressed unless we are to remain locked in a cosy loop which sees language as the sole element in political interaction, with certain discourses achieving dominance in some wondrous way, and which takes no account of the fact that political activity does give rise to a whole series of socio-economic consequences which affect people's lives. If we look no further than language, we need take no account of the unequal distribution of wealth, of the way in which prosperity for the few on both the national and the international scale is bought at the expense and misery of the many, nor do we need to consider other forms of social injustice or the threats to our very human existence posed by the arms race and man-made environmental devastation (for which the term 'ecocide' has been coined). Language does indeed have a role to play, but political critique (and political action) cannot stop at linguistic critique.

One could argue, with Marx, that 'the ideas of the ruling class are in every epoch the ruling ideas', and that the power of the ruling class is ultimately founded in the economic power which put the ruling class in its position and enables it to pursue policies in its interest and to apply sanctions if its role is seriously challenged. The use of sanctions, however, is the ultimate measure, and ideally more subtle methods of social control are preferred, which can be glossed as 'ensuring the assent of the governed'. One such method is that of establishing the rulers' perceptions or world view as 'reality' or 'the truth' and by appealing to sets of allegedly common values or beliefs which are presented as being those of the particular polity ('our way of life', 'die freiheitlich-demokratische Grundordnung'). Although the establishment of a particular world view can be attained by non-linguistic means (e.g., physical coercion and terror), a more lasting effect can be achieved by establishing the dominance of a particular discourse through such channels as the mass media and the education system. In his review of Noam Chomsky's *Deterring Democracy*, a *Guardian* reviewer was reminded of a story one told by 'a New York academic friend ... of a puzzled visit by a group of Russians touring the US ... They had criss-crossed the United States, they said, reading the newspapers and watching the television coverage of a free society, and discovered that all the opinions on vital issues were the same. "In our country," they said, "to get that result we have a dictatorship, we imprison people, we tear out their fingernails. Here you have none of that. So what's your secret – how do you do it?" The answer, of course, is that it is done by 'manipulation of opinion' and 'the Orwellian abuse of language.'[44]

In the process of maintaining a dominant discourse, the inertia of the governed probably has an important part to play, which is presumably what Greiffenhagen means when he talks of the political role of language as an 'as an institution which relieves individuals of the excessive need for making decisions'. As Shapiro puts it, reflecting the Sapir/Whorf hypothesis that our perceptions and world-view are conditioned by the language in which we are socialised: 'Insofar as we do not invent language or meanings in our typical speech, we end up by buying into a model of political relations in almost everything we say without making a prior, deliberate evaluation of the purchasing decision'.[45]

Lest it be thought that an excessively cynical view of politics is being purveyed here, which sees everything in terms of political *control*, we must hasten to add that the conscious subscription to a common discourse, and thus the conscious acceptance of its underlying system of beliefs and values, also ha've a central part to play in the creation of *solidarity*.

Furthermore, the establishment of a dominant public discourse does not necessarily signify that 'the hearts and minds' of the population have been won; the dominant discourse has to be credible, i.e., it must bear some relation to popular perceptions. The observation has often been made that the gulf between public discourse and private perception was a significant feature under the Stalinist regime of the erstwhile German Democratic Republic; when the discrepancy became so great that the first defensive reaction – the retreat into the private sphere of the *Nischen-gesellschaft* – no longer appeared adequate, one of the forms that the revolution took was that of a direct challenge to the dominant discourse: the now famous slogan 'Wir sind das Volk' reinter-preted one of the key terms of the public discourse and reclaimed it for those to whom it had allegedly always belonged, but who were unable to identify with it. It would of course be naïve to ascribe excessive significance to this one slogan, which would have remained ineffectual without the thousands of people stand-ing round the banner bearing it; the mass exodus of citizens from the GDR was a far more potent factor, but when the end did come, it was in the form of a linguistic act – an announcement that the borders of the GDR were opened – which in its effect was probably more devastating than the fanfares before the walls of Jericho.

Establishing dominant discourses/Establishing rules of discourse: political conflict as a conflict of competing discourses – either at macro-level (linguistic colonialism) or at micro-level

The establishment of a dominant discourse can proceed in a variety of ways and on a number of levels.

At the macro-level – i.e., the inter-language level – we find the imposition of a complete national language as the medium of government, administration, education and official public discourse, a process which could be classified as 'linguistic colonialism'; at the same time, competing languages are suppressed or supplanted. Such 'competing' languages may either be indigenous (e.g., Welsh, Gaelic, Polish) or other 'colonial' languages (e.g. Dutch/English in South Africa or German in Namibia). The result can either be an, at times, uneasy co-existence of the competitors or the dominance of one, with the other, if it continues to exist, becoming a symbol of resistance and the striving for 'national independence'.

'Linguistic colonialism' will not be of great concern to us in the present study, although elements of it will be seen in Chapter 3 in the discussion of late–nineteenth–century views of the 'world role' of the German language and fascist views of the role of the German language as an instrument of conquest and domination. The converse, however, in the form of attempts to establish or re-establish the German vernacular in the face of the dominance of French and Latin, will form an important element in the discussion of the role of language in creating national solidarity.

At the micro-level – i.e., the intra-language level – three mechanisms can be identified in attempts to achieve linguistic dominance: naming, referencing and signifying.

By 'naming' we understand the efforts of a particular group to establish its own terminology in a way that will enable it to create presuppositions favourable to its purposes. Examples of this are legion, and conflicts of terminology are particularly prevalent under conditions of linguistic polarisation such as those obtaining between two German-speaking states from 1949 to 1989/90.

'Referencing' and 'signifying' can be viewed as complementary aspects of the process of 'ascribing meaning'. 'Referencing' is understood as the attempt to stake a claim to positively loaded terms and to dispute the political opponent's right to use the

terms (e.g., 'democracy', 'freedom', 'peace-loving') while at the
same time trying to establish negatively-loaded terms (e.g., 'communist', 'capitalist', 'unpatriotic') and to ascribe them to the
political opponent.

'Signifying' is taken to refer to the claim that a particular group
is in sole possession of the 'true' meaning of a word, and that the
opponent is 'misrepresenting' or 'abusing' the 'true' meaning. A
variation on this is the reinterpretation of terms from the opponent's discourse in an attempt either to discredit them or to
harness them for one's own purposes.

The mechanisms outlined here have been presented so far as
having an 'external' orientation, as representing the attempt by
one group to establish the dominance of its discourse as an aid
towards establishing or maintaining power. They do, however,
also have an internal orientation when they are used as a means of
creating or maintaining group solidarity. The existence of a 'common language' is an important tool for forging group identity,
whether at the national or sub-national level, and particularly at
the group or party level can perform much the same function as
the wearing of uniforms.

Instances of the ways in which 'referencing' and 'signifying'
can be used will be demonstrated in Chapter 5 in the discussion of
the 'semantic battles' of the 1970s and in Chapter 6 in the
'competition' for the 'right' to bear the title of 'peace-movement'
in the nuclear arms debate of the early 1980s.

Types of political meaning – denotational, associative (deontic)

Before leaving this section, which deals with some aspects of the
'meaning' of key political terms, it is perhaps useful to dwell for a
moment on the types of meaning to be found at the word level
and relate these to the more general discussion of the relationship
between language and 'reality' conducted earlier.

Following Leech (1974), meanings can be divided into three
main categories or types – 'conceptual', 'associative' and 'thematic'; it is the first two of these on which we shall concentrate
here.

'Conceptual' meaning refers to the denotation of a term, and
here problems immediately present themselves for both refer-

encing and signifying. Attempts to circumscribe the conceptual meaning of a term often take the form of a definition, but as any definition – even of a seemingly simple object – involves making a selection from the myriad properties which make up the object, an exhaustive definition can never be supplied. A comprehensive definition of a 'chair' for example would not only cover all the physical properties of the object in question, but would also not only have to include all the uses to which 'chairs' have been put and – presumably – to which they might potentially be put, but also contain statements on the social status and value of chairs. Naming and defining a chair is a relatively simple exercise compared with the problems posed by more complex phenomena where disagreement can arise about the reference of a term. While out walking with a young German friend, he asked 'Siehst Du den Dackel mit den zwei Hunden da drüben?' ('Can you see the dachshund over there with the two dogs?'). The suggestion was obvious: a 'Dachshund' does not belong to the category of dog, so in this case perception involved a re-categorisation of the sign 'dog' with a resultant shift in reality.

Political definitions can be of two kinds, depending on whether the linguistic act of naming precedes or succeeds the creation of the phenomenon defined. Let us take as an instance of the first type a political institution – the *Deutscher Bundestag*. The institution owes its existence to a number of texts (for example the constitution or *Grundgesetz*) which created it and defined its composition and functions, so that theoretically at least it should be possible to provide an exhaustive definition, as the existence of the institution depends on the original legal definitions given. This situation, however, only applies to a relatively small number of specialist terms in the fields of government, law and public administration.

If the attempt at definition succeeds the creation of the phenomenon (or the existence of the term), the problems indicated above increase exponentially, particularly if the 'phenomenon' is an abstract or an ideal which will ultimately defy exhaustive definition, so that either a partial definition has to be established (using the term 'partial' as a derivative of both 'part' and 'party') or the term is left conceptually undefined. The ability to establish dominant definitions is an important means of exercising political control.

'Freedom', 'peace', 'democracy', 'equality' are instances of
terms which defy definition, but which have a significant role to
play in political discourse, representing as they do ideals and
values to which many polities subscribe. Against them can be set
words such as *Chaot*, 'imperialist', 'militarist', *linksradikal*, which
have an equally important role to play in the defamation of
political opponents or the disqualification of opposing views.
Such terms – the negative and the positive – function by virtue of
their associations rather than by their conceptual content. Their
appeal is to emotion (and prejudice) rather than to the intellect.
They are very often deployed in antagonistic discourse, and it is of
such terms that participants will attempt to 'take possession',
determining less their definition than their reference. The 'control' of terms such as 'freedom', 'peace', 'democracy', 'equality',
and *Chaot*, 'imperialist', 'militarist', *linksradikal* do have an important part to play in the exercise of social control, but they are also
significant in the creation of solidarity.

In summary then, we can state that the power to determine
both names and signification and to establish definitions, in other
words to control both denotative and associative meanings and
thus to create realities is a significant factor both in the exercise of
political control and the creation of solidarity.

The relationship of language and socio-economic context

We have discussed some aspects of the relationship between
'language', 'power' and 'solidarity', and it is now time to return to
the question of the relationship between language and socio-
economic context. It is necessary to do this for the reasons indicated above, that we cannot deny that political activity does
give rise to a whole series of socio-economic consequences which
affect people's lives and that ultimately we cannot ignore these
consequences.

It is suggested that the relationship between language and its
socio-economic context is one of interdependence, and that the
interaction between them takes place on two main levels.

Firstly one can consider the relationship in terms of interpretation and presentation. The elements of the socio-economic context (e.g., ownership of the means of production, distribution of
wealth, power relationships) need to be mediated or interpreted,

but as was suggested before, the process of interpretation and presentation of the context is then itself constitutive of the reality which is being presented. Except possibly in the case of academic discourse, the interpretation and presentation of a reality is not altruistic; it serves the interests of those presenting it, who will seek to establish their reality as the dominant one, perhaps by ascribing to it such qualities as 'truth' or 'objectivity'.

The interpretation and presentation of the socio-economic context is not restricted to material aspects, but is buttressed by a system of beliefs and values (e.g., 'freedom', 'equality of opportunity', 'the market', the identification of 'friends' and 'foes') which provide the conceptual framework for the interpretation and determine its orientation. The underlying system of beliefs and values is an important element in the political culture of a body, and it is this system which, following Shapiro,[46] we shall term 'ideology'.

An example of such an underlying framework could be seen in the discourse of the nuclear arms race during the period of confrontation between the two 'superpowers', the USA and the USSR. The underlying Western perception was that the 'free' society of the West was living under the constant shadow of potential Soviet military aggression, and it was this belief which determined the perception of the nature and role of the military hardware deployed. Soviet thermonuclear means of mass destruction were construed as the 'threat' against which the West was forced to defend itself, and within the construction of strategy, Western (principally US) thermonuclear means of mass destruction were presented as a 'deterrent' to aggression. On the international scale, the build-up of thermonuclear means of mass destruction was accompanied by a conflict of discourses, with both sides presenting themselves as potential victims of aggression (which is why both name their politico-military coordinating institution the 'Ministry of *Defence*', even though the majority of weapons deployed were clearly of an 'offensive' capacity). This topic is one which will be taken up again in Chapter 6.

The relationship between language and socio-economic context is dynamic, not static; the socio-economic context is constructed as a reality through the acceptance of ideologies and the establishment of perceptions. The 'reality' which is thus constructed is then used as a legitimation for further action (which may be either linguistic or non-linguistic) designed to affect the socio-economic context, which then has to be re-constructed. In other words, there is a constant process of interaction taking place between text and context.

The attempt to create and establish political realities has two main functions. The first is the maintenance of existing power structures and thus of preserving continuity, and the second is that of altering power structures, i.e., initiating change. The relevant discourses are in constant conflict within the dialectic of continuity and change. A good example of this conflict in Western political culture can be observed in the discourses of election campaigns,[47] and the conflict can also be seen clearly in the views of German conservative language critics in the 1970s, which will be discussed at greater length in Chapter 5.

The second level on which language and socio-economic context interact is also connected with processes of change, but here both the language as a set of systems and the context are subject to change. The two sides of the argument are firstly that language change and changes in patterns of communication require material conditions which are favourable to such change, and secondly that socio-economic change presupposes the existence or creation of the communicative conditions favourable to the change. Thus language stands in a Janus-like relationship to changes in the socio-economic context, both creating the conditions required for the change to come about, and reacting and adapting to the change. A fuller discussion of this relationship will be presented in Chapter 2, which deals with the interaction under the conditions of German industrialisation in the 19th century.

Linguistic perceptions

So far, the discussion has been restricted to attempts to identify the roles and functions of language in the political process and to define relationships between linguistic and non-linguistic action. The view of politics on which the discussion has been based is that of an area of human communication comprising both linguistic and non-linguistic symbolic acts directed towards the creation of solidarity and the exercise of power.

There is a further dimension of the relationship between language and politics which now needs to be considered, and which will play an important part in the ensuing chapters. The practice of politics is to a large degree conscious and reflective, and among political actors and observers there is a general awareness that communication and language have a major, if not a central role to play. Two consequences emanate from this realisation: the first is that there is conscious reflection and deliberation on this role of language and communication, and the second is that such reflection often results in deliberate language policies and strategies aimed at establishing or challenging dominant discourses on both the inter-language and intra-language levels. Thus, although there might be fundamental objections to talking about the 'language of politics', there can be no doubt about the need to discuss the 'politics of language'. A consideration of the field of 'language and politics' must deal not only with the functions and roles of language in the political process, but also with perceptions of such roles and functions.

A consideration of linguistic perceptions, policies and strategies is of particular relevance for German, which is a highly politicised language, i.e., one with speakers who have an acute realisation of its political significance, as evidenced in the appreciation of the role of language in establishing a sense of national identity and in the efforts to 'purify' the language from alien elements as an act of liberation from foreign domination, as we shall see in Chapter 3. Linguistic sensitivisation in German political culture has manifested itself in the formation of an appreciable body of *Sprachkritik*, which at various times has not only concerned itself with actual language use but has also served as the basis for programmes of linguistic and political action. One example of the linking of reflection and practice can be seen in the development of *Germanistik* as an academic discipline and the political activities of *Germanisten* in the nineteenth century, which will form part of the discussion in Chapter 3.

Policies and strategies directed towards establishing dominant discourses at the intra-language level which will be dealt with in the following chapters include the overt control over the mass media established by the German fascists post-1933 (Chapter 4), the language conflict between German East and German West post-1945, the *semantische Kämpfe* of the 1970s and attempts to criminalise oppositional movements in the 1980s (Chapters 5 and 6).

Overview of relationships between language and politics

Following the preceding discussion, we are now in a position to summarise the relationship between language and politics which forms the basis for analysing aspects of the socio-cultural history of German in the following chapters.

A dualism of politics and language is rejected, as this is seen to represent a dualism of expression and content which, in its turn, presupposes the existence of a 'reality' independent of perception. In politics in particular, the human actor is a part of the reality, and cannot be divorced from it. The theoretical position being presented here is that language is constitutive of reality, and that political realities are very much linguistic constructs.

Language is seen primarily less as an underlying system than as language-in-text, through which certain communicative functions are realised, i.e., actions are performed.

Political activity is viewed as an area of communication comprising both linguistic and non-linguistic actions with socio-economic antecedents and consequences. Political action is primarily *linguistic* action, covering a wide range of activities from the telling of political jokes as an oppositional act to a formal declaration of war; even when non-linguistic action is predominant, it is based on and accompanied by linguistic action (e.g. regulation, justification, sanction).

Political action in both its linguistic and non-linguistic manifestations serves the three main functions of regulation, persuasion and bonding; these are directed towards preserving the integrity of the body politic, towards the establishment, legitimation and exercise of power – or with the converse, the challenging, disqualification and frustration of power – and towards the creation and maintenance of solidarity.

The role of linguistic action within the political process is twofold. Firstly it serves to establish dominant perceptions of reality and their discourses (including collective symbols and metaphors), together with the converse process of challenging dominant perceptions and discourses, and to prepare, legitimise and justify the socio-economic consequences of political action. Secondly it defines and creates group identity (at either the national or the sub-national level) and determines membership of the group by establishing common discourses either at the inter-language level (where the use of a particular language can itself become a political statement) or at the intra-language level, where different varieties can be linked with either high status or low status.

The relationship between language and the socio-economic environment is such that in the (fictitious) steady-state, a society will have developed certain communicative needs which are constitutive of social structures and processes. Changes in the socio-economic environment require changes in the communicative environment and in social structures and processes; socio-economic change then determines new communicative needs which must be met for further socio-economic change to come about. Thus communicative change and socio-economic change are continuously feeding into each other.

Communicative change can lead not only to changes in language use (e.g., the development of new text-types, the relative decline of certain discourses) but can also effect changes in the form and distribution of language structures and existential forms of the language (e.g., the relationship between standard and dialectal varieties).

In summary, then, we are proposing a view of language as an integral element of political activity, not just as a mirror and accompaniment to a politics which exists outside and independent of language.

Notes

1 'Fachsprache erscheint als: das Mittel einer optimalen Verständigung über ein Fachgebiet unter Fachleuten; sie ist gekennzeichnet durch einen spezifischen Fachwortschatz und spezielle Normen für die Auswahl, Verwendung und Frequenz gemeinsprachlicher und grammatischer Mittel; sie existiert nicht als selbständige Erscheinungsform der Sprache sondern wird in Fachtexten aktualisiert, die außer der fachsprachlichen Schicht immer gemeinsprachliche Elemente enthalten.' W. Schmidt, 'Charakter und gesellschaftliche Bedeutung der Fachsprache', *Sprachpflege* 18, 1969, p. 17

2 'politische Binnen- oder institutionsinterne Kommunikation', 'institutionsexterne Kommunikation' and 'öffentlich-politische Kommunikation' G. Strauß, U. Haß and G. Harras, *Brisante Wörter von Agitation bis Zeitgeist*, Berlin, New York, 1989

3 Strauß *et al.*, *Brisante Wörter*, p. 30

4 An example can be found in the following extract from a letter requiring certain information from a citizen: 'Diese Angaben sind zur Berechnung der Höhe des Förderungsbetrags erforderlich. Zur Abgabe dieser Erklärung als auch der erforderlichen Nachweise sind Sie gem. § 47 Abs. 4 i.V.m. §60 des 1. Buches SGB gesetzlich verpflichtet, unabhängig davon, ob Unterhalt geleistet wird oder nicht. '(Landratsamt Ansbach, 5.9.90). Lexically, this extract is marked by a number of technical terms – e.g., *Förderungsbetrag* – and syntactically by the impersonal construction in sentence 1 and the double passive in the second sentence, particularly in the subordinate clause. The striking conventional characteristic is the use of abbreviations in the main clause of sentence 2 (gem. = gemäß, Abs. = Absatz, i.V.m. = in Verbindung mit, SGB = Sozialgesetzbuch)

5 'ideologische Einmischungen, z.B. mit Wortbildungen wie *Volksaktie, soziale Marktwirtschaft* oder *Bürger in Uniform*. Solche Ausdrücke werden primär im Hinblick auf die Öffentlichkeit gebildet und gehören deshalb eher zur öffentlichen (Meinungs)Sprache.', Strauß *et al.*, *Brisante Wörter*, p. 31

6 'Für den Bereich der öffentlich-politischen Kommunikation ... ist meinungs- oder ideologiesprachlicher Gebrauch charakteristisch und mit ihm das gesamte ideologische Vokabular. Die Meinungssprache vermittelt Deutungen, die in bestimmter, oft ideologischer Sehweise von der Wirklichkeit gegeben werden.' Strauß *et al.*, *Brisante Wörter*, pp. 31–2

7 J. Klein (ed.), *Politische Semantik. Beiträge zur politischen Sprachverwendung*, Opladen, 1989

8 '– Insofern der gesamte Bereich der Politik in Wörtern formuliert ist, stellt sich die Frage nach der Gliederung des politischen Wortschatzes...
– Insofern die politische Auseinandersetzung in Wörtern ausgetragen wird und teilweise auch um die Wörter selbst gestritten wird, stellen sich die Fragen nach der Kampffunktion von Wörtern und nach Typen des Kampfes um Wörter ...
– Insofern der einzelne Kampf um Wörter meist nur Teil eines umfassenden politischen Ringens um die Vormacht ganzer Wortfelder ist, werden die Begriffe des "dominanten politischen Wortfeldes" und des "konnotativ integrierten Wortfeldes" eingeführt, mit deren Hilfe dann die Schwerpunkte der Entwicklung seit den Gründungsjahren der Bundesrepublik diachronisch skizziert wird.' Klein, *Politische Semantik*, p. 4

9 *Institutionsvokabular, Ressortvokabular, allgemeines Interaktionsvokabular* and *Ideologievokabular*

10 *Ideologiesprache, Institutionssprache* and *Fachsprache des verwalteten Sachgebiets*, W. Dieckmann, *Sprache in der Politik. Einführung in die Pragmatik und Semantik der politischen Sprache*, Heidelberg, 1969, p. 50

11 'Eigene fachsprachliche Züge enthält am ehesten das politische Institutionsvokabular.', Klein, *Politische Semantik*, p. 5

12 'Bezeichnungen für die staatlichen **Organisationen**, die politischen Institutionen und deren Untergliederungen: *Bundesstaat, Parlamentarische Demokratie, Bundesrepublik Deutschland* ...
– Bezeichnungen für staatliche und politische **Rollen**: *Mandat, Amt, Bundespräsident, Bundestagspräsident(in)* ...

– Bezeichnungen für **kodifizierte Normierungen** politisch institutionellen Handelns: *Charta der Vereinigten* (sic) *Nationen, Grundgesetz* ...
– Politik-spezifische Bezeichnungen für politische **Handlungen, Prozesse** und **Zustände:** *freie, gleiche und geheime Wahlen,* ... *Volksbegehren, konstruktives Mißtrauensvotum.*', Klein, *Politische Semantik,* pp. 45-6

13 'Politik bezieht sich auf alle öffentlich relevanten Bereiche. Politische Sprachverwendung integriert daher in vielfältiger Weise Vokabular aus den verschiedenen Fachsprachen der zahlreichen Sachbereiche, für die politische Entscheidungen getroffen werden und für die es Ressorts gibt.' Klein, *Politische Semantik,* p. 6

14 'Sprache in der Politik ist tief durchtränkt von allgemeinsprachlichen Bezeichnungen für menschliche Interaktion und ihre verschiedenen Aspekte. ... Dazu gehört auch ein umfangreiches Vokabular zur Bezeichnung sprachlicher Handlungen.' Klein, *Politische Semantik,* p. 7

15 'Das Ideologievokabular umfaßt die Wörter, in denen politische Gruppierungen ihre Deutungen und Bewertungen der politisch-sozialen Welt, ihre Prinzipien und Prioritäten formulieren.' Klein, *Politische Semantik,* p. 7

16 see p. 29 below

17 'Die Tatsache, daß sich in den Lexemen des Ideologie-Vokabulars die grundlegenden politischen Orientierungen – und damit "Meinungen" – einer politischen Gruppierung zeigen, könnte zu dem Schluß verleiten, Ideologiesprache mit Meinungssprache gleichzusetzen. Doch Ideologiesprache ist nur eine Teilmenge der politischen Meinungssprache.' Klein, *Politische Semantik,* p.10

18 e.g., Strauß *et al.*, *Brisante Wörter,* p. 31

19 Klein, *Politische Semantik,* p. 11

20 Klein, *Politische Semantik,* p. 4

21 '(Denn) die Schlagwortforschung leidet unter einem Übel, das für den modernen Linguisten viele der Untersuchungen zu dem – größeren "Komplex Sprache + Politik" ungenießbar machen muß, darunter nämlich, daß "diesem Forschungsgebiet ein sprachinternes Spezifikum fehlt: Es gibt kein distinktives Merkmal, daß die Sprache der Politik von anderen unterscheiden würde". So W. Herrlitz in der Rezension eines der Bücher, die zu den von der Forschung am häufigsten rezipierten des Komplexes gehören, W. Dieckmanns "Sprache in der Politik".' W. Wülfing, *Schlagworte des Jungen Deutschland. Mit einer Einführung in die Schlagwortforschung,* Berlin, 1982, p. 11

22 '... politisches Handeln und Reden (geschieht) im Rahmen aufgabenorientierter, häufig strategischer Sprachspiele... Der Zugang zu solchen Sprachspielen ist dabei nicht direkt über die Annahme eines politischen Wortschatzes als eines Fach- oder Sonderwortschatzes zu erwarten, sondern über die Untersuchung kommunikativer Situationstypen oder Textsorten der unterschiedlichen Funktionsbereiche.'Strauß *et al.*, *Brisante Wörter,* pp. 29-30

23 'Mit dem bloßen Text als einer geordneten, strukturierten Folge sprachlicher Zeichen erfassen wir aber noch nicht die "Wirklichkeit" des Textes. Jeder Text "verwirklicht" sich erst in einem komplexen Sinn- und

Handlungszusammenhang.' H. Grünert, 'Politische Geschichte und Sprachgeschichte', *Sprache und Literatur in Wissenschaft und Unterricht*, 14. 2. 1983, p. 44

24 G. Leech, *Semantics*, Harmondsworth, 1974

25 Leech, *Semantics*, p. 49

26 Leech, *Semantics*, p. 48

27 'Jeder Text "verwirklicht" sich erst in einem komplexen Sinn- und Handlungszusammenhang. Damit meine ich das ganze Bedingungsfeld des Textes, seine kommunikative Vorgeschichte und Intention, seine Handlungsbeteiligten und Handlungsbetroffenen, individual- und sozialpsychische Bedingungen, Situation, soziales Umfeld und allgemeine Herrschaftsbedingungen.' Grünert, 'Politische Geschichte und Sprachgeschichte' , p. 44

28 I.e. using extra-linguistic criteria to define and analyse linguistic phenomena

29 F. Palmer, *Semantics. A new outline*, Cambridge, 1976, p. 154–5

30 'Das regulative Sprachspiel', 'Das instrumentale/begehrende Sprachspiel', 'Das integrative Sprachspiel', 'Das informativ-persuasive Sprachspiel'. Grünert, 'Politische Geschichte und Sprachgeschichte', pp. 51–5

31 'Die politischen Texte lassen sich in vier Handlungstypen einteilen, die sich allmählich in wechselseitiger Beziehung mit Typen politischen Handelns herausgebildet haben: regulativ-stabilisierend, prospektiv-verändernd, integrativ und publizitär-persuasiv.' K. Bochmann (ed.), *Eigenschaften und linguistische Analyse politischer Texte*, Berlin, 1986, p. 11

32 'Politische Texte ... dienen in regulativ-stabilisierender Funktion der Machterhaltung. ...
Texte in prospektiv-verändernder Funktion entstehen vor allem da, wo politisch-soziale Subjekte ihre Forderungen stellen, Wünsche und Bitten vortragen, ihren Willen bekunden oder ihre Ansprüche geltend machen. ...
Wenn die Texte mit integrativer Funktion zur Stabilisierung und/oder Abgrenzung von politischen Gemeinschaften beitragen, die Texte mit regulativ-stabilisierender und solche mit prospektiv-verändernder Funktion unmittelbar politische Handlungen darstellen, so dienen die Texte des *publizitär-persuasiven* Handlungstyps vor allem der Motivation, Vorbereitung und Koordination des politischen Handelns, zur politischen Bewußtseinsbildung nicht nur innerhalb politischer Gemeinschaften, sondern auch zur Meinungsbildung und Ausweitung des Konsens über die politische Gemeinschaft hinaus.' Bochmann (ed.), *Eigenschaften und linguistische Analyse,* pp. 12–13

33 'Sprache ist nicht nur ein wichtiges Mittel des Politikers, sondern das Element, in dem sein Beruf sich vollzieht. Was er auch tut, auf welchem Felde er auch wirkt, stets arbeitet er mit dem geschriebenen, gehörten oder gesprochenen Wort. ... Das Leben des Politikers ist ... Umgang mit dem Wort.' M. Greiffenhagen (ed.), *Kampf um Wörter – Politische Begriffe im Meinungsstreit*, Munich/Vienna, 1980, p. 9

34 'ein zu enger Begriff des Politischen als "staatlichen oder auf den Staat bezogenen Handelns und Redens" (ist) zu korrigieren. Vielmehr sehen wir Politik als in sich differenzierten Großbereich der Kommunikation, in dem

über Angelegenheiten öffentlichen Interesses gehandelt wird, in dem Meinungen gefaßt werden und Prozesse ablaufen, die der Herstellung und Durchsetzung verbindlicher oder auch umstrittener gesellschaftlicher Entscheidungen dienen.

Politisches Handeln ist somit auf weite Strecken sprachliches und kommunikatives Handeln oder bedarf doch zumindest der sprachlichen Vermittlung. Strauß *et al.*, *Brisante Wörter*, p. 29

35 J. Steele, 'Going on to the next party', *The Guardian*, 26 August 1991, p.19

36 'Sprache ermöglicht dem Menschen das Leben in Gruppen.' Greiffenhagen, *Kampf um Wörter*, p. 11

37 'Sprache ermöglicht dem Menschen das Leben in Gruppen. Sie tut das auf folgende Weisen …
1. als intellektuelle Wirklichkeitserfahrung,
2. als Institution, die den einzelnen von Entscheidungsüberforderungen entlastet,
3. als Träger gesellschaftlicher Normierung,
4. als Instrument gesellschaftlicher Kontrolle.' Greiffenhagen (ed.), *Kampf um Wörter* , p. 11

38 M. Shapiro, *Language and Political Understanding*, New Haven and London, 1981, p.20

39 'Die Sprache, das Wort, dient nicht nur dazu, einen Gedanken auszudrücken und nach außen in Erscheinung treten zu lassen, um dem anderen den bereits fertigen, noch nicht ausgesprochenen Gedanken zu übermitteln. In der Sprache formulieren wir den Gedanken, und indem wir ihn formulieren, formen wir ihn auch. Die Sprache ist mehr als das äußere Werkzeug des Gedankens. Sie ist im Prozeß des Denkens als Form, die mit seinem Inhalt verbunden ist, mitenthalten.' S.L. Rubinstein, *Sein und Bewußtsein*, s'Gravenhage 1971, p.150 – after Dieckmann *Politische Sprache, politische Kommunikation*, pp. 43–4

40 Shapiro, *Language and Political Understanding*, p. 11

41 Shapiro, *Language and Political Understanding*, p. 20

42 Shapiro, *Language and Political Understanding*, p. 20

43 Fritjof Capra, *The Turning Point. Science, society and the rising culture*, New York, 1983, pp. 86–7

44 S. Louvish, 'A loud foghorn in the mist of newspeak', *The Guardian*, 4 July 1991

45 Shapiro, *Language and Political Understanding*, p.231

46 '…an ideology is … a coherent set of beliefs, attitudes and values on the basis of which persons interpret human relations and construct their own position and choices'. Shapiro, *Language and Political Understanding*, p. 200

47 For an analysis within the UK context, see M. Townson, 'Manifestations of Policy', *Englisch-Amerikanische Studien* Heft 3,4/88, pp. 407ff

2 Language and socio-economic change in nineteenth-century Germany

Introduction

In the opening chapter, we suggested that a relationship of inter-dependence and a process of interaction exists between language and its socio-economic context. The aim of the present chapter is to use nineteenth-century developments in the German language as a case study to demonstrate some of the interrelationships and interactions which obtain between language development and socio-economic and socio-cultural change.

Nineteenth-century Germany has been chosen for two main reasons. In Germany, the nineteenth century was a period charac-terised by major socio-economic and political change, being marked by the shift from a territorially fragmented feudal society with a rural base and oral modes of communication to a centralist, technologically advanced capitalist nation-state in which the written mode gained in importance. Language change in the nineteenth century is well documented, with a large body of textual data on which to draw. Paradoxically, however, it is a period which, until recently, has been largely ignored by language historians. None of the 'classic' twentieth-century accounts of the history of the German language from Behagel[1] to Eggers[2] devoted much attention to linguistic developments in the nineteenth century, and it is suggested that there are perhaps three main reasons for this apparent neglect.

The first two, which are very closely linked, are that these accounts, particularly of developments in the eighteenth century, tended to concentrate on the literary language. As Eric Blackall[3] and others have shown, the standardisation of the literary lan-guage can effectively be regarded as having been completed by

1800, with the process being documented and expedited by seminal works such as Gottsched's *Grundlegung einer deutschen Sprachkunst* (first published in 1748, with a sixth edition by 1776) and Adelung's *Versuch eines vollständigen grammatisch-kritischen Wörterbuches Der Hochdeutschen Mundart* (first published 1774). Thus, the nineteenth century has often been seen as a consolidation phase in which no radically new systemic developments took place. It was in such systemic developments, i.e., in the reconstruction and development of linguistic *forms*, that historical linguistics was more interested – and here the influence of the neo-grammarians makes itself particularly strongly felt. There were, of course, further moves towards formal standardisation, both in orthography (Duden) and in pronunciation – or, to be more precise, orthoepics (Siebs). Those formal changes which did take place, particularly in the evolution of urban koines (*Umgangssprachen*), affected registers with which linguistics had not hitherto concerned itself, and which were not amenable to the methods of geographical dialectology, which traditionally worked from the predominantly rural base which characterised much of feudal German society prior to about 1810.

The third possible reason is, somewhat paradoxically, that the nineteenth century is regarded primarily as the century in which historical linguistics was put on a 'scientific' footing – and thus attention has concentrated on the reception of the historical efforts of nineteenth-century linguistics and possibly on questions of the status of the German language rather than on the historicity of the language in the nineteenth century itself. This tendency is then strengthened by the way in which nineteenth-century German linguistics paid relatively little attention to recording contemporary language usage, and in which those attempts to deal with the contemporary language were, for reasons which will be discussed later, largely concerned with questions of the 'purity' of the language. The lack of interest in synchronic language usage was determined by the view, prevalent before the neo-grammarians, of language as an organism which obeyed its own laws of development and decay, which motivated the desire of linguists to turn away from the contemporary language to earlier stages which displayed 'youth', 'freshness' and 'vigour'.

The traditional emphasis of historical linguistics on formal developments meant that texts were regarded mainly as invento-

ries of forms, with the result that their textuality was ignored. As
we have already indicated, however, language use is transmitted as
text, and it is the types and forms of text which allow conclusions
to be drawn about cultural continuity and change, not the features
of language as an abstracted formal system. Our views of language
variation and change are functions of the types of text studied,
and it is suggested that the neglect of nineteenth-century linguistic processes in the classic accounts was due in part to a failure to
consider a sufficiently wide range of texts and in part to a failure to
take account of the textuality and contextuality of the data. The
nineteenth century saw the genesis, development and expansion
of a number of text types which both reflect and bring about important changes in the communicative environment; as Joachim
Schildt has shown,[4] the establishment or predominance of linguistic phenomena is due at least in part to the text-types in which
they occur, so that accounts of language change must be related to
more general changes in the communicative environment.

It is the increasing realisation of the importance of *text* as being
more than the (possibly 'incomplete') source of data for a construction of the underlying formal system of language that supports much of the enhanced interest currently being shown in
socio-cultural aspects of language change, as reflected for example
in the work by Schildt and recent work by Maas.[5] For Maas, the
objective of a socio-cultural language analysis is the reconstruction of an historically-determined language practice, which is
conditioned by the social contradictions which it articulates, and
therefore a linguistics has to reconstruct these contradictions.[6]

From the aspect of linguistic theory, we are thus turning away
from the (possibly artificial) distinction between '*langue*' and '*parole*' propagated by structuralist linguistics in the wake of de
Saussure, and we are definitely turning our backs on Chomsky's
aggregated fiction of the 'ideal speaker-hearer in a homogeneous
speech community' to concentrate on actual communicative interaction in a heterogeneous society.

An awareness of the importance of the socio-economic context
for the historical development of language is one which, in recent
years, was at the heart of studies in the history of the German
language conducted in the GDR (here the name of Joachim Schildt
can stand for many others) and has come to play an increasing
role in West German *Sprachgermanistik*, with the call for a 'prag-

matic history of language'.[7] It is no coincidence that this 'pragmatic history' has concerned itself to a large degree with the development of the German language in the nineteenth century.

By concentrating on the wider aspects of language development, we are reforging the link with a view of *Germanistik* as *Kulturwissenschaft* which inspired much of the nineteenth-century work in the subject, and which, for example, lay behind the understanding and definition of the term *Germanist* not only by Jacob Grimm, but also by other representatives of the subject, as evidenced for example by Hermann Bausinger's account of the views of Moriz Heyne, who held that the task of German philology was to record the whole spiritual and intellectual development of the nation, and not just that recorded in literature.[8]

The view of language that we are promoting here is one in which the way language itself is used becomes an historical document – in other words, language is not simply the medium through which historical evidence is transmitted, but is itself part of that evidence. Thus the analysis of language assumes added significance as an instrument of social, economic and political analysis – and language assumes a wider cultural, or even ethnological, significance. It is, however, important to stress again that what we are talking about is not so much language as a system, but language as it is used. Eugenio Coseriu attempted to resolve the dichotomy of *langue* and *parole* by postulating a third level of *usage* as an intermediary norm of textual realisation,[9] and it is usage in this sense with which we are concerned here. What is not being propagated here is the kind of content analysis which Weisgerber and others conducted, trying to relate specific grammatical phenomena to cultural features (for example in Weisgerber's article 'Der Mensch im Akkusativ'[10]).

A case study of the interaction between language developments and socio-economic change in the nineteenth century is, however, not only of 'pragmatic' significance but can also furnish valuable theoretical insights into processes of language change, as language history provides a valuable source of data on language change and variation and on the links between linguistic and socio-cultural history.

An approach which viewed language only as evidence of socio-economic and socio-cultural change would however fail to recognise the role of language in the processes of such change; to repeat the theoretical position which is being advanced here, language is not just a reflection of a social reality external to itself, but is also constitutive of that reality. As the reality is one which is subject to change, language has a role to play in that change; socio-economic and socio-cultural change implies communicative change, and unless the communicative conditions are such that change can be facilitated, then the change will not take place. Thus, not only must a theory of language change take account of the role of socio-economic and socio-cultural change, but theories of socio-economic and socio-cultural change must also take account of the role of communicative and linguistic change.

The nature and theory of language change

For linguistic theory, the study of language history provides a valuable source of data on the mechanisms of language change, and on processes of language variation, for which a theory of language must allow.

Language is subject to the dialectic of continuity and change which is central to all human institutions, and indeed to life in general. As Polenz suggests, language is fundamentally unstable because of its variability, and the balance between different variants can easily be upset.[11]

Mattheier stresses the social aspects of change by regarding language change as a form of social action in which speakers are testing their language against their communication requirements.[12]

If language is indeed characterised by variability and change, then a theory of language must allow for change, i.e., a theory of language must also subsume a theory of language change.

In a survey of theoretical aspects of language change, Mattheier discusses the conditions which must be met by a satisfactory theory of language change. He sees language change as a form of linguistic action, which can be either internally or externally motivated. Any comprehensive theory of language change must take account of both the communicative-functional and the articulatory-perceptive aspects, and a theory which fails to take consider both types of change is seen as deficient.[13]

Table 1 Aspects of a theory of language change

Actions of linguistic change			
	Linguistic actions (without individual intentional change)		Intentional actions
Articulatory-perceptive apparatus	Language as an instrument and as a deposit of earlier language actions	Social conditions for language actions	
		Social, situational and regional conditions	
		Formation of variants through processes of re-defining patterns of linguistic action in response to constantly changing social, situational and regional conditions	Intentional formation of variants with the aim of effecting language change
		Goal-orientation of varieties through general processes of social change with communicative relevance, changes in communication maxims and language value-structures	Language policy, Language planning, Language education, Language standardisation, Language critique, Language evaluation
Articulatory-perceptive theories of language change/ 'Sound shift theories'	System-oriented or structuralist theories of language change	Theories of language change oriented towards communicative functions or social situation and dialect	Theories of language change with direct social orientation

Source: K. Mattheier 'Allgemeine Aspekte einer Theorie des Sprachwandels', in W. Besch, D. Reichman and S. Sonderregger (eds), *Sprachgeschichte*, 1984/85.

Mattheier suggests that actions of linguistic change can either be non-intentional or intentional; the motivation for non-intentional change can be either language-internal or external, while intentional change is externally motivated. Internally motivated change is primarily causal (i.e., determined by the language system and processes such as co-articulation, analogy and redundancy) whereas externally motivated change is primarily final (i.e., determined by the ends which linguistic communication seeks to serve).

The category of intentional change is an important one; it includes language planning and language policies, with such features as terminological innovation and linguistic standardisation, but has often been neglected.[14]

We can postulate that the failure to afford adequate theoretical consideration to intentional change is probably a result of prevailing views either of language as an organism obeying its own laws or of language as a reflection of a material base; such views ignore the constitutive role of language in social activity.

The model which Mattheier presents of aspects of a theory of language change[15] (Table 1) gives priority to the non-intentional/intentional distinction and derives the resultant categories from it.

In our analysis, we shall be concentrating on those aspects of change covered by the last two columns, examining intentional change and socially and situationally motivated non-intentional change (communicative-functional change).

Survey of relevant changes in German socio-economic environment in the nineteenth century

If we are to consider the interaction between language change and social change, it is useful to remind ourselves at this point briefly of the main socio-economic and socio-cultural changes in the nineteenth century, and particularly of those which can be regarded as relevant for linguistic change over the same period.

Basically, what we are concerned with are the changing patterns and conditions of communication resulting from the development of a largely individual-based agrarian feudal economy to an institution-based industrial capitalist economy.

Whether the term 'revolution' is an appropriate one for the processes under review is only of marginal concern, but we can probably subscribe to the view put forward by Jaeger that the

Industrial Revolution had a more radical effect on everyday life than any other complex event in recent history.[16]

Among the radical changes were a rapid growth in population, increasing urbanisation, new forms of transport and other inventions and innovations, especially the development of industrial means of production with its attendant technicalisation. The effects of such a revolutionary process also shook the traditional social order.[17]

This last point is one with which not all commentators might agree, and one could cite here the failure of the German bourgeois revolution to upset the established power structures with which the bourgeoisie finally threw in its lot. Kitchen, for example, draws the following conclusion from his analysis of socio-economic change in nineteenth-century Germany:

Industrialisation failed to bring bourgeois democracy to Germany, just as it failed to do so in Japan or Russia. In its place was Bismarck's subtle, cynical and often brutal Bonapartist dictatorship hidden from the eyes of so many historians by the constitutional trappings and universal suffrage that failed to fool his contemporaries. Industry had been effectively modernised ... but the social structure remained essentially unchanged [18]

and Böhme comments as follows: 'Thus, the economic reorganisation of the Prusso-German state in 1879 meant a refounding of the state on the basis of principles which were pre-industrial, estate-oriented and autocratic'.[19]

Without wishing to become embroiled in historical controversy at this stage, it is important to point out that the form of political culture developed during the nineteenth century has important consequences for political discourse, and to the political culture belongs the construction of social relationships.

Of importance too for the development of political discourse and patterns of communication is the redrawing of political boundaries and power relations and the creation of political institutions, which Jaeger omits from his list, but to which Kitchen refers as 'constitutional trappings and universal suffrage'. We shall return to this point later.

Let us now come back to Jaeger's list and establish some of the *realia*.

Population explosion

From 1800 to 1900 the population of Germany increased by some 250 per cent from 23 to 56.4 million, a rate of growth which outstripped that of both France and England.

Urbanisation

Despite the high rate of overall population growth, the growth in the rural population was relatively low, from 17 to 22 million (29 per cent), as a result of migration to the urban areas. The trends are illustrated by figures quoted by Bechtel, who points to a change in the definition of a 'large city': whereas in 1808, this was applied to a town with at least 10,000 inhabitants, by the mid-century the term *Großstadt* denoted an urban community of 100,000 or more. In 1850 only 5 cities qualified for the title, but the number increased to 8 by 1870, 26 by 1890, 33 by 1900 and 45 by 1910, with an attendant increase in the number of medium-sized towns. The rate of increase was higher in Germany than other European states.[20]

The process was, however, still a relatively slow one: in the 1870s Germany was still primarily an agricultural state; in terms of the number of those employed, industry did not achieve parity with the primary sector until the early 1890s.

Urbanisation was only one aspect of the large-scale migration which took place during the century; there was a shift of population from the eastern areas to Berlin, the industrial areas of Central Germany, and finally in the Rhineland and Westphalia.[21] The main axis of economic activity became concentrated along a line from the Ruhr to Berlin and Upper Silesia.

New forms of transport

For Germany this means principally the development of the railways, which not only helped overcome the territorial fragmentation of Germany and improve the mobility of the population and the movement of goods, but also acted as one of the main motors of the first phase of industrialisation up to about 1860. The length of track in use increased from 500 km in 1840 and 8000 km in 1855 to 28,000km by 1875. The increased mobility made possible by advances in transport were bound to have an effect on patterns of communication.

Inventions and innovations

Here we can count such factors as developments in mining and steel production (for example, the opening of the deep mines of the Ruhr and the introduction of the Bessemer and Siemens-Martin processes), the intensification of agriculture and the growth of the chemical industry, the development of telegraphy and Werner Siemens' discovery of the principle of the electric dynamo, which had a revolutionary potential as significant as the invention of the steam engine.

Industrial mass production and the attendant technicalisation of labour

This not only affected the working conditions of the industrial workers, with an increasing division of labour (specialisation) and alienation, but also required novel forms of industrial organisation (development of an administrative bureaucracy) and constitution (e.g., the development of joint-stock companies – *Aktiengesellschaften*) and new modes of economic thought. In addition, it placed demands on the education system which the classical patterns of the grammar school (*Humanistisches Gymnasium*) and the traditional universities were unable to meet. Here we can mention the spread of universal education and the development of the *Polytechnikum* and the engineering academies (the precursors of the *Technische Hochschulen*).

Industrialisation, specialisation and technocratisation also placed new demands on public administration, which was forced to take on an increased regulatory role, which led not only to a quantitative increase in the number of civil servants, but also to a qualitative change with an increase in the number of specialist ministries.

Political organisation

Even if power structures did not essentially change all that much over the century, there can be no doubt that there were far-reaching changes in the political map of Germany during the century. In 1800, the 'Holy Roman Empire' comprised some 314 sovereign imperial territories and 1,475 imperial knights. Society retained an estate structure where individual classes were sharply distinguished from each other. The predominant form of government was still that of absolutism, without formalised constitutions. Although the ideas behind the French Revolution were received in Germany, it took the force of Napoleonic arms to introduce them, albeit for only a short time.

The *Heiliges Römisches Reich Deutscher Nation* formally ceased to exist in July 1806, to be superseded after the defeat of Napoleonic France by the *Deutscher Bund*, the constitution of which represented a step backwards in Germany's political development, with the restoration of conservative and monarchic forms of government.[22]

Any cautious initial steps there may have been towards political liberalisation were quickly stopped by the notorious Karlsbader Beschlüsse of 1819, and further symbolic attempts at liberalisation such as the Hambacher Fest of 1832 and the Frankfurter Wachensturm of 1833 were quickly nipped in the bud.

The years after the Congress of Vienna saw a process of concentration and centralisation within the Deutscher Bund. Sixty years after the dissolution of the Holy Roman Empire under the force of French arms, the Second German Empire was founded in the wake of the success of Prussian arms against Denmark, Austria and France; although a confederative structure was maintained, there was no doubt that the creation of the Second Empire cemented Prussia's hegemony. The years after 1871 saw internal consolidation followed by attempts at external expansion, both in Central Europe and overseas, with the German Empire increasingly seeking to challenge the 'traditional' maritime power of Britain. The move towards external expansion was a response partly to the depression which set in from about 1873 onwards, when excessive productive capacity strove for outlets beyond Germany's borders, and partly to the social tensions arising within Germany, which the German government attempted to defuse by providing an alternative focus of attention. The social tensions were due at least in part to the rise of the working class as a 'fourth estate' which was effectively cut off from participation in the political process.

In terms of political organisation, the years following the Congress of Vienna saw the establishment of formal constitutions in the German states with varying degrees of parliamentary participation, and a growing involvement of the state in social and economic affairs. This involvement was both regulatory and direct; two examples of direct involvement are to be found in the social legislation of Bismarck's administration following the imperial decree of 1881 that the damage caused to society was not to be repaired exclusively by the repression of the excesses of the Social Democratic movement, but also by promoting the welfare of the workers[23] and in the entrepreneurial role of the state in such areas as rail transport, mining and metals. Henderson sees in the industrial activities of the Prussian state an expression of an underlying autocratic and paternalistic culture: 'Tradition died hard in Prussia, and the notion that the country was a vast estate to be managed by the King and his advisers survived into the modern age of steam-engines and railways.'[24]

Economic policy throughout the century was marked by a tension between liberal and protectionist approaches, with the lines between the two camps being drawn in different ways at different times. By the end of the century, however, the macroeconomic landscape was marked by protectionism and by industrial concentration and cartellisation.

In summary, then, although basic power structures may not have changed much in the course of the century, with agrarian feudalism being superseded by industrial feudalism, there were far-reaching changes in patterns of economic activity, in demographic structure and social conditions, and in at least the externals of political organisation and public administration. All of these changes created and were dependent on new patterns of communication, which were mainly realised by linguistic means.

Prerequisites for industrialisation and their realisation

Having sketched in the main outlines of socio-economic development, we can now turn to the changes brought about in the communicative environment and relate these to the socio-economic change. The changes in patterns of communication can be approached by looking at some of the material prerequisites for industrialisation and examining the communicative prerequisites and consequences of their realisation.

Material prerequisites and their realisation

It is possible to identify four necessary material preconditions for the changes brought about by the industrialisation of Germany: 1, the availability of a pool of cheap labour, 2, an adequate capital base, 3, technical innovation and training, and 4, secure markets. The fulfilment of these conditions can be summarised as follows:

Labour

The beginning of the nineteenth century saw the formal ending of feudalism (which took place in Prussia in 1810). Welcome though such a development may have been, it did mean that not only were the obligations of the subjects towards their feudal lord cancelled, but also the obligations of the feudal lords towards their subjects. The rights of the feudal subjects included a security of tenure (*Bauernschutz*), and the abolition of this right had a number of far-reaching consequences. It enabled the landowners to organise agriculture on a more 'industrial' basis with a reduced workforce, and the options facing rural workers were bleak; they could either stay on the land and try their luck as waged labourers (and risk sliding further down the social scale as day-labourers) or they could leave the land and face an uncertain future in the expanding urban centres. The other option was emigration, and the nineteenth century saw the development of all three scenarios.

Capital

The capital base was secured with a combination of state aid (which was perhaps of particular importance for the development of the railway system) and the growth of the *Aktiengesellschaften*, with its attendant rise in the power and influence of the banks, as both providers of capital and determiners of business policy.

Technical innovation

The pattern of technical development can be traced from the transfer of existing technologies (particularly steam technology and railway engineering) from more advanced industrial societies – particularly Great Britain – through the adaptation and refinement of these technologies to the development of new technologies (particularly in the fields of electrical engineering, telecommunications, and chemical engineering).

Secure markets

A sufficiently large domestic market was achieved through the process of national unification. (Although it is not being suggested that this materialistic motive was the sole driving force behind German unification, it is interesting to note that the institutional forerunner of the German *Reich* was an *economic* union – the *Zollverein*.)

These, then, were the primary conditions which had to be met, and the fulfilment of which was to have a profound effect on patterns of communication in the nineteenth century and beyond.

The communicative environment

Language varieties

At the beginning of the nineteenth century, it is possible to distinguish four main varieties within which the German language operates: the literary language, regional *Umgangssprachen*, urban *Umgangssprachen* and territorial and local dialects. Schildt speaks here of *Existenzformen* of the language, which he sees as being characterised by use within a particular territorial area by a socially determined class of speakers to perform specific communicative functions within a specific mode (oral or written) with a definite systemic structure.[25]

The labels used for the varieties follow those used by Schildt and others[26], but a word needs to be said about the label 'literary language' for the 'standard language' or High German. At the end of the eighteenth century, the literary language is to all intents and purposes identical with the standard language, which was also establishing itself as the language of academic discourse. High German had, however, not yet gained wide currency as a 'public' language in other areas such as state administration; administration was still very much a 'private' affair of the autocratic courts, and the communication was mainly internal. In the course of the century, however, the public domain grew, and that, together with changes in the literary registers, means that by 1900 it will be necessary to make a distinction between the 'standard language' and the 'language of literature'.

Following Schildt's criteria, we can schematise the relationship between the four main varieties as shown in Table 2.

Table 2 Relationship between the four main varieties of the German language

Variety	Geographical spread	Social spread (no. of users)	Mode	Structure
Literatursprache	'National'	Narrow: aristocracy/ 'Bildungsbürger'/ intellectuals	Written	Codified
Umgangssprache (1)	Regional	Less narrow : landed aristocracy/bourgeoisie	Oral	Open
Umgangssprache (2)	Urban	Wider : petty bourgeois/artisans	Oral	Open
Territorialdialekte	Rural district	Wide : 'peasants'	Oral	Open

Inasfar as the relationships between the four categories are concerned, we can postulate relatively little cross-fertilisation, although *Umgangssprache* (1) drew on both the literary language and the rural dialects.

When we come to examine the language changes which occur under the conditions of industrialisation, it will be necessary to examine not only the possible emergence of new varieties and the internal changes within the varieties, but also the relationship of the varieties to each other. It is also necessary to consider the communicative environment within which the language varieties operate; Mattheier[27] distinguishes here between *innere Sprachgeschichte*, meaning systemic changes within the language, and *äußere Sprachgeschichte*, changes in the communicative environment, which he sees as being closely linked to each other in the nineteenth century. Changes in the communicative environment (*äußere Sprachgeschichte*) in their turn are closely related to socio-economic change. 'External' history comprises five main areas: the changing patterns of variants, media history, the history of text types, the history of meanings, and the history of linguistics and the study of language history. In each of these areas, linguistic developments are closely linked with the history of the German speech community and its members. Shifts in the patterns of variants relate to social change occasioned by modernisation processes, media developments are connected with the revolutionary changes in the storage and transmission of text, new text types arise to deal with the manifold changes in social institutions, changing views of the world link with semantic change, and the changing position of language in society occasions changes in the role of the observers of language.[28]

In the following sections, we shall be examining the linguistic and communicative changes under the first four of these categories; the consideration of the fifth category will form part of the subject-matter of Chapter 3.

Development of the body politic

With reference to new patterns of political activity and organisation, we can point to the rise of constitutionalism and parliamentarism as significant factors in nineteenth-century Germany. These both generated new terminologies and – more importantly – gave rise to new patterns of discourse as political activity shifted to the public arena. Linked with the shift of political activity to the public domain was an increased level of popular participation in political processes – although in view of what was said before, it would be an exaggeration to claim that democratic principles became firmly established in nineteenth-century Germany.

The movement towards the role of 'the people' as sovereign, and the progress of politics from the private concern of absolute aristocratic rulers to a matter of general public interest and concern can be illustrated with five short texts spanning the years from 1784 to 1919 – i.e., bracketing our period of interest.

In 1784, Friedrich II had issued an edict that denied the right of any subject to take any public stand on affairs of state; politics was a matter for the princes and their courts.[29]

With the restoration of 1815, the *Deutsche Bundesakte*, proclaimed by the 'souveräne Fürsten und freie Städte Deutschlands' (Sovereign Princes and Free Cities of Germany), does at least acknowledge the existence of their subjects as individuals – though not as a collective 'public' – but any rights these may have derive from the beneficence of the princes, as laid down in Article 18, which still regards 'subjects' as the passive recipients of the political decisions of their political 'masters'.[30]

The abortive effort to create a Second Empire in 1849 was marked by an attempt to break out of the subject-monarch schema and establish the legitimation of a parliamentary body which had the right to proclaim a constitution.[31]

How far ahead of its time this attempt was in terms of *realpolitik* is demonstrated by the Imperial Constitution of 1871, which still maintains the sovereignty of princes to form an alliance 'for the protection of their territory and for the welfare of the German people'.[32]

At least, however, the people have progressed from the explicit state of 'subjects', and there is some acknowledgement of their membership of a body politic, not just a collection of individuals.

It was not until 1919, however, with the apparent total collapse of the old order, that the 'spirit' of 1849 is incorporated into a valid constitution which the German people give themselves, and in which 'the people' are constituted as the sovereign ('all power emanates from the people').[33]

The nineteenth century is marked then by a gradual popularisation of the political process, with politics becoming a matter of increasing public interest and concern, which is a further manifestation of the development of a mass society.

With increased participation in the political process, the century sees a development of the concept of the public sphere (*Öffentlichkeit*), and growing attention is paid to public opinion, and to attempts to control or influence it. Whereas in 1793 Georg Forster could write that there was no public opinion in Germany,[34] by 1819 the Brockhaus devotes the first German encyclopedia entry to *Oeffentlichkeit*. In the meantime, in 1813 Friedrich Wilhelm III had issued an appeal 'An mein Volk!', the first time that a Prussian king had adressed a direct appeal to the people and acknowledged their possible role as political actors.

Chances of raising the level of political participation and

furthering the development of a public domain received a setback after the Restoration with the proclamation of the Karlsbader Beschlüsse of 1819, the intention of which, according to Franz Schneider, was to hinder communication and thus prevent the formation of a body of public opinion.[35]

The body of public opinion that did arise after 1815 was seen by both its proponents and the authorities as progressive oppositional potential directed against what was regarded as the repressive power of the monarchs, as Jürgen Schiewe states in his study of Carl Gustav Jochmann.[36]

There was, of course, an increase in the level of public political debate, as evidenced above all by the Assembly in the *Paulskirche*; although this National Assembly shared many of the characteristics of a parliament, it lacked that recognition and power as an organ of state which would have allowed it to assume the mediating function between state and society which Habermas sees as one of the characteristics of a parliament.[37]

Parliamentarism in nineteenth-century Germany displayed a truncated development compared with England, for example. The Paulskirche Assembly regarded itself as sovereign, but never enjoyed sovereignty; the forms of debate and the ideology of 'reasonableness' were there, but the power was not, and when, after 1871, a Reichstag was established with at least some powers, the development of that body had already progressed beyond the concept of a parliament as a place of reasoned debate to that of a parliament as a conflict of interests. This change in the function of parliament reflects a more general change in patterns of public debate from 'reasoned discussion' to 'negotiation' between conflicting interests.[38]

The 'interests' are represented on the one hand by the public administration, and on the other by political parties and interest groups, both of which gain power at the expense of the power of parliament.[39]

The rise of political parties and interest groups occasions an increase in public persuasive discourse – in both advertising and in the political propaganda put out by the state, the political parties, and the various interest groups which arose with the progress of industrialisation and with the formation of federations of industrialists and others. In this connection, Jaeger points to the power of industrialists' associations, and sees the years following the foundation of the Empire as the era in which such interest groups maximised their power.[40]

Such organisations, however, also pursued more general political (and militarist) aims: 'The imperialism and militarism of the 1890s was marked by the growing importance of the interest groups that mobilised mass support for imperialism and the navy programme'.[41]

Education

Industrialisation, the changing role of the state, the emergence and political role of a new bourgeoisie, and the development of working-class consciousness all created new educational demands, which were met by increased educational provision at all levels in nineteenth-century Germany. Under the heading of 'technicalisation' we shall later refer to the growth in demand for technical education and training; at this point we shall turn to more explicitly linguistic matters.

Habermas sees the new bourgeoisie – the middle classes – of the nineteenth century defined by education and property, with the stress on the latter; Schiewe regards education as the determining factor, arguing that Habermas' approach does little to explain developments between the restoration and about 1850. Both would agree, however, that the precursor to the formation of political public opinion is a literary public sphere.[42,43]

The combination of a literary base and growing political awareness, coupled with the rise of German nationalism, had a profound effect on the status of the German language. We shall be considering the role of the German language as a national symbol in Chapter 3; at the present juncture we shall be concentrating on educational aspects of the language's status.

With the shift from the triglossia of the period up to the eighteenth century (with Latin as the language of scholarship, French as the language of aristocratic privilege, and German as the language of administration and day-to-day communication) towards the established monoglossia of the nineteenth century, Standard German (which was generally understood as being the *literary* language) enhanced its status as a symbol of educational privilege, as a level of education evidenced by a command of the standard language was the necessary prerequisite for a post in the growing state bureaucracy, with the upward social mobility which this brought with it.

The nineteenth century saw a gradual shift from Latin to German as the main vehicle of bourgeois education; German as a subject in secondary schools (*höhere Schulen*) acquired increasing significance – for instance, between 1856 and 1891, the time devoted to German classes was raised by 30 per cent, which, coupled with an increase in the secondary-school population (which went up by some 330 per cent from 1822 to 1864) meant that the spread and level of advanced formal training in the native language became an important cultural factor.

German teaching at secondary level concentrated on three main areas: literature, grammar and rhetoric.[44] The resultant effects were firstly a spread in the reception of the works of classical German authors and the establishment of reading habits, secondly a sensitivisation for the production of the written language, and thirdly the training of oral skills, which helped mark the transition of the standard language from a primarily written medium to a written and oral medium. The development of a rhetorical tradition in the standard register meant that with the emergence of new public discourses – e.g., in parliaments – this register assumed an oral dimension beyond the theatre in which it had traditionally been rooted.

Given that language develops through the interaction of text producers and text users, and that the history of language is also the history of language use, the opening up of literary texts to new circles beyond the tradtional privileged educational classes was bound to affect the form and function of the literary language and to lead to the production of new types of popular literary text, particularly so as there was also a change in the expectations of the reading public.[45]

It does seem possible to hypothesise that certain changes in literary style through the nineteenth century, including the adoption of 'non-standard' forms, evolved in response not only to changing socio-economic patterns but also to changing patterns of readership.

The further development of the literary language of literature cannot, however, be explained solely and directly through changing socio-economic conditions and changing patterns of readership – if this were the case, it would be extremely difficult to account for much of early twentieth century German literature. To explain the changing patterns of literary language, we must also have regard to the socio-cultural status of the language itself. With the increasing institutional canonisation of the classical literary language in the course of the nineteenth century, its predominant social role became one of an instrument of the educational prestige of the bourgeois establishment, culminating in 'the presentation of the pathetic-elitist literary style of German Classicism as a model in German language teaching in late nineteenth century grammar schools and its deployment as a formal register in Wilhelmine Germany in the style of Schiller with quotations from the German classics'. [46] The forward development of the literary language can be seen as a reaction against this hijacking of the literary language, as creative writers refused 'to persist as models for the bourgeois establishment, with the result that they switched to everyday language and (later) to word-play and alienation'. [47]

The institutionalisation and canonisation of the classical literary language not only resulted in the search for new forms of literary expression, but also provoked a reaction within the establishment against linguistic developments in the new types of non-literary text which were being produced to meet new communicative needs (e.g., in journalism, technology and administration). The view that the classical literary language was the yardstick against which all language use had to be measured gave rise to a new type of language purism (beside the *Fremdwortpurismus* dealt with in the next section) which manifested itself in a growing body of conservative *Sprachkritik* (e.g., Wustmann's *Sprachdummheiten*) and in the institutionalisation of *Sprachkritik* with the creation of quasi-official organisations (such as the Allgemeiner deutscher Sprachverein – 1885) dedicated to preserving the 'purity' of the German language.

Besides the advances in secondary education and changes in bourgeois language concerns, the nineteenth century also saw an increase in elementary education, with the progressive introduction of compulsory schooling and the resultant expansion of the *Volksschule*. The effects, however, were not as dramatic as one might perhaps have expected; the illiteracy rate in Prussia was still around 12 per cent in 1871, and even towards the end of the century, schooling finished for a significant minority at the age of twelve. Education for the working classes was viewed from the utilitarian standpoint that future factory workers should only be taught what they needed to enable them to fulfil their economic role.[48]

Instruction was given in the mother tongue, with literature and grammar playing an important role, but again the syllabi were content with minimum standards.[49]

Pupils' progress in German was also hampered by the gulf between their native dialect and the norms of the standard language, and children mainly left school with only a passive command of High German (which would presumably enable them to understand the orders given by their later superiors). Those who left elementary school were often aware of their deficiencies, and the efforts of the workers' educational associations in the nineteenth century were directed towards overcoming these educational deficits. The fact remains, however, that the educational gulf persisted, with a minority leaving secondary school with a linguistic and communicative potential which was denied to the majority who were restricted to elementary schooling.[50]

Effects of industrialisation – lingustic pre-requisites and consequences

Urbanisation

The migration from the countryside to the growing industrial conurbations sketched above meant an increased contact between the speakers of rural dialects and urban colloquial speech and had a dual effect on the spread and status of the various language varieties. The first of these was a reduction in the number of people for whom their native rural dialect was the sole or principal means of communication, and this led to far-reaching changes in both the structure and status of dialect. Concomitant with the 'decline' of rural dialects was the development and expansion of the urban koines (*Umgangssprachen*) as an essential vehicle of communication among the new urbanites – who came from a variety of dialect backgrounds – and between the new urbanites and the longer-established city-dwellers. It would be a travesty to suggest that the new urban migrants simply 'shook off' their old rural dialects and somehow assumed a 'new' urban dialect, because in reality the structures and processes involved were far more complex. Firstly there is the point that the new urbanites did not simply sever all links with their rural origins, and indeed it would be a gross over-simplification of the patterns of labour movement to suggest that the new industrial workers all lived in the cities; a large number maintained their residential base in their villages, and commuted to the factories in the cities, thus operating in two communicative environments – a pattern that could, for example, still be observed in villages around the industrial conurbation of Ludwigshafen-Mannheim into the early 1970s. [51] In this way, elements of urban speech were also imported into the rural environment. Secondly there is the factor of the attitudes of the established city-dwellers towards the 'new urbanites' and their concern for the status of their urban dialect.

Thus it was that the original urban dialects developed towards a 'new' interlanguage to meet the changing communication needs within the growing industrial conurbations. The need for the 'interlanguage' was determined both by social contact – many of the 'migrants', for example, were young and unmarried, and their choice of possible sexual and marital partners was not, as had probably hitherto been the case, restricted to speakers of their particular rural dialect – and by the requirements of the workplace, where labour had to be coordinated and supervised. Overall, the urbanisation of society and the development of industrial forms of production led to an increase in contact between varieties; for example, members of the urban proletariat had contact not only with other members of their class from different language backgrounds, but also with members of the bourgeoisie acting in supervisory and management roles in industry and as representatives of the state bureaucracy. Within the workers' educational movements, members of the working class will also have been exposed to the intellectual discourse of the enlightened bourgeoisie and to the language of literature. This last point will be taken up again under the heading of politicalisation.

Technicalisation

The development of new technologies and industrial processes in the nineteenth century reflects the increasing role and enhanced status of the natural sciences, furthering trends in patterns of language and communication which can be observed since the Middle Ages, with the increasing status and influences of the specialist languages of science and technology, as Uwe Pörksen has pointed out.[52]

It was in the nineteenth century that in the German universities the natural sciences 'liberated' themselves from their previous subordinate existence to the arts and medicine, and independent science faculties were founded. In this context, it is also significant to note that the study of natural sciences had not moved from its previous Latin base to a German base until the second half of the eighteenth century, so that in the nineteenth century there was a double impetus behind the linguistic expansion from this quarter.

The expansion of science and technology led to a massive increase in specialist terminologies, and the development of industrial means of production meant that large numbers of people required at least some command of the specialist vocabularies to perform their economic role. At the same time, the growing realisation of the importance of science and technology meant an enhanced social and cultural status for the natural sciences, which was reflected in the adoption and adaptation of specialist terms within the 'common core' of discourse and in the acceptance of scientific terminology in other disciplines.

A good example of this acceptance can be seen in the development of linguistic terminology in nineteenth century Germany. Although Jacob Grimm contrasted 'soft' subjects such as linguistics and history with the 'exact sciences'[53], neither he nor other linguists were averse to adopting scientific metaphors in their description and analysis of language. Here it is interesting to observe how for the first part of the century advances in anatomy and biology determined views of language as an 'organism', and how this view was then superseded around mid-century by psychological and physiological approaches, at about the same time as the holistic views propagated by Grimm and Bopp were being rejected in favour of the more 'atomistic' approach of the neogrammarians, at least partly in an attempt at legitimation by aping the methods of the natural sciences.

Thus at the lexical level, the onward march of science and technology led to an expansion of specialist terms, with specialist terms then being adopted – often as metaphors – in other areas, but not simply as means of denotation, but also as a reflection of the increased importance of science and technology both within the economic base and – to an increasing degree – as a surrogate world view for religion. The process was not, however, unidirectional – i.e., from the specialist language to the common core; in some areas at least, terms from the common core were taken as metaphors into specialist vocabularies (e.g., Darwinism, psychoanalysis) and there given new, specialised meanings.

Neither was the quantitative and qualitative rise of specialist vocabularies limited to science and technology; new forms of economic organisation (for example the rise of the joint-stock company – *Aktiengesellschaft*, in the nineteenth century) and state intervention and administration (e.g., in the area of welfare policy and education) also gave rise to new terminologies, which again were not restricted to the specialist user.

Advances in science and technology and changing forms of economic and social organisation not only led to an expansion in specialist vocabularies, but also – and perhaps more importantly – gave rise to new text-types, or at least led to an increase in the currency of certain text-types, which today we regard as an indispensable element within the discourse of an advanced industrial society, and which must be considered in an investigation into linguistic variation and change in nineteenth century Germany.

There are various ways of categorising 'technical' texts; here it will suffice to distinguish between those texts intended for specialist 'internal' communication and those intended for 'external' communication, whereby in the case of external communication it is perhaps useful to distinguish between individuals and institutions (particularly of the state) as addressees.

Internal communication in the scientific and technical field includes such texts as laboratory reports – including articles in specialist journals – technical documentation, operating instructions, standards specifications (from 1860 onwards, for example, the Verein deutscher Ingenieure was responsible for establishing industrial standards in certain areas). In the commercial and administrative area, internal communication encompasses the whole field of socio-communicative interaction within companies and commercial organisations, for example business correspondence, internal memos, guidelines and reports, and financial accounts.[54]

External communication directed towards individuals in

science and technology takes in the whole field of popularisation – as seen, for example, in the development of *Fachprosa* and encyclopaedias in the course of the nineteenth century – but will also include texts for use in formal education, with the development of the textbooks required for the spread of technical education.

An example of an external text addressed to the state is to be found in patent applications; although the history of patents can be traced back to the Renaissance, the first 'modern' patent legislation in Prussia was passed in 1815, and the first *Reichspatentgesetz* was enacted on 25 May 1877.

A study of external communication in commerce must consider such texts as share prospectuses and advertising, which really 'took off' in the nineteenth century with increasing literacy and wider newspaper readership, aided by developments in printing technology, particularly the invention of the rotary press.

The progressive industrialisation in nineteenth-century Germany generated an increased need for effective communication – and here it is significant to note that two of the motors of German industrialisation, namely railways and the advent of telecommunications, were important factors in meeting this need – and that not only the speed and quality, but also the volume of communication increased over this period. The new types of text indicated above were not the preserve of a select few, but enjoyed wide circulation, which meant that not only were more people involved in text production, but also that more were engaged in text reception and in reacting to texts, and that thus these 'new' texts had a more general impact on discourse, affecting areas outside their immediate fields and influencing general socio-communicative interaction. In socio-cultural terms, the nineteenth century saw the movement towards a 'mass society', as evidenced by the development of methods of 'mass production', of 'mass movements' and 'mass media'.

Politicalisation

As we have already seen, the term 'political' is notoriously difficult to define; for present purposes we shall relate it to three areas.

Firstly we shall look at the changes in the corpus of the language arising from the terminologisation of new forms of socio-economic organisation and at the discursive changes brought about by new patterns of political activity. Secondly we shall examine some of the innovation and change occasioned by the need to analyse the socio-economic and socio-cultural changes on a meta-level. Thirdly we need to consider the status of the German language itself as a symbol and instrument of changing values and power structures, and attitudes towards it. We shall consider this third point in the following chapter, when we shall be considering the role of the German language in the creation of national solidarity.

With reference to the first two points, we can observe how the technological innovation and socio-economic structural change which marked the nineteenth century not only created new inherent communicative needs, but also gave rise to a body of critical analysis, as contemporaries strove to come to terms with the new structures at a meta-level, and here too the development of the German language affords a valuable insight into the processes at work as the 'new' disciplines of sociology and political economy became established.

Language change is reflected not only in the creation of new terms, or in shifts of meaning, but also in the frequency with which certain key-terms occur and the level of profile which they assume. An example of this with reference to the change from the supranationalism of the Enlightenment to the nationalism of the nineteenth century is given by Straßner, who shows how terms such as 'reason' and 'humanity' are superseded by 'nation', 'people' and 'German-ness'.[55]

At the same time as these terms were assuming increased prominence, new terms were being introduced, either as neologisms or loan-words, as new institutions were being created – such as *Bundesrat*, *Zollverein*, *Nationalversammlung*, *Verfassung* – and new bodies of political theory developed. Three such key-terms, which still influence much of our twentieth century political discourse, were *liberal* (*Liberale*, *Liberalismus*), *sozial* and *konservativ*, the first having entered German at the beginning of the nineteenth century, with the other two dating back to about 1830, whereby the specialisation of *sozial* in its relationship to *Sozialismus* did not become established until around the mid-nineteenth century, whereas *liberal* and *konservativ* were adopted immediately in their political or politico-economic sense. The century also saw the introduction or coming to prominence of terms such as *Kommunist* (often applied indiscriminately to a person with radical views) and *Demokrat*, which did not always enjoy the high status it has in the late twentieth century; for example, in 1852 the Prussian rail minister von der Heydt issued an order that all 'democrats' should be dismissed forthwith from the railways – shades of the *Radikalenerlaß* promulgated under the Brandt administration in 1974!

Critical analysis

The socio-economic changes through the nineteenth century gave rise to a body of critical analysis, as contemporaries strove to come to terms with the new structures at a meta-level, and here too the development of the German language affords a valuable insight into the processes at work as the 'new' disciplines of sociology and political economy became established.

Without in any way wishing to play down the body of liberal and conservative political theory developed during the century, it can be argued that it was the development of socialist and Marxist politico-economic theory which had the greatest intellectual and linguistic impact.

The justification for this claim is twofold, being on the one hand that it was socialist theory which took fullest account of the social changes and the changing class structure evolving through the change from feudal agrarianism to capitalist industrialisation, and on the other that it was this theory which established the identity of a working class as a 'fourth estate' and helped this working class to find its identity, with all the resultant social and cultural changes which this involved.

At the lexical level we find such innovations as the specialisation of the terms *Arbeiter*, *Klasse*, *Kapital*, the occurrence of such terms as *Sozialdemokrat*, *Streik*, *Aussperrung*, *Arbeitskampf*, *Arbeiterbildungsverein*, *Gewerkschaft*, and the establishment of key political terms such as *Solidarität*. At the same time, other words undergo significant changes in meaning; it is not possible to go into detail here, so that a brief mention of the semantic evolution of the term *Volk*, with its shift from the associations of 'lower classes' (*niederes Volk*, *Gesinde*) towards a more populist connotation will have to suffice.

Important though these lexical changes are – and it is in the lexis that language change is at its most apparent – it is the changing patterns of text production and reception which are of far greater significance for the social structures of language use.

The postulation of a homogeneous working class, and the growing self-awareness of this class, not only manifests itself politically in the development of a labour movement with new forms of party-political and trade-union organisation but is also of cultural significance in that the labour movement develops a strong educational element with the formation of workers' educational associations (the movement was founded in 1844). The result of the German labour movement's educational efforts was, as Kitchen states, that 'The SPD was to enable the German working class to have the best organised and most politically educated party in Europe'.[56] The interesting point about these educational associations, which had as their objective the educational betterment of the working class, is that their efforts were not only directed towards political education and a study of political, economic and social texts in the narrower sense of the term, but that they also had a more general cultural mission and concerned themselves with a study of literary texts – including texts of classical German literature.[57] The mid-century saw, too, the establishment of the first *Volkshochschulen* (analagous to the development of the Workers Educational Association in Britain), part of whose remit was also to contribute to the educational betterment of the working class.

As we turn from the internal status of the German language to a consideration of what we have termed its 'external' status, we must leave a number of questions open – for example to what extent the development of conservative purism was due to a misunderstanding of the historical nature of language, to what extent the preoccupation of 'professional' linguisticians with the reconstruction of past forms of the language meant that only 'amateurs' dealt with contemporary developments, and to what extent this linguistic conservatism can be interpreted as a manifestation of the general conservative ideology of the Prussian state in the last quarter of the century – but as questions which suggest their answers.

Unification

The growth of national awareness in the nineteenth century (which was by no means solely a German phenomenon), coupled with the need for as large a secured domestic market as possible, were important motivating factors behind the move for German 'unification'. Although the final step in the move from political polycentricity to monocentricity was not taken until the enactment of the Weimar constitution in 1919, for present purposes the 'refoundation' of the German *Reich* in 1871 can be regarded as the political culmination of a process of economic integration which started some fifty years previously.

In contrast to linguistic developments in states with a long-standing centralist tradition such as England and France, where the centre of linguistic influence and innovation was established at a relatively early stage, the development of German proceeded in a polycentric fashion, and even today there is evidence of this polycentricity in the wider acceptance accorded to different regional standards within the Germanophone world compared for example with the predominance and enhanced social status of the Southern English standard in Britain.

When discussing the role of the German language in the process of unification – and the role of the process of unification in the development of the German language – it is useful to distinguish between the *status* of the language on the one hand and efforts towards the regulation of language *corpora* on the other, whereby one can roughly postulate that status relates more closely to the first of the above roles, while corpus regulation is more closely linked to the second.

In the first instance, it is necessary to examine the role of the German language as a national symbol, and in the second to look at official or quasi-official moves towards linguistic standardisation. As a third element straddling these two areas comes the question of language purism, itself linked with changing patterns of linguistic borrowing in the nineteenth century.

With the growth in the volume, extent and significance of written communication as a prerequisite for the effective functioning of a modern industrial state, it is not surprising that the two main efforts at linguistic standardisation in the nineteenth century were both connected with the written language – the attempts at spelling standardisation and reform, the best-known manifestation of which was perhaps Conrad Duden's proposals published in 1872 and debated at the 1876 Berlin Conference, and Theodor Siebs' efforts at orthoepic standardisation from 1898 onwards.

Conclusion

It was the intention of this chapter to indicate some of the relationships between language history on the one hand and socio-economic and socio-cultural history on the other, using as an example the development of the German language and German linguistic culture in the nineteenth century.

The changes observed in the language cover firstly its dia-system, particularly in the area of socially determined variation (Mattheier's *Variantenverschiebung*), with a decline in the extent and status of the predominantly rural dialects, the growth of urban koines (*Umgangssprachen*) as a vehicle of social interaction in the growing industrial centres, and an increase in both the status and coverage of educated (literary) German (*Hochsprache*). In addition, increased mobility (both geographical and social), the extension of educational provision, and increased contact between social classes, determined at least in part by the demands of division of labour, meant that there was more contact between the regional and social varieties.

Secondly, there are shifts in the modes of discourse (Mattheier's 'Media history'), with an increase in the significance and currency of the written language, which is both a consequence and a motor of higher standards of literacy. Connected with this are changing perceptions of the status and role of the standard language, which then also affect the form of the language of literature.

Thirdly, one can point to an increase in the number and circulation of socially relevant text-types (Mattheier's 'History of text-types'), and the growth of the public domain with the development of a wide-reaching 'public language'.

Fourthly, one sees a striking growth in the number and currency of specialist registers in the areas of science, technology, and public and business administration, and the entry of more specialist terms into everyday language interaction.

Fifthly, the process of language standardisation assumes wider significance, and is linked with an increased level of awareness of both the internal and the external status of the German language (partly covered by Mattheier's 'History of linguistics').

The evidence presented supports the hypothesis that there is a two-way interactive relationship between linguistic change and socio-economic and socio-cultural change. Although changes in the modes of production of goods and services could not directly or indirectly account for all of the changes that can be registered in the German language in the nineteenth century, the industrial revolution in Germany, with the shift from feudal agrarianism to capitalist industrialism, did create or promote new communicative needs which occasioned changes in the patterns of linguistic interaction.

Notes

1 O. Behagel, *Geschichte der deutschen Sprache*, Strasbourg, 1911

2 H. Eggers, *Deutsche Sprachgeschichte*, Hamburg, 1963-77

3 E. Blackall, *The Emergence of German as a Literary Language*, Cambridge, 1959

4 J. Schildt, 'Die Bedeutung von Textsorten für eine Theorie des Sprachwandels', *Zeitschrift für Germanistik* 2.87, pp. 187–98

5 U. Maas, 'Der kulturanalytische Zugang zur Sprachgeschichte', *Wirkendes Wort* 2/87, pp. 87-104

6 'Der Gegenstand einer kulturanalytischen Sprachbetrachtung (oder auch sprachsoziologisch – die Differenzen liegen bei unterschiedlichen Akzentuierungen) ist die Rekonstruktion der *Sprachpraxis* in ihrer historischen Bestimmtheit. Daraus folgt, daß der Sprachprozeß eben auch von den gesellschaftlichen Widersprüchen bestimmt ist, die sie artikulieren – oder anders gesagt: daß die Sprachwissenschaft diese Widersprüche aus den ihr zugänglichen Quellen zu rekonstruieren hat.' Maas, 'Der kulturanalytische Zugang', p.89

7 Cf. P. v. Polenz 'Sozialgeschichtliche Aspekte der neueren deutschen Sprachgeschichte', and D. Cherubim, 'Sprachentwicklung und Sprachkritik im 19. Jahrhundert. Beiträge zur Konstitution einer pragmatischen Sprachgeschichte', in Th. Cramer, (ed.), *Literatur und Sprache im historischen Prozeß – Band 1: Literatur, Band 2: Sprache*, Tübingen, 1983

8 'Im letzten Viertel des 19. Jahrhunderts erklärte Moriz Heyne, der als Germanist in Basel und Göttingen tätig war, die Aufgabe der deutschen Philologie liege in der Erfassung "des gesamten Geisteslebens unserer Nation und seiner Entfaltung soweit es uns in Denkmälern überliefert. Diese

Denkmäler sind nicht bloß solche der Litteratur, sondern auch solche der Kunst, des Gewerbes, der mündlichen Überlieferung".' H. Bausinger, 'Sprache in der Volkskunde', H. Brekle and U. Maas (eds), *Sprachwissenschaft und Volkskunde. Perspektiven einer kulturanalytischen Sprachbetrachtung*, Opladen, 1986

9 E. Coseriu, 'System, Norm und "Rede" in: E. Coseriu, *Sprache, Strukturen und Funktionen*, Tübingen, 1970, pp. 193-212

10 L. Weisgerber, 'Der Mensch im Akkusativ', *Wirkendes Wort*, viii, 4, 1958

11 'Sprache ist grundsätzlich nicht stabil, sondern veränderlich, weil sie variabel ist. ... Zwischen den vom Sprachsystem zur Verfügung stehenden Varianten und den (die freie Variabilität einschränkenden) *Sprachnormen* besteht ein sozial funktionierendes Spannungsverhältnis, das leicht zu Veränderungen im Verhältnis zwischen den Varianten führen kann.' P. v. Polenz, 'Grundsätzliches zum Sprachwandel', *Der Deutschunterricht*, Jg. 38, 4, 1986, p. 6

12 'Sprachliches Handeln als soziales Handeln läuft über situativ gesteuerte Re-Definitionsprozesse von erlernten bzw. erworbenen Sprachhandlungs-mustern ab. In diesen Re-Definitionsprozessen ist ein Wandlungsprozeß organisch angelegt.' K. Mattheier, 'Allgemeine Aspekte einer Theorie des Sprachwandels', in W. Besch, O. Reichman and S. Sonderegger (eds), *Sprachgeschichte. Ein Handbuch zur Geschichte der deutschen Sprache und ihrer Erforschung*, Berlin, New York, Vol. 1 1984, Vol. 2 1985, p. 724

13 '(Eine angemessene Sprachwandeltheorie) muß die beiden hauptsächlich konkurrierenden Sprachwandeltheorien integrieren, nämlich die kommuni-kativ-funktionale Theorie, die Coseriu (1958/74) umrissen hat und die artikulatorisch-perzeptive bzw. innersystematische, besonders auf den Laut-wandel abzielende Theorie, die sich sowohl bei den Strukturalisten und Generativisten als auch bei Lüdtke und in den Konzepten zum "natürlichen" Lautwandel findet.' Mattheier, 'Allgemeine Aspekte', p. 724

14 'Intentionale Sprachveränderungshandlungen werden in den meisten Sprachwandeltheorien in den Randbereich gerückt. Wenn man sich jedoch den Gesamtbereich derartiger Handlungen vergegenwärtigt, dann wird deutlich, wie wichtig intentionale Sprachveränderungshandlungen für den Sprachwandel sind. Hierzu gehören einmal alle bewußten Sprach-schöpfungen, seien sie literarischer oder fachsprachlicher bzw. werbe-sprachlicher oder auch sprachspielerischer Art. Weiterhin gehört die Durchsetzung und Verallgemeinerung sprachlicher Normen während des Spracherziehungsprozesses dazu. Intentionale Sprachveränderungs-hand-lungen sind auch bewußte Abwertungen bestimmter Varietäten und Aufwer-tung anderer sowie alle anderen Arten sprachplanerischer oder sprach-politischer Maßnahmen wie etwa Sprachregelungen, Terminologisierungen usw.' Mattheier, 'Allgemeine Aspekte', p. 725

15 After Mattheier, 'Allgemeine Aspekte' p. 729

16 'Die industrielle Revolution verwandelte die Lebensbedingungen und Lebensformen der Menschen radikaler als jeder andere Ereigniszusammen-

hang der neueren Geschichte.' H. Jaeger, *Geschichte der Wirtschaftsordnung in Deutschland*, Frankfurt, 1988, p. 82

17 'Bevölkerungsexplosion, Verstädterung, die neuen Verkehrsmittel, eine Vielzahl von Erfindungen und Neuerungen, vor allem aber die fabrik-industrielle Massenproduktion von Wirtschaftsgütern und die damit verbundene Technisierung der Arbeit trugen zu dieser Verwandlung bei. Das Umsichgreifen eines derart revolutionären Prozesses erschütterte auch die traditionelle Gesellschaftsordnung.' Jaeger, *Geschichte der Wirtschaftsordnung*, p. 83

18 M.Kitchen, *The Political Economy of Germany 1815-1914*, London, 1978, p. 138

19 H. Böhme, *An Introduction to the Social and Economic History of Germany. Politics and Economic Change in the Nineteenth and Twentieth Centuries*, transl. by W. R. Lee, Oxford 1978, p. 71 (orig. *Prologomena zu einer Sozial- und Wirtschaftsgeschichte Deutschlands*, Frankfurt, 1972)

20 'Die preußische Städteordnung hatte noch 1808 eine Stadt mit 3500 Bürgern eine mittlere, eine mit 10 000 Bürgern eine große Stadt genannt. Seit der Jahrhundertmitte rechnete man bei Großstädten mit mindestens 100 000 Einwohnern. 1850 zählte man erst 5 Großstädte, 1870: 8, 1890: 26, 1900: 33, 1910: 45. Etwa ebenso schnell nahm die Zahl der den Großstädten nahe-stehenden Mittelstädte zu ... es gibt zu denken, daß im übrigen Europa die Wohnorte mit mehr als 40 000 Einwohnern von 1880 – 1900 nur um rund 70% zunahmen, in Deutschland dagegen um 130,5%.' H. Bechtel, *Wirtschafts- und Sozialgeschichte Deutschlands*, Munich, 1967, p. 327

21 Cf. Böhme, *An Introduction*, p.76

22 'Die führenden monarchisch-konservativen Kräfte in Europa – Österreich, Rußland und Preußen – nahmen den endgültigen Sieg über Napoleon und das revolutionäre Frankreich zum Anlaß für die Wiedererrichtung einer restaurativen Staats- und Gesellschaftsordnung.' Jaeger, *Geschichte der Wirtschaftsordnung*, p. 44

23 'die Heilung der sozialen Schäden (sei)nicht ausschließlich im Wege der Repression sozialdemokratischer Ausschreitungen, sondern gleichmäßig auf dem der positiven Förderung des Wohles der Arbeiter zu suchen', after Bechtel, *Wirtschafts- und Sozialgeschichte*, pp. 371–2

24 W.O. Henderson, *The State and the Industrial Revolution in Prussia 1740 – 1870*, Liverpool, 1967, p. xix

25 'Sprachliche Existenzformen sind in der Regel gekennzeichnet durch – einen bestimmten territorialen Geltungsbereich, – eine sie vorrangig tragende, sozial determinierte Sprecherschicht, – spezifische Funktionen, die sie in der sprachlichen Kommunikation einer Gesellschaft ausüben, – eine bestimmte Existenzweise (mündlich oder schriftlich), – ein bestimmtes Sprachsystem mit einer spezifischen Struktur. ' J. Schildt, 'Sprache und Sozialgeschichte', in D. Cherubim and K. Mattheier (eds), *Voraussetzungen und Grundlagen der Gegenwartssprache. Sprach- und sozialgeschichtliche Untersuchungen zum 19. Jahrhundert*, Berlin, 1989, p. 32

26 E.g., in J. Schildt *et al.*, *Die Auswirkungen der industriellen Revolution auf die deutsche Sprachentwicklung im 19. Jhdt.*, Berlin, 1981

27 K. Mattheier, 'Industrialisierung der Sprache. Historisch-soziologische Überlegungen zur Sprache im Industriebetrieb des 19. Jhdts', *Wirkendes Wort*, 2/87, pp. 130–44

28 'Durch (das) öffentliche Interesse an sprachlichen Entwicklungen und Veränderungen ist die innere Sprachgeschichte anders als in anderen Epochen im 19. Jahrhundert eng mit der äußeren Sprachgeschichte verknüpft. Diese äußere Sprachgeschichte umfaßt in besonderer Weise fünf Teilbereiche: die Sprachgeschichte als Geschichte der Variantenverschiebung, die Sprachgeschichte als Mediengeschichte, die Sprachgeschichte als Textsorten-geschichte, die Sprachgeschichte als Geschichte von Bedeutungen und die Sprachgeschichte als Geschichte der Sprachwissenschaft und der Sprach-geschichte. In jedem dieser Teilbereiche ist die Sprachgeschichte eng mit der allgemeinen Geschichte der deutschen Sprachgemeinschaft und ihrer Sprecher verbunden: durch die Variantenverschiebung mit den gesellschaft-lichen Veränderungen im Zusammenhang mit dem allgemeinen Modern-isierungsprozeß, durch die Medien mit den revolutionären Veränderungen im Bereich von Speicherung und Transport von Sprache, durch die Textsortengeschichte mit den vielfältigen Wandlungen in den gesellschaft-lichen Institutionen, durch die Bedeutungsgeschichte mit zentralen sozial-und geistesgeschichtlichen Veränderungen beim Erfassen der Welt und durch die Wissenschaftsgeschichte mit dem eigenen Standort innerhalb der sich wandelnden Verortung der Sprache in der Gesellschaft.' Mattheier, 'Industrialisierung', p. 133

29 'Eine Privatperson ist nicht berechtigt, über Handlungen, das Verfahren, die Gesetze, Maßregeln und Anordnungen der Souveräne und Höfe, ihrer Staatsbediensteten, Kollegien und Gerichtshöfe öffentliche, sogar tadelnde Urteile zu fällen.', after J. Habermas, *Strukturwandel der Öffentlichkeit. Unter-suchungen zu einer Kategorie der bürgerlichen Gesellschaft*, Darmstadt/Neuwied, 1962, p. 40

30 'Die verbündeten Fürsten und freien Städte kommen überein, den Untertanen der deutschen Bundesstaaten folgende Rechte zuzusichern...', after Grünert, 'Politische Geschichte und Sprachgeschichte', p. 49

31 'Die deutsche verfassungsgebende Nationalversammlung hat beschlossen und verkündigt als Reichsverfassung ...', after Grünert, 'Politische Geschichte und Sprachgeschichte', p. 48

32 'Seine Majestät der König von Preußen im Namen des Norddeutschen Bundes, Seine Majestät der König von Bayern usw. ... schließen einen ewigen Bund zum Schutze des Bundesgebiets und des innerhalb desselben gültigen Rechts sowie zur Pflege der Wohlfahrt des deutschen Volkes.', after Grünert, 'Politische Geschichte und Sprachgeschichte', p. 48

33 'Das deutsche Volk, einig in seinen Stämmen und von dem Willen beseelt, sein Reich in Freiheit und Gerechtigkeit zu erneuern und zu festigen, dem inneren und dem äußeren Frieden zu dienen und den gesellschaftlichen Fortschritt zu fördern, hat sich diese Verfassung gegeben:

§ Das Deutsche Reich ist eine Republik.

Die Staatsgewalt geht vom Volke aus ...', after Grünert, 'Politische Geschichte und Sprachgeschichte', p. 48/9

34 'so gibt es auch keine deutsche öffentliche Meynung' G. Forster, 'Über die öffentliche Meinung', in G. Forster, *Sämtliche Schriften*, Berlin, 1974, Vol. 8, p. 365, after J. Schiewe, *Sprache und Öffentlichkeit. Carl Gustav Jochmann und die politische Sprachkritik der Spätaufklärung*, Berlin, 1989, p.171

35 'Die Karlsbader Beschlüsse sollten verhindern, daß sich die bürgerliche Gesellschaft politisch formiert. Sie sind der Versuch, eine fundamentale geistige Entwicklung, die in breitesten Schichten Fuß gefaßt hatte, durch Kommunikationsunterbindung zu sistieren und rückgängig zu machen.' F. Schneider, *Pressefreiheit und politische Öffentlichkeit*, Neuwied/Berlin, 1966, p. 244

36 '"Öffentlichkeit" repräsentierte im restaurativen Deutschland gerade nicht die politische Wirklichkeit, sondern ihr Gegenbild. ... "Öffentlichkeit" wird ... nicht nur zu einem politischen "Schlagwort", sondern zum Schlüsselwort einer progressiven Denkart, die ihre Kraft aus der Opposition zu einer als repressiv empfundenen Realität bezieht.' Schiewe, *Sprache und Öffentlichkeit*, p. 169

37 Cf. Habermas, *Strukturwandel*, 'Im Maße einer wechselseitigen Durchdringung von Staat und Gesellschaft verliert die Öffentlichkeit, und mit ihr die als Staatsorgan etablierte Öffentlichkeit, das Parlament, gewisse Vermittlungsfunktionen ...', p. 216

38 'Die Öffentlichkeit wird mit Aufgaben eines Interessenausgleichs belastet, der sich den klassischen Formen parlamentarischer Einigung und Vereinbarung entzieht; ihm sieht man gleichsam die Herkunft aus der Sphäre des Marktes noch an – er muß buchstäblich "ausgehandelt", durch Druck und Gegendruck auf Abruf erzeugt werden.' Habermas, *Strukturwandel*, pp. 216–17

39 'einer Positionsschwächung des Parlaments entspricht eine Stärkung von Transformatoren vom Staat zur Gesellschaft (Verwaltung) und umgekehrt von der Gesellschaft zum Staat (Verbände und Parteien)'. Habermas, *Strukturwandel*, p. 216

40 'Nachdrücklicher und wirkungsvoller als die (Handels-)Kammern und ihre Spitzenorganisationen haben die Wirtschaftsverbände die Interessen des Unternehmertums gegenüber der Öffentlichkeit und den politischen Gremien zu fördern versucht. Die große Zeit der Verbände begann in Deutschland ... nach der Reichsgründung von 1871.' Jaeger, *Geschichte der Wirtschaftsordnung*, p. 70

41 Kitchen, *The Political Economy*, p. 236

42 'Der Prozeß, in dem die obrigkeitlich reglementierte Öffentlichkeit vom Publikum der räsonierenden Privatleute angeeignet und als eine Sphäre der Kritik an der öffentlichen Gewalt etabliert wird, vollzieht sich als Umfunktionierung der schon mit Einrichtungen des Publikums und Plattformen der Diskussion ausgestatteten literarischen Öffentlichkeit.' Habermas, *Strukturwandel*, p. 63

43 'Genau dieser Wechsel von poetischem Entwurf zu einer als historischen Notwendigkeit empfundenen Forderung, ein Wechsel, der zunächst im Bewußtsein und dann auch im Handeln des Bürgertums stattfand, bezeichnet den Übergang von literarischer zu politischer Öffentlichkeit. Das in der Aufklärung vorgeprägte und durch die Antike-Rezeption in der Klassik entworfene Ideal einer bürgerlichen Individualität und nationalen Gemeinschaft fand seinen Niederschlag zunächst nur in der Literatur.' Schiewe, *Sprache und Öffentlichkeit*, p.168

44 For a full discussion, see G. Kettmann, 'Die Existenzformen der deutschen Sprache im 19. Jahrhundert' in Schildt *et al.*, *Die Auswirkungen*, pp. 35-97

45 'Da das lesende Publikum den Anspruch auf Wiedererkennung seiner eigenen Existenz in der Literatur stellte, wurden die poetologisch festen Typen entlassen, um dem bunten Personal der Straße den Einzug in die Dichtung zu gewähren.', H. Schlaffer, 'Beiträge zur Naturgeschichte der bürgerlichen Gesellschaft. Physiologie und Roman im 19. Jahrhundert' , Cramer, *Literatur und Sprache*, Vol.1, p. 303

46 'die Pädagogisierung des pathetisch-elitären Literaturstils der deutschen Klassik im Deutschunterricht der Gymnasien des späteren 19. Jahrhunderts und seine Anwendung in Festreden der Wilhelminischen Zeit, vor allem als Schillerimitation und mit Klassikerzitaten.' Polenz, 'Sozialgeschichtliche Aspekte', p.16

47 'mit ihrer Sprache weiterhin Vorbilder für das Bildungsprestige des bürgerlichen Establishments zu produzieren, mit der Konsequenz des Ausweichens in die Alltagssprache bzw. (später) in Sprachspiel und Sprachverfremdung.' Polenz, 'Sozialgeschichtliche Aspekte', p.17

48 '(Die speziellen Lehrplanziele der Volksschule) weisen ... deutlich darauf hin, daß man sich an Mindestforderungen, nicht aber an zielstrebigem Wissensaufbau orientierte: man bot in der Regel gerade soviel, wie ein zukünftiger Fabrikarbeiter zum Bewältigen seiner Aufgaben an Wissen benötigte.' Kettmann, 'Existenzformen', p. 51

49 'Zu dem Mindestangebot an grammatischer Bildung gesellte sich in der Volksschule ein ebensolches auf dem Gebiet der Literatur.' Kettmann, 'Existenzformen', p. 52

50 'Trotz aller sichtbar werdenden Kritik am Entwicklungsstand und an der Praxis des Deutschunterrichtes an höheren Schulen steht eines selbst bei einem summierenden Überblick außer Frage: Ihren Schülern wurde mit ihm insgesamt ein Bildungsangebot gemacht, das für die Beherrschung der Muttersprache einen Schlüssel in die Hand gab, der dem weitaus größeren Teil der Schuljugend verwehrt blieb.' Kettmann, 'Existenzformen', p. 52

51 I am grateful to Herr Ulrich Zipf, *Hausmeister* in the Institut für Deutsche Sprache in Mannheim, for confirming the accuracy of this observation

52 'Unsere Geschichte ist seit dem Mittelalter zunehmend von den Naturwissenschaften bestimmt, die naturwissenschaftlichen Fachsprachen sind daher ein wesentliches Moment neuzeitlicher Sprachentwicklung'. U. Pörksen, 'Deutsche Sprachgeschichte und die Entwicklung der Natur-wissen-

schaften – Aspekte einer Geschichte der Naturwissenschaftssprache und ihrer Wechselbeziehung zur Gemeinsprache', Besch, Reichman and Sonderegger (eds), *Sprachgeschichte*, Vol.1, p. 86

53 'Viel sanfter und zugleich viel träger ziehen die ungenauen wissenschaften nach sich, es gehört schon eine seltnere vorrichtung einzelner naturen dazu, um sie an deutsche geschichte oder an die untersuchung deutscher sprache innig zu fesseln, während wir die hörsäle der chemiker und physiker wimmeln sehen von einer dem zeitgeist auch unbewust huldigenden jugend.' J. Grimm, 'Über den werth der ungenauen wissenschaften', in *Kleinere Schriften*, Bd.VII, Hildesheim 1966

54 Cf. Mattheier, 'Industrialisierung'

55 'Insgesamt traten Begriffsfetische wie *Nation, Volkstum, Volksgeist, Deutschtum, Deutschheit* in der ersten Hälfte des 19. Jahrhunderts an die Stelle der für das 18. Jahrhundert noch bestimmenden Begriffe wie Vernunft, Humanität und Menschheit.' E. Straßner, *Ideologie – SPRACHE – Politik. Grundfragen ihres Zusammenhangs*, Tübingen, 1987, p. 129

56 Kitchen, *The Political Economy*, p. 130

57 In this connection it is interesting to observe that the Reclam *Universalbibliothek*, the success of which can at least in part be explained by its success in meeting the need for cheap texts arising from a vastly expanded educational provision, published its first volumes in 1839

3 Phatic functions: the German language as a political metaphor and instrument

In the previous chapter, we considered the interrelationship of socio-economic and communicative change; among other things, we discussed the spread of public discourse and ways in which the standard language both evolved in response to new communicative needs and became more widely disseminated. The emphasis was placed very strongly on material aspects of linguistic and communicative change.

It is now time to turn to more idealist concerns and discuss the ways in which the status and function of the German language evolved and in which *perceptions* of its role developed.

The main language function which we shall be addressing is the phatic, but the phatic on a national scale, i.e., we shall be examining the ways in which the German language operates as a 'bonding' agent. For this we shall examine how the concept of a *national* language emerged, and consider the changing images of the German language as a political symbol embodying and promoting national solidarity. We shall also investigate the role which was ascribed to the language as an instrument both of political emancipation and liberation and of nationalist assertion.

The perception and role of the German language as an instrument and symbol of both political emancipation and national identity can be traced back to Martin Luther, with whose activities a first climax was reached, but the developments were disrupted by the political events which culminated in the Thirty Years' War. In the present study, however, we shall be concentrating on an essentially uninterrupted development covering events over a period which, for the sake of convenience, can be marked as beginning in 1687, the year in which in Leipzig Thomasius posted what is generally regarded as the first notice to appear in German on the notice-board of a German university, and ending in 1941, when the German fascist empire was at the height of its power, with the publication of the five volumes of the propagandistic work *Von deutscher Art in Sprache und Dichtung*.[1]

It is suggested that for Germans, their language is a particularly powerful political symbol, and we shall start with a consideration of the origins of 'deutsch' and the light this might throw on the matter under discussion. Then we shall proceed to the eighteenth century, to consider how this period marks the culmination of efforts to establish German as an effective means of public communication, before going on to consider the German language as a symbol not only of national unity but also of political progress in the nineteenth century; finally, we shall investigate the ways in which perceptions of the role of the German language assumed more sinister overtones, as it changed from being a symbol of unity to becoming a tool of national expansion and conquest.

The political significance of the German language as a symbol of German nationhood – the origins of 'deutsch'

The equation of language and nationhood is of course not a specifically German phenomenon, neither is the enlistment of language as a national symbol; 'languages in competition' or 'in conflict' can be found in many polities, as was indicated in Chapter 1, and language conflicts have served as a *casus belli* before now.

However, the relationship between the Germans and their language was from the beginning a peculiar one, because in a way it can be claimed that 'the Germans' as a nation are defined by their language.

Even a cursory glance at European languages will show a wide variety of names both for 'the Germans' and their language, and among the major European nations, Germany is the only one where the members' own label for nation and language is not

shared by the majority of others. Consider nationality/language
adjectives in some major European languages (Table 3).

**Table 3 Nationality/language adjectives in some major European
languages**

English	French	Italian	Spanish	Russian	German
English	anglais	inglese	ingles	anglijskij	englisch
French	français	frances	frances	francuzskij	französisch
Italian	italien	italiano	italiano	italijanskij	italienisch
Spanish	espagnol	spagnolo	español	ispanskij	spanisch
Russian	russe	russo	russo	russkij	russisch
German	allemand	tedesco	alemán	nemeckij	deutsch

   Language names are in the main derived either from the names
of tribes or peoples – e.g., 'English' from 'Angles', or from geographical areas – e.g., 'Latin' from 'Latinum'. The various terms for
'German' illustrate this: 'German' is of geographical origin, and
the Romance 'allemand', 'alemán' are derived from the name of
one of the Germanic tribes. Three of the terms for German,
however, fall into neither of these categories: 'tedesco' and
'deutsch' – which are in fact etymologically linked – and
'nemeckij'. The significant point about all these as nationality
adjectives is that they are of linguistic and not regional or ethnic
origin, and that all three arose as a result of language contact (or
competition). The traditional etymology of 'nemeckij' (and Polish
'niemiecki', Bulgarian 'nemski', etc.) is that the Slavs (the word
derives from 'slovo' = 'word') were 'the speaking ones', in contrast
to the 'non-articulate' (derived from 'nemb' = 'mute')[2].
   For our purposes, the history of the word 'deutsch' is of even
greater interest. There is – understandably – a large body of literature on the etymology and shifts in meaning of 'deutsch' – for
example in 1970 the Wissenschaftliche Buchgesellschaft devoted a
volume in its *Wege der Forschung* series[3] to the question – which is
still surrounded by a fair measure of controversy, as can be seen
from some of the conflicting opinions published since 1970.[4] However, without going into the controversies in great detail, it is still
possible to identify the issues on which there is consensus.
   Etymologically, 'deutsch' appears to be based on an adjective
derived from Germanic *þeudo = people (to be seen in Gothic

'þiuda', Anglo-Saxon 'þéod' etc). The first extant instances, however, are found from 786 in the Medieval Latin form 'theodiscus' = 'the vernacular'.

It is widely assumed that 'theodiscus' is a Latinised form of a Germanic *þeudiska; by the mid-eleventh century, 'theodiscus' had largely been superseded in Latin texts by 'teutonicus'. By this time, however, the vernacular form – variously rendered as 'thiudisc' or 'diutisk' – had established itself in written texts, referring also initially to the *language*. In the eleventh century, there is then a shift in reference; a text from around 1025 contains the phrase 'terra Theodisca'[5], and the Anolied (late eleventh century) refers to 'Diutischin sprechin, Diutischin liute, man, laut'. The *Kaiserchronik* (c. 1155) uses a substantivisation to refer to 'die Diutiscen', and a Hessian version of the legend of Pilate from 1170 uses the phrase 'tutisch volk'. Around the turn of the thirteenth century, Walter von der Vogelweide could use the adjective in an extended meaning in the phrase 'tiuschu zuht'.[6] Then, by the end of the fifteenth century, the 'national' connection had become sufficiently strong for the name of the Empire to be expanded to 'Das Heilige Römische Reich Deutscher Nation'.

Whether, as Weisgerber suggests, the term 'deutsch' arose as a result of language conflict on the western borders between Romance and Germanic before moving eastwards, or whether it developed simultaneously over a wider area to denote the distinction between Latin and the (a?) vernacular does not need to concern us overmuch here. Neither is it central to our argument whether, in the latter case, there was a difference in meaning between the Western and South-Eastern (Bavarian) uses of the term. Two points are, however, of significant interest. The first – and minor one – is that there is a body of philological opinion (represented by Weisgerber) which sees a 'national consciousness' arising from language conflict. The second – and major one – is that in the definition of 'deutsch' the language is prior, i.e., it can be strongly argued that 'die Deutschen' are defined originally by their language, and that in this they differ from the majority of other European nations.

Whilst not wishing to postulate a 'strong' hypothesis that this priority of language has affected the German 'collective unconscious', it does give added meaning in the German context to Grimm's contention put forward at the Frankfurt *Germanisten-*

versammlung in 1846 that 'a nation is the totality of people who speak the same language'.[7] There is in German history a long tradition of regarding the German language as a major constituent of nationhood – not least because the course of German history left few other defining characteristics. This tradition has helped shape the national consciousness and attitudes towards the German language, and it is to some of the manifestations of this consciousness that we shall now turn.

Linguistic purism

The development and political role of a German standard

The development of what Habermas terms a German 'literary public sphere' (*literarische Öffentlichkeit*)[8] in the 18th century is necessarily paralleled by changing perceptions of the status, role and function of the German language in the move from triglossia to monoglossia referred to in Chapter 2.

With the move from a 'literary public sphere' to a 'political public sphere' (*politische Öffentlichkeit*) in the nineteenth century, there is then a further shift in these perceptions, with an attendant shift from the humanist ideals of the eighteenth century Enlightenment to nationalist concerns by the mid-nineteenth century, as indicated by the increasing dominance of concepts such as *Nation*, *Volkstum*, *Deutschtum* traced by Straßner to which we also referred in Chapter 2.

Alan Kirkness sees changing linguistic attitudes reflected in perceptions of the 'purity' of the German language and the reception accorded to foreign words, both of which have had an important part to play in German linguistic culture from the seventeenth century onwards.[9] Kirkness distinguishes three main periods of language purism, which it is worth bearing in mind here: the first phase encompasses the seventeenth and eighteenth centuries, which he sees as being marked by a general *Sprachpurismus*, followed by a transitional phase from about 1789 to 1819, leading into a third phase of *Fremdwortpurismus* in the nineteenth and twentieth centuries.

Concepts of 'purity' such as those described by Kirkness must however be viewed in a wider communicative and socio-cultural context, as they are indicative of more general linguistic and political concerns.

The main concern of language theorists and critics in the sevententh and eighteenth centuries was to assert the status of the German language and to form it into an effective communicative instrument; the attempts to ensure the 'purity' of the language were directed towards the establishment of a national standard, free not only of superfluous foreign elements but also of archaisms and dialect forms.

In the first half of the seventeenth century, the efforts of the Baroque poets such as Harsdörffer, Zesen and Opitz were directed towards the creation of a *literary* standard on a par with Latin and Greek. Their puristic concerns were mainly morphological and lexical; Martin Opitz, for example, in his *Buch von der deutschen Poeterei* (1624) demands that words should be 'pure and clear', following the usage of High German with standardised forms. He also rejects the use of foreign words, as these offend against the principles of purity and clarity.[10]

Opitz is making three main points here; the first concerns the adherence to an accepted norm which, among other things, is marked by its morphological integrity (second point) and by its freedom from alien elements (third point). The freedom from alie forms, for which Opitz claims classical antecedents,[11] is, however, not being propagated as an end in itself, but as protection for the readers against anyone who happens to have picked up a few foreign words, which he probably does not even understand, and insists on using them at every opportunity,[12] and in the interests of general clarity.[13] That the main concern of the desire for purity is clarity is demonstrated by the continuation of the text, where Opitz lays down that everything must be avoided which can impede clarity and understanding, and shows an appreciation of the need for syntactic unambiguity. [14]

If the concern of Baroque poetics was with the elevation of the German literary standard, that of the early Enlightenment was with the establishment of German as a language of academic discourse to supplant Latin – this, with the gift of hindsight, being an essential prerequisite for the creation of a political public sphere at the beginning of the nineteenth century.

At the end of the seventeenth century, Latin was still the language of academia; a first blow for German had been struck by Christian Thomasius who, in 1687, posted a notice at Leipzig *in German*, announcing his intention of delivering a course of lectures *in German*[15], an action which Eric Blackall sees as an eminently political act: 'His fixing of the notice in the vernacular to the university screens was a symbolic gesture reminiscent of Luther's nailing his theses to the door of the church at Wittenberg. It was a gesture to flout authority.'[16]

The effect of the movement towards German was such that by the third decade of the eighteenth century, German had become established as the medium of spoken academic discourse, and in the course of the century German also attained dominance in the written medium as well, as is shown in an analysis of the relation of German to Latin publications contained in the catalogues from the Leipzig Spring Fairs of 1740, 1770 and 1800 (Table 4)[17]

Table 4 Relation of German to Latin publications at Leipzig Spring Fairs of 1740, 1770 and 1800

Year	Total publications German/Latin		Sciences German/Latin		Mathematics German/Latin	
1740	545	209	4	8	10	3
1770	981	163	31	14	23	3
1800	2442	102	108	21	53	1

Source: Pörksen, *Deutsche Naturwissenschaftssprachen*, 1986.

What we observe here is firstly an increase in the absolute number of publications, and secondly a considerable rise in the volume of German-language texts relative to Latin. The two trends are linked, because a rise in the volume of German publications led to an increase in the size of the potential readership, which in its turn then created the demand for more publications.

Some five years before Thomasius' defiant act, Leibniz had published his *Ermahnung an die Teutsche, ihren verstand und sprache beßer zu üben, sammt beygefügten vorschlag einer Teutsch gesinnten Gesellschaft* (probably 1682/3). Leibniz' main concern was to establish German as the primary medium of communication in the interests of general enlightenment. His emancipatory objective is subsequently taken up by others, and we can follow a line of development into Kirkness' 'transitional phase' with the works of Campe, for example, who sought to realise his pedagogic mission in educational administration; the emancipatory movement is also represented into the nineteenth century by progressive bourgeois intellectuals. Jacob Grimm, for example, understood the development of the German national language not solely as a manifestation of the 'German spirit' in the interests of national unity, but also as an antidote to the particularist and reactionary interests of the restored aristocratic order which treated its subjects like goods and chattels.[18]

Leibniz' objective is enlightenment, and the love of wisdom and virtue, which he perceives as a patriotic duty.[19] He analyses the present parlous state of the German language, which he ascribes to the gulf separating scholars and people, who – quite literally – do not speak the same language, and he attacks the former on two counts. Firstly they are lacking in creativity and originality,[20] and secondly they write in foreign languages.[21] The use of Latin is condemned precisely because it excludes large sections of the population from the fruits of learning and prevents the renewal of the German language.[22] Here Leibniz draws comparisons with English, French and Italian, all of which have developed a strong vernacular tradition, for which the Germans must also strive.[23]

Thus, while Leibniz does not discount the part played by external influences in Germany's decline – and he lists the Thirty Years' War and the lack of a capital or cultural centre as being contributing factors – he strongly maintains that there will be no improvement and restoration of Germany's reputation and dignity without due care being taken of the language.[24]

The Emperor and princes can be relied upon to make their contribution towards restoring Germany's fortunes,[25] but intellectual renewal will only be brought about by the concerted efforts of everybody (i.e., every intellectual).[26]

With this general appeal to his peers, Leibniz is setting a marker for a public role for the 'ordinary citizen'.

In his other critical linguistic text *Unvorgreiffliche Gedancken betreffend die Ausübung und Verbesserung der Teutschen Sprache* (most probably written in 1697), Leibniz undertakes a critique of the present state of the German language and attempts to define those areas in which he perceives the language to be deficient.

Once again, Leibniz is motivated by the rationalism of the Enlightenment. He asserts that language is a reflection of reason, and that if a people value reason, then they will also pay due attention to the exercise of their language.[27] He maintains that science has been invigorated in Germany and the art of war developed, and expresses the wish that reason should also come to fruition and take its rightful place.[28] At the same time, he again sees the strengthening of the language as a patriotic duty, as the failure to care for the native language and the adoption of foreign tongues leads to subjugation and a loss of liberty.[29]

In his analysis of the present state of the language, Leibniz finds that the main strength lies in the discourse of the tangible and practical, [30] – these having been the very areas with which Latinate intellectuals had not concerned themselves. The downside is that it is in those very areas of academic discourse, in the discourse of the abstract and the ideal, that the German language is weak.[31]

Emancipation through language – linguistic critique in the Enlightenment

If Leibniz' analysis is correct, then the political consequences are serious, because it means that the emerging 'new bourgeoisie' are deprived of the means of self-expression and self-definition and do not command a discourse which will allow them to engage in public debate and thus to contribute to the formation of a public sphere. Thus, although Leibniz does not state this explicitly, the development of the German language in the areas of weakness which he identifies is a prerequisite – though not a guarantee – of political emancipation.

The combination of the emancipatory tradition of the Enlightenment and the establishment and propagation of a German standard is represented in the works of two further writers whom we shall consider here – Joachim Heinrich Campe and Carl Gustav Jochmann – in order to illustrate some of the linguistic concerns of the German Enlightenment.

Joachim Heinrich Campe (1746-1818) studied theology and held a variety of ecclesiastical and teaching posts (including one as private teacher to Alexander and Wilhelm von Humboldt) before turning to a short-lived career in educational administration from 1786 to 1790, during which time he not only edited a sixteen-volume educational encyclopaedia but also founded a publishing company (the Braunschweiger Schulbuchhandlung) and co-edited the *Braunschweigische Journal*. His writings, which increasingly attracted the unwelcome attentions of the censors, were marked by a commitment to education, particularly to political education. An admirer of the initial achievements of the French Revolution, which he observed at first hand on a number of visits to Paris, he was particularly impressed by the standard of public discourse in France, marvelling for example at the way in which even manual workers were able to engage in informed political discussion.[32] The prerequisites for this he perceived in the constitution of the French language and the state of the French communicative environment, in which a truly common language was available for the conduct of public discourse.

Despite his enthusiasm for the French Revolution, Campe had serious doubts about its 'exportability' to Germany, fearing that the Germans were not yet ready for such an upheaval. His analysis of the reasons points to the desolate state of the communicative environment, which he sees as being marked by a low level of public discourse, which in its turn is a result of the miserable state of German, with the majority of speakers being alienated from many aspects of their language. It is this realisation which leads him to direct his efforts towards a reform of the German language, and in particular to campaign for a liberation of German from alien elements, which for him are one of the main obstacles to a political and social debate in which all may engage. In other words, he wants to give the language back to the people.

One of the main vehicles for his campaign was his *Wörterbuch zur Erklärung und Verdeutschung der unserer Sprache aufgedrungenen fremden Ausdrücke,*[33] in which he proposed German terms in the place of the many xenologisms in the German language of his day. In the Preface to his dictionary, Campe is concerned to stress that he does not view linguistic purism as an end in itself, but as a means to an end, and in his essay *Ueber die Reinigung und*

Bereicherung der Deutschen Sprache,[34] published as an appendix to the Preface, he expresses his astonishment that the purist argument always has recourse to an abstract ideal of purity rather than considering the practical uses of linguistic purity – as if the language users existed for the sake of the language, rather than the other way round![35]

For Campe, linguistic purity is an essential prerequisite for two things – for universal education and meaningful philosophy.[36]

With respect to the latter, Campe's argument runs that the overloading of philosophical discourse with Latinisms and Graecisms not only deprives the majority of the opportunity to participate in philosophical debate, but is also detrimental to the quality of the debate itself in that it conceals the vacuity of much of the discussion.[37]

Campe's general case against xenologisms rests on two linked arguments, the one semantic, the other morpho-phonological. For him, the 'Germanness' of a word is a matter of both content and form: firstly, it should be comprehensible to all Germans, and secondly its formation and sound pattern should coincide with that of other German words.[38]

As far as the meaning is concerned, Campe contends that a monolingual German is unable to relate to the meaning of a xenologism or to connect the word to other semantically related words of different origin. Thus, the foreign word becomes completely arbitrary, disconnected from the rest of the lexis, and therefore difficult to retain and deploy.

With respect to the form, Campe argues that foreign words detract from the homogeneity of the language, thus weakening both its essential nature and its links with its speakers (so that language and language community become alienated from each other). He subscribes to the commonly-held view of language as an organism which should be allowed to develop naturally from within. The link between speakers and language is so strong for Campe that he sees the permeation of the language with foreign words as weakening the national character, with Germans ceasing to fulfil their 'natural function' as Germans if they allow their language to become a 'chequered mixture of foreign and native sounds and words'. [39]

Campe's argument from homogeneity is however pragmatic rather than idealistic; an 'organic' homogeneous language can be more easily learnt and more effectively used, since it displays a more uniform set of rules with fewer exceptions.

Campe's basic intentions are reminiscent of those we observed in Leibniz – the desire to open rational and reasoning discourse to as many of the people as possible; both of them inveigh against Latinisms which exclude so many from that discourse. What distinguishes Campe from Leibniz (apart from the fact that all his works are written in German!) is firstly his view of language as a homogeneous organism, secondly his more direct pedagogical commitment directed towards improving the general communicative environment in the interests of political enlightenment and emancipation, and thirdly the way in which, with his dictionary, he attempted to implement a programme of Germanisation, some of the results of which are still with us today.[40]

The guiding principle behind Campe's Germanification programme is that all those words which should form part of the educated citizen's vocabulary should be in German,[41] and he details those fields which he considers relevant: ethics, religion (as distinct from theology), law, parts of philosophy, natural science, medicine, business and literature.

In many respects, the linguistic critique of Carl Gustav Jochmann (1789–1830), a late representative of the Enlightenment, shows apparent similarities to that of Campe, but in fact his analysis and critique is far more radical; Campe believes that he can effect linguistic change by systemic reform at the word level, particularly by purging the German language of foreign words, whereas Jochmann sees the need for a radical reform of the ways in which communication structures are configured in Germany. The titles of Jochmann's two main works, *Über die Sprache*[42] and *Über die Öffentlichkeit*[43] already indicate the direction of his thinking.

There are two main lines to Jochmann's thought in his critique of the present state of the German language. Firstly – like Campe – he finds that the majority of German speakers are effectively alienated from their language and debarred from intellectual discourse. Together with Campe, he sees the absence of political openness and freedom reflected in the absence of a common public discourse, and in an argument strongly reminiscent of Leibniz (whom he quotes approvingly on a number of occasions), he maintains that national greatness and material prosperity are ultimately dependent on intellectual achievement, constituted and mediated through language.[44] Indeed, he goes so far as to claim that without intellectual mastery, even the material base is put at risk.[45]

Like Campe, Jochmann rejects foreign terms, which he sees can be used to conceal rather than to inform, and he adduces the same argument against the use of xenologisms (particularly for abstract concepts), namely that they are not integrated into the lexical structure of the language. His argument against foreign words is not a nationalistic one, i.e., xenologisms are rejected not simply because they are foreign, but because firstly they are not readily comprehensible, and secondly many speakers cannot relate to them; the excessive use of them shows a lack of commitment to the German language which will ultimately lead to intellectual and material impoverishment.

Jochmann's main contention is not, however, that the German language *qua* language is deficient as a system; in contrast to Campe, he sees the problem less in the language itself than in the manner in which it is used, and thus he introduces a strong *socio*-linguistic perspective. Although, for example, he admits that languages are structured differently, each with its own strengths and weaknesses, some offering greater scope than others, he does not consider that any language is intrinsically incapable of clear expression.

The determining factors for Jochmann are the 'spirit' or 'will' of the users of the language and the communicative conditions under which it is used, and it is here that his critique of the current state of the German language pivots.

For Jochmann, language is essentially a social phenomenon, and its main function is to work as an instrument for social development.[46] Linguistic change and social change go hand in hand, the one feeding on and into the other, and as an example of the type of radical socio-cultural change which he means, Jochmann cites Luther and the Reformation. In the ensuing period, however (up to the time at which Jochmann was writing), he maintains that the linguistic potential which Luther had established failed to be realised, for reasons which were not inherent in the language, but were to be found in its use, or rather in its users.[47]

Four factors are identified as contributing to this state of affairs. Firstly there is the fact that, after Luther, German remained a

'bookish' language, which established itself as a vehicle for literature and science, but did not lend itself to more general public
debate and to the establishment of an active oral tradition; the
only places in which the language was heard – as opposed to read
– was in the home and from the pulpit.[48] The upshot was that the
Germans gradually lost control over their language; what oral
public discourse there was took place either in French or in Latin.

Part of the reason, and this brings us to the second factor
obtaining against the establishment of an active linguistic culture
in Germany, was the lack of commitment to the German language
of those who today would be called 'opinion-leaders'. Here,
Jochmann cites the examples of Charles V and Frederick the
Great, and reminds his readers that it was only over the previous
fifty years that the use of the mother tongue ceased to be proscribed in higher education,[49] and that the intellectuals started
using German, even though it was only 'as a stop-gap between
foreign expressions'.[50] In Jochmann's eyes, the German language
had become nothing more than a receptacle for foreignisms, and
was thus incapable of being established as a valued asset for its
'owners'.

The third and fourth factors both relate to facets of the socio-
communicative environment. Firstly, Jochmann identifies the
lack of a common discourse, which manifests itself in the gulf
between 'learned' discourse and that of the rest of the population,
and secondly he sees German political culture as one which is not
based on dialogue or on reasoned political debate, this being both
the consequence and the cause of the lack of a common discourse.
He points with admiration at France and England (both countries
which he knew at first hand), where a common discourse has led
to a general understanding of the factors determining social
progress, whereas in Germany he sees such phenomena as only
having been 'demonstrated, or at best commanded, but seldom
understood'.[51] For Jochmann, public life and 'communication' is
restricted to the chancery or the orderly-room, the parade ground
and the church,[52] and none of these institutions lend themselves
to reasoned dialogue and debate. The view of the chancery, the
parade-ground and the official church as the determining social
institutions in Germany points clearly to an imbalance of power,
to an asymmetry of communication which Jochmann tellingly
characterises with the phrase 'Lords and serfs are seldom good

communicators'.[53] Ultimately, it is this imbalance of power which is going to act as one of the main barriers to a discourse of equality, and it is at this point that the full political impact of Jochmann's language critique becomes clear. A high level of social development and a sophisticated political culture are dependent on and constitutive of a lively linguistic culture. Jochmann's message is that a community which neglects its language is doomed to mediocrity and intellectual poverty.

Jochmann concludes his essay *Über die Sprache* with a passionate appeal for political emancipation and the active involvement of all citizens in the social and political life of the community; he returns for the last time to his two main themes, the divorce of the language of scholarship from everyday discourse and the asymmetry of political power relations, both of which stand in the way of the full flowering of the German language. His final message is that when the Germans have discovered themselves and have confidence in their own capabilities, then they will also discover their language.[54]

Many of Jochmann's views on language appear remarkably modern – for example his insistence on language-in-use as the touchstone of his critique and the links he draws between language and social structure foreshadow much linguistic sociology and socio-linguistics. At the same time, however, he had in some ways already been overtaken by events. *Über die Sprache* appeared anonymously thirteen years after the restoration of German monarchism had made a mockery of the Enlightenment's demand for a political system based on reason, and nine years after the Karlsbad Edicts had been promulgated in an attempt to prevent the very type of reasoned discussion which Jochmann was propagating.

At the same time, the next 'great event' after the Reformation (namely the French Revolution and the overturning of the 'old order' in Germany in 1806 and the brief interlude before its restoration) had seen a rise in national and nationalist sentiment which was at variance with the universal humanitarian ideals of the Enlightenment. Although the move towards emancipation continued, it was an emancipation in the sense both of national liberation and of liberation of the nation from the feudal order as restored.

Finally, the rise in national feeling, and the desire of Germans to rediscover their identity, had led to a search for Germany's roots, a search which included an increasing scholarly concern with the origins and history of the German language.

If the main concern of Leibniz, Campe and Jochmann was to establish an effective intellectual and political discourse in Germany in order to generate an articulate body of informed public opinion, then that of their successors in the nineteenth century was to establish the unity of the German language as a symbol, instrument and generator of the unity of the German nation. This is not to say that 'national' concerns played no part in the deliberations of Leibniz and Campe, and even less is it to deny that the works of writers such as the Grimm brothers had emancipatory or didactic objectives – indeed, the contrary is the case – but the main thrusts of linguistic concern in the two centuries were different.

The increasing preoccupation with the status and role of the German language in the second half of the eighteenth century reflects a growing awareness of German nationhood and a desire for unity on the part of the emerging progressive middle classes. Around the turn of the century, the existence of a common German *literature* began to be adduced as evidence for the existence of a German nation which transcended the boundaries of the myriad of kingdoms and petty princedoms which made up 'Germany'. It was about this time that the concept of a *Nationalliteratur* began to establish itself.[55] The perception of a 'national' literature written in the 'national' language assumes an identification of language and nation which was seen as a wider identification of the German nation as originally a cultural and linguistic entity, which as Eric Hobsbawm has pointed out,[56] distinguishes German (and Italian) nationalism from the English and French manifestations.

Two important points need to be made about this growing national awareness. The first is that, although the process was perhaps accelerated by the trauma of French occupation in the years following 1806, its origins precede the Napoleonic Wars. Secondly, the process was very much the concern of the emerging middle classes (Habermas' 'literary public sphere') who perceived national unification as a counterbalance to the power of the particularism of the princes who had so often been responsible for foreign invasions of German soil.[57]

Thus there are two strands which must be considered when examining the role played by the German language; the first is its status as a symbol of the unity of the German nation *per se*, and the second its status as a symbol of unity set against the particularism of the established aristocratic order.

If Leibniz, Campe, Jochmann and the lexicographers and grammarians of the eighteenth century had been concerned to standardise the contemporary language and to establish an effective discourse in the mother tongue, the philologists of the nineteenth century, influenced at least in part by the interests of the Romantics in earlier stages of German literature, turned their attention towards the history of the German language. Again, however, the interest in language history, although undoubtedly influenced by the pioneering work of William Jones and others, was not pursued solely for academic reasons; rather it is a reflection and part of more general social and political concerns. Here it is worth reminding ourselves that one of the arguments which we shall be following in the present study is that concerns of language study, and in particular of linguistic critique, are strongly influenced by and constitutive of more general political concerns. Earlier stages of the German language were seen to represent a 'golden age' of unity and youthful vigour in which 'language and people were one', but which now no longer obtained, and the political motives behind the study of German-language history were to evoke that spirit of the Golden Age to remind the Germans of that unity which they now were lacking.

The linkage between philological and historical interest and political activity can be illustrated very well using the example of Jacob and Wilhelm Grimm – particularly the former.

Jacob's early interest in law, which he studied under Savigny in Berlin, soon gave way to a growing interest in ancient German culture and literature, and especially in the history and development of the German language, which he saw as the cultural band unifying the German people – 'ein volk ist der inbegriff von menschen, welche dieselbe sprache reden' ('a nation is the totality of people who speak the same language'), as he had declared at the Frankfurt *Germanistenversammlung* in 1846. Nowadays, Grimm is probably remembered best for his philological achievements – as an editor of ancient texts, as a language historian, after whom the First or 'Germanic' Sound Shift is named, as a grammarian, and above all as the lexicographer who, together with his brother Wilhelm, launched the ambitious programme for a *Deutsches*

Wörterbuch[58]. His biography, however, reminds us of the close links which existed in the first half of the nineteenth century between *Germanistik* and emancipatory political activity. In 1829, after holding various posts in Hesse, he accepted an appointment as Librarian and Professor at the University of Göttingen (in the kingdom of Hanover); he identified himself with the protests against the *coup d'état* by the King, who in 1833 tried to annul the constitution, an act of defiance by Grimm which cost him his post when, together with his brother and five others, he was dismissed in 1837. In 1846 and 1847, Grimm was Honorary President of the *Germanistenversammlungen* in Frankfurt and Lübeck (which were seen by some both inside and outside Germany as eminently 'political' gatherings) and in 1848 he was elected to the National Assembly in Frankfurt. In this connection, it is worth noting that he was not the only *Germanist* to be elected to that body, which might help to explain why there was no *Germanistenversammlung* in 1848. Grimm regarded his philological and political activities as fully consistent with each other; in the Introduction to the *Deutsches Wörterbuch* he sees the desire for national unity as the main motive force behind both care for the mother tongue and the exercise of philology, for German language and literature are the only bond holding the nation together.[59]

Thus the German language becomes a symbol of national unity; the dominant metaphor is that of the language as an organism incorporating the spirit of the German nation, and the objective of *Germanistik* is perceived as a patriotic one, to demonstrate the historicity of the German language and evoke a 'golden age' of youth and vitality, where language and people were one, and not yet alienated from each other.

It is, however, not only as a *symbol* of national unity that the German language acquires significance; Grimm goes further to argue that the development of the language uniquely mirrors the development of the people and is the manifestation of their 'spirit' or 'soul'.[60]

As an example of the way in which Grimm sees language history and 'national' history as being linked, Robins cites his views of sound shifts: 'Grimm applied the ideas of Herder on the close relationship between a nation and its language to the historical dimension of language, seeing indeed in the sound shift to which he gave his name an early assertion of the independence on the part of the ancestors of the German peoples.'[61]

Grimm's historical perspective is, however, not restricted to the past; the German language fulfils a programmatic need, with both an external and an internal orientation. Internally, there is a need for linguistic consolidation and standardisation – not, however, for reasons of rationalisation and efficiency, but as an act of bourgeois emancipation. Grimm sees Germany as a nation unnaturally divided by the machinations of petty princes which can only be united in peace and tranquillity if the various dialects come together to form a unified whole.[62]

It is this view of Germany as a nation unnaturally divided by the machinations of petty princes which clearly marks Grimm's political position and motivates his overt political activity, for example as a member of the Assembly in the Paulskirche. His view of a unified German nation is not of one within the established political order, but of one with a clear democratic form.

The objective pursued by Grimm and the early *Germanisten* was not only to evoke the unity of a (mythical?) past and to establish the unity of the German language as a symbol of the unity of the German people, but also to restore to the German people their language in all its richness. The concept of the *Sprachnation*, the nation defined and represented by its language rather than by any political entity, led to the German language being regarded as a supreme national value which became endowed with almost religious significance, as is evidenced by a passage from the Introduction to the *Deutsches Wörterbuch*, which seems to suggest that the dictionary should assume a role previously held by the family bible.[63]

At the same time, however, the external orientation of Grimm's historical perspective as put forward at the Frankfurt *Germanistenversammlung* in 1846 contains – perhaps unwittingly – the seeds of future nationalist-expansionist views of German language and *Geist*; if the people are defined by their language, then they will set their own boundaries wherever they take their language.[64]

The view of *Germanistik* as an eminently political discipline, and one which espoused not only the cause of German unification, but also that of potential German expansionism, was one which did not just obtain in Germany. It was shared, for example, – though not with any joy – by the Dane C. Hinrichsen, who wrote in 1848 that the *Reichstag* in Frankfurt was nothing more than an overt manifestation of the 'Germanism' which had been inherent in the Germanistic assemblies such as that in Lübeck.[65]

In 1829, Grimm had been appointed to a chair in German at Göttingen, an appointment which reflected the 'institutionalisation' of *Germanistik* in the first half of the nineteenth century; the first appointment to a professorship in German had been that of von den Hagen in Berlin in 1810, which was followed by his translation to a post (and later a chair) in Breslau. The lending of official support to German Studies faced the authorities with a dilemma; on the one hand they acknowledged the 'patriotic' role which the historical study of German could play in the struggle to liberate 'Germany' from the French, but on the other they were faced with the progressive republican views which many *Germanisten* espoused and which motivated their work. In the course of the century, however, both the ethos of the discipline and its thematic and methodological foci underwent a gradual change, so that from being a movement for patriotic liberation and political emancipation it became a pillar of Prussian conservatism in the service of the state establishment.

The initial dilemma is shown by the treatment of the Brothers Grimm in Göttingen, but they were not the only *Germanisten* to fall foul of the authorities: in a study of 100 biographies of *Germanisten* from the first half of the nineteenth century, Müller discovered that no fewer than twenty-six had been the subject of political or legal persecution.[66]

In the course of the century, the discipline of *Germanistik* underwent a gradual transformation dictated both by methodological and thematic developments within the discipline itself and by its social and cultural standing.

Internally, the development was marked by a clear move away from the holistic approaches to language history propagated by Grimm and others in favour of a more 'exact' and backward-oriented atomistic approach designed to bring *Germanistik* closer to the methods of both classical philology and the 'exact sciences' and thus to establish its academic credentials.

What happened externally was that, putting it briefly, the relationship between language as an expression of the 'national spirit' and a German state as a political organisation was reversed. In the first half of the nineteenth century, the predominant view was that the function of a unified German state was to serve the cause of 'national spirit' and its language; after the failure of the 'bourgeois revolution' of 1848, the 'national spirit' and the German language were progressively pressed into the service of the German state,[67] with a degree in *Germanistik* becoming an entrance qualification for the state service, and the study of German in schools being regarded as serving the 'national interest'.

The internal change is clearly reflected in Scherer's work, and the new external orientation is documented for example both in the introduction to Scherer's history of the German language, where he writes of *Germanistik*'s 'bold venture' in setting up a system of 'national ethics'[68] and in Hildebrand's introduction to the fifth volume of Grimms' *Deutsches Wörterbuch* (published in 1873), which establishes the priority of *Realpolitik* over *Idealpolitik*: now that German statesmanship and military endeavour have procured a new lease of life for the nation, the study of history is to teach coming generations how to maintain it, and the study of German philology has to provide its spiritual life-force.[69]

Education

The increasing institutionalisation of *Germanistik* and the shift in its orientation towards a state-led nationalism were accompanied by a change in the social status of *Germanisten* and in their career prospects. At the turn of the century, it had been the study of theology which allowed members of the (lower) middle classes a degree of social mobility and an enhancement of their social status; the role played by theology was later assumed by the study of the classics, with the study of classical philology opening the path to a teaching career in the Gymnasium. The rise of *Germanistik* from around mid-century, when the first *Germanistische Seminare* were founded, led to 'competition' between *Germanistik* and Classics, with the institution of state examinations in German opening the way to a teaching career.

At the same time, as we have already seen in the previous chapter, the amount of time devoted to German classes was raised by 30 per cent, which, coupled with an increase in the secondary school population, not only meant that the spread and level of advanced formal training in the native language became an important cultural factor but also led to enhanced career prospects for *Germanisten*. The final 'dominance' of German over Classics is documented in a speech by Wilhelm II in 1890, when he decreed that German was to form the basis of the Gymnasium, whose role was to educate nationally-minded Germans, and not young Greeks or Romans.[70]

Although, as we have seen in the previous chapter, the increased attention paid in schools to competence in the mother tongue was in part a response to the changing communicative environment and the demands placed on communication skills, the 'official' ethos and justification for the subject, particularly after 1871, was to be found on a completely different plane, one which mirrors the changing perceptions of the cultural and political role of *Germanistik*.

In the same way that Scherer saw *Germanistik* as providing a system of national ethics, so the teaching of German in schools was to imbue the pupils with the spirit of 'German-ness' that was incorporated in the German language. The guidelines for the teaching of German in Prussian high schools of 1901 laid down that the teaching of German was to have an academic purpose, but was also to serve a superior objective, that of education towards a 'spiritual, determined and joyful German-ness'. In this, the teaching of German was seen as being on a par with the teaching of religion and history.[71] The 'nationalist' motive behind the teaching of German was one which survived the First World War; for example, the guidelines for the teaching of German in Prussian high schools of 1925 still decreed that the function of German teaching was not only to train pupils in the skills of speaking and writing German, but was also to teach them to 'feel, think and will in a German manner'.[72]

Purism revisited

As we have already seen, the initial concerns of language purists from the Baroque poets to Campe were to establish an effective and comprehensible German standard in literature, science and politics, with increasing emphasis being placed on the creation of a public political discourse; Carl Gustav Jochmann can be said to have represented the culmination of this strand of purism.

With the growing view of the German language as a symbol of national unity and the move away from the emancipatory concerns of the first generations of *Germanisten*, linguistic purism ceased to be regarded as a means to an end, but became an end in itself. Foreign words were now no longer to be rejected because of their incomprehensibility or because they excluded sections of the population from certain discourses, but solely because of their foreignness, which was seen as detrimental to German 'Geist' as reflected in the language. With this new phase of purism, which arose around the middle of the nineteenth century, and for which Joseph Brugger[73] can stand as one of the main representatives, strong racist elements began to make themselves felt. At this stage, however, popular support for the movement was lacking, and interest in it ebbed.

After the Prussian victory over France and the establishment of the Second Empire, however, a new phase of purism was ushered in, which was marked by two features which had hitherto been lacking – official implementation and widespread public support. Hitherto, language purism had been seen as an act of liberation, and as such had been the concern of individuals or small informal groupings. With the constitution of a unified German state, the 'Germanification' of the German language became an expression of national supremacy and self-confidence. In the wake of the wide-ranging administrative reforms necessitated by the foundation of the Second Empire, imperial authorities decreed that the replacement of foreignisms by 'native' German terms was to be official policy. Thus in the administration of transport, postal services, education and the military, a wave of 'Germanification' set in, which had far-reaching effects not only on official texts but also on public discourse generally.[74] Parallel to these official efforts, private initiatives were set up, and here particular mention should be made of the Deutscher Sprachverein (later the Allgemeiner Deutscher Sprachverein), founded in 1885 by Professors Riegel (Brunswick) and Dunger (Dresden). The objectives of the association reflect the linguistic and ethical functions ascribed to the German language in education, to free the German language from unnecessary foreign elements, to maintain and restore the 'true spirit' and 'proper essence' of the German language, and thus to help strengthen German national awareness. The Association, with its slogan of 'No foreign word when a good

German expression is available' ('Kein Fremdwort für das, was deutsch gut ausgedrückt werden kann'), recruited members from throughout the Empire and beyond,[75] numbering some 11,000 by 1891, and claiming 45,000 members by the start of the First World War. Much of the following discussion will be based in the main on the activities and publications of the Allgemeiner Deutscher Sprachverein, and this for three reasons. Firstly, the Association presents a focus of activity for language purists and therefore provides a convenient forum for analysis, even though its activities and opinions were hotly contested in some academic circles. Secondly, the membership – or at least the executive – of the Association contains a large number of 'opinion-formers' from education and the civil service, and also includes a number of prominent *Germanisten*, including Behagel and Siebs; thus it can fairly be claimed that the Association, though not a mass movement in the modern sense of the word, does reflect an influential body of linguistic opinion and enjoyed at least the passive support of the authorities (Bismarck, for example, was elected an honorary member). Thirdly, the Association was concerned with the status of Germanhood and the German language, and one of the thrusts of its activities was directed towards public discourse, so that it can fairly be regarded as a 'political' linguistic organisation.

The main targets of the language purists had previously been Latin (particularly in the seventeenth and eighteenth centuries) and French (particularly in the nineteenth century), partly because it was from these two languages that the main foreign influences had come, and partly of course because French had been viewed as the language of an occupying power and a political rival. Towards the end of the nineteenth century, however, attention shifted somewhat towards Anglicisms, and it is suggested that there were two main reasons for this, one of them eminently political.

The first, pragmatic, reason was that with industrialisation and Britain's technical and industrial superiority in the nineteenth century, there was an increase in the amount of borrowing from English, so that English 'incursions' into the German vocabulary became more visible.[76]

It is suggested that the second, idealist, reason was that, with the triumph of German arms over French arms in 1870/71 and the establishment of a strong German nation-state, France was no

longer regarded as Germany's principal political rival, but that
England was now cast in this role, with the result that a 'threat'
was seen to be emanating from the English language.

As an illustration of the more militant 'new spirit' of language
purism towards the end of the nineteenth century, we shall look at
two numbers of the monthly periodical of the Allgemeiner
Deutscher Sprachverein from November and December 1899,
paying particular attention to two articles from the December
number and the announcement of a competition in November.
The two articles, by the founder member H. Dunger [77] and the
editor of the journal, O. Streicher,[78] both concern themselves with
questions of the role and status of English and can be viewed as
representative of the views of the Association. We shall have to
consider not only the linguistic and political arguments advanced,
but also examine the metaphors and imagery which constitute the
arguments.

In academic terms, Dunger's article 'Wider die Engländerei in
der deutschen Sprache' is far more substantial than Streicher's
piece. Dunger reports on the increase in the number of Anglicisms
entering German and also records the enhancement of the social
status of English in Germany, which has replaced French in
popular estimation and public usefulness.[79] His report, however,
serves a deeper purpose, which is to remind his readers that the
'struggle' against xenologisms is not yet over, furthermore it is not
only the old 'enemies' which must be repulsed, but new 'foes'
have also appeared on the scene, insolently trying to effect an
entry into the German language; principal among these intruders
are the English.[80]

The English xenologisms are rejected because they are seen as
detracting from the 'purity' of the German language, even if there
is a genetic link between German and English, which is 'flesh of
our flesh'. Four main sets of images convey Dunger's perception of
the German language.

It is seen first as a living organism, either animal or vegetable,
which is subjected to the assaults of parasites or weeds,[81] and here
Dunger propagates the 'organic' view of language which enjoyed
wide currency throughout the nineteenth century.

Secondly, language is perceived as a building – the talk is of the
'venerable halls' of the German language, which are invaded by
'mobs' of foreigners;[82] the image of the 'house' is one which can be

traced back to the Bible, and here the use of 'halls' with the epithet 'venerable' carries distinct religious overtones, with the language being perceived as a shrine or sanctuary.

Thirdly, the language is conceptualised as a 'territory' which is 'invaded' or 'swamped' by foreign hordes,[83] and it is here that the imagery is at its most militaristic.

Fourthly, there is a reference to the 'naturalisation' of foreign words in German, behind which is the concept of the language as a polity with rights of citizenship.

Behind all these metaphors lies the assumption that the German language possesses a 'purity' which is under threat, and also that the German language is superior to those languages trying to gain entry into it, as evidenced for example by the perception of foreign language elements as 'parasites' or 'weeds'. Given the close link that is postulated between 'language' and 'nation' or *Volk*, such imagery is inherently racist, and is reminiscent of that used (not just in Germany) against migration, particularly of those from different ethnic backgrounds.

Streicher's piece is more strident, more militant than Dunger's, and more overtly 'political'. In it, he inveighs against a view put forward by a Professor H. Diels in June 1899 that England was destined to be the universal language of the future. Streicher accuses Diels of being prepared to sacrifice the richness and glory of Germany's linguistic heritage and to submit to the domination of a foreign power, an act which is tantamount to treason and must be resisted.[84] Apart from the general line of Streicher's argument, there are three elements in his piece which are of particular relevance for our purposes.

The first is Streicher's self-reflection on the purpose of language purism. Diels had advanced the argument that the adoption of foreign words in German is a welcome development which leads to the internationalisation of the German language, and attacked the nationalistic purism which would have all foreign words removed from the German language. For Streicher, the adoption of foreign words is despicable and undignified,[85] and the fight against xenologisms a valiant act of salvation for Germany's national spirit from despicable self-degradation and confusion.[86]

The second element is overtly racist. One of Diels' arguments in favour of English as an international language is that, by combining both Germanic and Romance elements, English has a certain international character. This is anathema to Streicher, who rejects the idea of a *Mischsprache* and argues that such a *Mischmasch* would be deeply offensive to German national feeling.[87]

Thirdly, Streicher's piece contains a programmatic element. He believes Germany can only achieve greatness from the strength of its own resources and that the process of national renewal is not complete; it is the avowed aim of the Allgemeiner Deutscher Sprachverein to promote this process, in collaboration with other associations with similar aims.[88] For an example of how the Allgemeiner Deutscher Sprachverein feels it can help, we need to turn to the previous number of its journal. In it, the Sprachverein offers a prize of 1,000 marks for a dictionary of German nautical vocabulary. The motivation behind the prize is to support the German people's newly-awakened longing for the sea, as Germany's future lies in its maritime power if it is to participate in the carving-up of the world among the nations of Europe.[89] There can be no doubt that the Sprachverein had correctly identified a trend of the age, which is expressed for example in the rise of naval associations towards the end of the nineteenth century and the popularity of sailor-suits in children's fashion. The interest in sea-power and the desire for a strong navy (for this is behind it all) was destined to provoke a clash with Britain, and – more importantly – marks a new direction in German politics; unification and internal consolidation is followed by the desire for expansion and the call for colonies, so that Germany can establish itself as a world power. In expansion as in unification and internal consolidation, the German language is perceived as having a role to play.

Expansionism

Grimm's reference [90] to a 'natural law' by which it is the language that sets the boundaries of a people could, under the circumstances of its formulation, be understood as a commitment to the unity of the German nation, no longer split by the machinations of petty princes. Under different circumstances, however, such as those obtaining after unification, it can assume a wider, more sinister significance.

The following section will treat the equation of nation and German language in three parts: from approximately the beginning of the twentieth century until half-way through the First World War, in the aftermath of the First World War, and then from the rise of fascism until the turning point of the Second World War in about 1942.

The main source for the first two parts will be the journal of the Allgemeiner Deutscher Sprachverein, with its clear and at times strident commitment to the German language as the clearest symbol and identification of German nationhood.

Two themes recur frequently in the pre-war numbers of the journal, the first being the status and development of the German language outside continental Europe, particularly in Germany's newly acquired 'protectorates' in Africa and elsewhere, and the second is the role of German as a world language, in keeping with Germany's new-found role as a world power.

With respect to the first, we find the Sprachverein's puristic concerns re-appearing in a new guise. There is still the worry that Germans are insufficiently secure of their 'Germanness' forcefully to establish the rights of their language and to combat xenologisms, but now the borrowings emanate not so much from French or English as European languages but firstly from competing colonial languages (particularly Afrikaans in the case of German South-West Africa) and secondly from the local vernaculars. In the Journal we find contributions with titles such as 'Deutsche Sprachpflichten gegen Südwestafrika',[91] which attempts to formulate a language policy for German South-West Africa, 'Das Deutschtum im Ausland',[92] 'Die deutsche Sprache in unsern Schutzgebieten',[93] 'Sprachnöte in Deutschafrika'[94] and 'Gegen das Neger-Englisch in Kamerun'.[95] Essentially, the argument that is advanced is that German colonies are part of Germany and therefore have the same obligations to preserve the purity of the German language.

The second theme, of German as a world language, appears in a number of articles which deal either with the establishment of the German language in specific parts of the world (e.g., 'Deutsches aus Amerika')[96] or with an overview of the global status of German (e.g., 'Ist Deutsch eine Weltsprache?').[97] In addition, there is a fairly regular column in the Journal entitled 'Vom Machtbereich der deutschen Sprache' which reports on 'triumphs' of the German language in such areas as the Russian Baltic provinces.[98]

It is perhaps worth taking a closer look at the article 'Ist Deutsch eine Weltsprache?',[99] as it contains a number of features which we shall encounter again later. Interestingly, it was written by a Swiss, a businessman from Zollikon-Zurich, rather than by a native German. The author rehearses the traditional arguments in support of his contention that German is a world language, e.g., geographical spread, number of speakers, trading status, status as a foreign language, and the status of German compared with other world languages, primarily English and French. The discourse is strongly influenced by an ideology of competition, in which the establishment of the German language is seen as an instrument in the establishment of more general German influence and power. The article ends with an appeal for support in the peaceful competition between languages ('im friedlichen und förderlichen sprachlichen Wettbewerb').[100]

That the competition is not always so peaceful becomes apparent in the Association's journal from September 1914 onwards, when the Allgemeiner Deutscher Sprachverein places itself in the forefront of the German war effort, as evidenced by the dedication of numbers of the journal, e.g., the May 1915 edition is dedicated to 'our warriors in the field' ('Feldnummer. Unsern Kriegern gewidmet'),[101] by the titles of articles, e.g., 'Der deutsche Krieg und die Ausländerei',[102] 'Der Krieg als Spracherzieher',[103] 'Deutscher Krieg und deutsche Sprache',[104] by appeals for gift subscriptions to the journal for soldiers at the front, and by the increased use of militaristic metaphor (e.g., 'Kampf gegen das Fremdwortunwesen').[105] The vision of German as a world language also reappears; however, whereas before, articles dealing with 'world languages' either addressed themselves to the status of English ('Englisch wird Weltsprache')[106] or presented German as a world language as a question ('Ist Deutsch eine Weltsprache?),[107] no doubt is left about the triumph of German arms also leading to the triumph of the German language in a leading article with the affirmative title 'Das Deutsche als Weltsprache'.[108]

With the defeat of the German and Austro-Hungarian empires, a new theme was introduced in the Allgemeiner Deutscher Sprachverein: the desire for expansion and a world role for the German language was succeeded by a fear for the continued existence of the language and a perceived need to conserve the language as the one symbol of nationhood remaining among the shambles of defeat, with more than one reference to the situation obtaining under French Napoleonic occupation. Four articles are of particular interest here: the first number of the Association's journal in 1919 opened with a passionate appeal to Germans to protect their language ('Aufruf an alle Deutschen – Bewahret, schützt eure Sprache'), which was followed in March by an open letter to the Government and the National Assembly 'Das Recht des deutschen Volks auf seine Sprache' demanding that the new constitutional documents and the names of state offices and agencies be in German, and by two relevant contributions in the July/August edition, 'Eine Sprache, ein Volk' and 'Deutsche Zukunft'.

The basic concern expressed in these contributions remains as before the resistance against an alienation of the German language through a flood of xenologisms – which are now not only called foreign words (*Fremdwörter)* but even hostile words (*Feindwörter)* – to which is added the fear that the victors of the war (particularly the Americans and the French) are determined to wipe out the German language in the territories under their control. If anything, although these four pieces were written in defeat, their tone – particularly in the first two – is more militant, more strident than that struck during the war years; it is not just a question of the Germans 'salvaging' their language and conserving it, but rather of nurturing it as the kernel of Germany's rebirth and future greatness, thus preparing the new wave of expansionism which was to follow, and in which a role was again to be ascribed to the German language.

Evidence of the spirit of militant language-led expansionism can be seen in a 'mission statement' (and the term 'mission' is used advisedly) contained in a letter written to the Emperor Wilhelm II on 15 November 1901 which is a truly striking example of the maxim of Germany as the saviour of the world ('Und es soll am deutschen Wesen/ einmal noch die Welt genesen'): 'And just as the German soul is indissolubly linked to the German language, so the advancement of mankind is bound to a Germany which will spread across the globe, establishing the sacred heritage of its language wherever it goes', [109] a testimony which is perhaps all the more noteworthy as it stems from the pen of a native-born Englishman who 'became' a convinced German and was one of the intellectual fathers of German fascist racist ideology – Houston Stewart Chamberlain.

Chamberlain provides an extreme example of the equation of language and nation/race, and thus it is not surprising that his views on language should be well-received both by influential elements within the Allgemeiner Deutscher Sprachverein and by fascist linguists.

The first reception accorded to Chamberlain in the *Zeitschrift des Allgemeinen Deutschen Sprachvereins* was in a review of his *Kriegsaufsätze* in September 1915,[110] which not only gratefully recorded his views on the supremacy of the German language, but also linked his campaign for the purity of the German people with the Association's campaign for the purity of the language, which Chamberlain saw as an important instrument in the establishment of German world domination. Partly at least as a result of this review article, which included an appeal for him to support the Allgemeiner Deutscher Sprachverein, Chamberlain did in fact become a member of the Association.

The next time Chamberlain featured in the journal was in 1932, when his reviewer of 1915 returned with a short piece on 'Chamberlain über deutsche Art und Sprache'[111] which consists in the main of extracts from the letter to the Emperor quoted above.

Then, in 1935, a more substantial contribution appeared[112] which was significant not only for its content but also for its authorship; Georg Schmidt-Rohr was one of the leading *Germanisten* of his age and an apologist for German fascism – and as such another example of the close links between linguistic and political culture in Germany. In his article, Schmidt-Rohr addresses the question of the extent to which it is still legitimate to regard the German language as a national identifier. His argument follows two main trains: the first is that Chamberlain, as one of the intellectual architects of German fascism, was also acutely aware of the significance of the German language in the definition of Germanhood, and the second is that the 'beloved Führer' himself was also aware of the role that language played in the definition and cohesion of the German people. The views expressed by Schmidt-Rohr are indicative of a final and extreme identification of language and people and of the way in which both the German language and those responsible for the academic study of it were pressed into the service of the German fascist ideology.

The particular brand of racism propagated by German fascism not only combined the features of any racism – i.e., the belief in the inherent superiority of their own 'race' and an attendant devalorising of other 'races' – but also embodied a militant expansionism and imposition of their own cultural values on others – ostensibly for the betterment of the world.

The belief in the superiority of the German, with the attendant fear of contamination, is one which has been inherent in much of the language-purist discussion since the nineteenth century; in German fascism it reaches its culmination when the 'purity' of language is inextricably linked with the 'purity' of 'race'.

At the beginning of the fascist era, the Allgemeiner Deutscher Sprachverein distinguished itself by the fervour with which it sought to remove not only 'foreign' words from the language but also endeavoured to purge it of allegedly 'Jewish' elements, in keeping with the spirit of the age. For a small instance of racist discourse in the purist discussion, we shall turn to a piece entitled 'Werden und Wesen der deutschen Sprache in alter Zeit. Die Fremdsprachenherrschaft und der Freiheitskampf der deutschen Sprache' by Klaudius Bojunga.[113] This publication probably predates the fascists' assumption of power, but is significant for that very reason, for it shows how the German fascists had recourse to ideologies already extant. Bojunga inveighs against the 'pollution' of the German language with foreign words and takes particular issue with a view put forward by a member of the Berlin Academy in 1918 that the existence of foreign words in a language is a sign of linguistic sophistication: 'For the Academy, Gypsy, Nigger-English and Yiddish-German are "highly-cultured languages", from which the Indian of Calidasa and Plato's Greek, Luther's Bible and Nietzsche's Zarathustra should hide with the uncultured purity of their language.'[114]

Here, the deliberate use of low-status examples on the one hand, coupled with derogatory designations, and high-status counter-examples, all coupled in an ironic presentation, clearly indicate the author's racist approach.

The title of Bojunga's piece, with its metaphors of domination and struggle, is typical of the spirit of militancy which pervaded much of fascist discourse; at the same time, however, we must be aware that militant and militaristic metaphors are not unique to this discourse: German, in common with other languages, fields an impressive array of military metaphors in a variety of fields.[115]

Given that the ultimate aim of German fascism was war and conquest, it is not surprising that military terms and metaphors play a significant role in fascist language use. As Seidel and Seidel-Slotty establish in their study of German fascist discourse, military expressions pervade all areas of discourse, whereby it is not just that military terms are to be found in increasing measure in non-military areas, but that the spirit of militarism and a violence of expression are prevalent everywhere.[116]

Two points here are of particular interest; the first is the phrase 'in increasing measure', which suggests that the military metaphor is not new; as the authors later point out, the German language is comparatively rich in such expressions . The second interesting phrase is 'in increasing measure in non-military areas', because this helps to answer the question of the extent to which fascist language use permeated fields outside the immediately political. A uniform answer cannot be given; it will be argued later that certain linguistic phenomena were probably of restricted currency. It is, however, possible to establish that at least some manifestations enjoyed wide currency, and to these belonged the use of military terms and metaphors.

Seidel and Seidel-Slotty echo an observation made – with vastly different intention – by Friedrich Panzer in his slim volume *Der deutsche Wortschatz* (1940). Panzer proudly points to the active use of military expressions in non-military contexts as a manifestation of the spirit of the age.[117]

One of these 'non-military contexts' is the discipline of *Germanistik* – or *Deutschwissenschaft*, as the linguistic purists preferred to call it.

Wendula Dahle (1969) has undertaken a profound and far-reaching study of both the use of military metaphor in Germanistik and the ideological function which representatives of the discipline saw for it. The title of Dahle's work, *Der Einsatz einer Wissenschaft*, itself a military metaphor, goes beyond the apparent remit of the sub-title *Eine sprachinhaltliche Analyse militärischer Terminologie in der Germanistik 1933-1945*. Referring to Panzer, she shows how many Germanists use terms such as 'hero', 'battle', 'front', etc., in professional texts in a deliberate attempt to establish a link between their discipline and the war effort, and points out that this is particularly apparent in contexts which do not require military terminology.[118]

Although some of the use of military metaphor can be attrib-
uted to the so-called *Zeitgeist*, this itself being evidence of the way
fascist ideology had permeated, *Zeitgeist* is by no means the sole
source or explanation. Neither is it sufficient to try and excuse the
militancy of such writing by pointing to the totalitarian nature of
the German fascist regime, which would brook not the slightest
deviation from the party line. Rather, the use of military metaphor
reflects the view Germanistik had of the mission – and this term is
used advisedly – which the discipline had to fulfil, this mission
being to underline the supremacy of German *Geist vis-à-vis*
inferior peoples and cultures. And it is through language that this
Geist, this *Kultur* is transmitted. Thus *Deutschwissenschaft* becomes
part of the *Bewegung*, the German language its image and its
instrument. *Germanistik* was not only to prepare the ground, it was
not only to fall in with the general ideology with the use of
military metaphor in Germanistic works; *Germanistik* itself becomes a military metaphor, an instrument of war. Thus, in the
preface to the anthology *Von deutscher Art in Sprache und Dichtung*,
Franz Koch could declare that total war was not just a military
struggle, but an intellectual and cultural battle on a massive scale.
For Koch, Germany stood before the massive task of imposing a
new spiritual order on Europe once it had been conquered by the
force of German arms.[119]

This 'intellectual and cultural battle' is to be fought with the
German language, which is not only a mediator and a means of
spiritual renewal (as Schönbrunn sees it in his *Sprache des deutschen
Soldaten* (1941)), where he maintains that military language never
serves simply to transmit thoughts but that its role is to raise
human qualities and convey the forces of will),[120] but is elevated to
the status of a weapon in its own right, as a 'sharpened sword to
defend the spirit of the nation'.[121] War is not only fought between
armies, is not solely a question of economic subjugation and the
devastation of territory. It is also a clash of languages, which enter
into combat, striving to establish and expand their territory while
denying the legitimacy of their rivals, and add their spiritual
weight to the force of arms,[122] because language is seen as the
epitome of race and nationhood. Thus the wheel turns full circle,
and again we observe the nationalistic views of language which
arose in the eighteenth and nineteenth centuries, and which in
Germany played their part in the movement for German unifica-

tion. In fascist Germany, as in the nineteenth century, German philology and linguistics again saw themselves as part of a national movement which they were called upon to serve. Given the belief in the close link between language and nationhood, it is perhaps inevitable that those who are most closely concerned with language find it difficult if not impossible to 'escape' from dominant political movements and trends, a line of enquiry which we shall be taking up again in Chapter 5.

Notes

1 G. Fricke, F. Koch and K. Lugowski, *Von deutscher Art in Sprache und Dichtung*, Stuttgart/Berlin, 1941

2 An alternative interpretation is, however, offered by O. Kronsteiner, 'Sind die *slovene* "die Redenden" und die *nemici* "die Stummen"? Zwei neue Etymologien zum Namen der Slawen und der Deutschen', P.Weisinger (ed.), *Sprache und Name in Österreich*, Vienna, 1980, pp. 339ff

3 H. Eggers, *Der Volksname deutsch*, Darmstadt, 1970

4 See for example I. Reiffenstein, 'Bezeichnungen der deutschen Gesamt-sprache', in Besch, Reichman and Sonderegger (eds), *Sprachgeschichte*, pp. 1716ff, and H. Thomas, 'THEODISCUS – DIUTISKUS – REGNUM TEUTONI-CORUM. Zu einer neuen Studie über die Anfänge des deutschen Sprach- und Volksnamens', *Rheinische Vierteljahresblätter*, 51, 1987, pp. 287ff

5 Reiffenstein, 'Bezeichnungen der deutschen Gesamtsprache', p.1718

6 After Reiffenstein, 'Bezeichnungen der deutschen Gesamtsprache', p.1719

7 'ein volk ist der inbegriff von menschen, welche dieselbe sprache reden', J. Grimm, *Kleinere Schriften*, Hildesheim, 1966 vii, 557

8 Habermas, *Strukturwandel*. The translations of *'Öffentlichkeit'*, *'literarische Öffentlichkeit'* and *'politische Öffentlichkeit'* are those proposed by Thomas Burger in his translation of Habermas, *The Structural Transformation of the Public Sphere*, Cambridge, 1989

9 A. Kirkness, 'Das Phänomen des Purismus in der Geschichte des Deutschen', in Besch *et al.* (eds) *Sprachgeschichte*, 290ff

10 'Die ziehrligkeit erfodert das die worte reine und deutlich sein. Damit wir aber reine reden mögen, sollen wir uns befleissen deme welches wir Hochdeutsch nennen bestens vermögens nach zue kommen und nicht derer örter sprache, wo falsch geredet wird, in unsere schrifften vermischen: als da sind, es geschach, für, es geschahe, er sach, für, er sahe ... So stehet es auch zum hefftigsten unsauber, wenn allerley Lateinische, Frantzösische, Spanische unnd Welsche wörter in den text unserer rede geflickt werden.' M. Opitz, *Buch von der deutschen Poeterei*, Wilhelm Braune (ed.), Abdruck der ersten Ausgabe

(1624), Tübingen, 1954, p. 24

11 'Da doch die Lateiner eine ſolche abschew vor dergleichen getragen, das in ihren verſen auch faſt kein griechiſch wort gefunden wird.' Opitz, *Buch von der deutschen Poeterei*, p. 24

12 'der nur drey oder vier außländiſche wörter, die er zum offtern nicht verſtehet, erwuſcht hat, bey aller gelegenheit ſich bemühet dieſelben herauß zu werffen' Opitz, *Buch von der deutschen Poeterei*, p. 24

13 'Wie nun wegen reinligkeit der rede frembde wörter unnd dergleichen mußen vermieden werden', Opitz *Buch von der deutschen Poeterei*, p. 27

14 'so muß man auch der deutligkeit halben sich für alle dem hüten, was unsere worte tunckel und unverstendtlich macht.' and 'Als wann ich ſagen wollte: Das weib das thier ergrieff. Hier were zue zweiffeln, ob das weib vom thiere, oder das thier vom weibe were ergrieffen worden' Opitz, *Buch von der deutschen Poeterei*, p.27

15 'Christian Thomas eröffnet der Studirenden Jugend zu Leipzig in einem Discours Welcher Gestalt man denen Frantzosen in gemeinem leben und Wandel nachahmen solle? ein COLLEGIUM über des GRATIANS Grund Reguln Vernünftig, klug und artig zu leben'. After U. Pörksen, *Deutsche Naturwissenschaftssprachen*, Tübingen, 1986, p. 46

16 Blackall, *The Emergence of German*, pp. 12–13

17 Jentzsch, 1912, reported in Pörksen, *Deutsche Naturwissenschaftssprachen*,1986, 50

18 'unbefugte theilung der fürsten, die ihre leute gleich fahrender habe zu vererben wähnten', Jacob Grimm, *Geschichte*, Widmung

19 'Können wir nun dieser Leute Zahl vermehren, die lust und liebe zu weisheit und tugend bey den Teutschen heftiger machen ... so achten wir dem Vaterland einen der größten Dienste gethan zu haben, deren privatpersonen fähig seyn.' Leibniz, *Ermahnung an die Teutsche, ihren verstand und sprache beßer zu üben, sammt beygefügten vorschlag einer Teutsch gesinnten Gesellschaft* published as *Wissenschaftliche Beihefte zur Zeitschrift des allgemeinen deutschen Sprachvereins*, 4. Heft 29, 1907, pp. 300ff

20 'Wir ſchreiben gemeiniglich ſolche bücher, darinnen nichts als zuſammen geſtoppelte abſchriften aus andern ſprachen genommen, oder zwar unſre eigne, aber oft gar ungereimte gedancken und unbündige vernunftſchlüſſe, deren iezo manche herumblauffende chartequen voll ſeyn, deren ungeſchicktes weſen ſo oftmahls mit der geſunden vernunft ſtreitet ...' Leibniz, *Ermahnung an die Teutsche*, p. 300

21 'In Teutſchland aber hat man annoch dem latein und der kunſt zuviel', Leibniz, *Ermahnung an die Teutsche*, p. 302

22 'bey der ganzen nation aber ist geschehen, daß diejenigen, so kein latein gelernet, von der wißenschaft gleichsam ausgeschloßen worden ... Daraus denn folget, daß keine Verbeßerung hierin zu hoffen, so lange wir nicht unser Sprache in den Wißenschaften und Haupt=materien selbsten üben', Leibniz, *Ermahnung an die Teutsche*, p. 304

23 'darauff dann auch alsbald in den ſchriften ſich ganz ein anderer glanz hervorgethan, der nunmehr bei denen Welſchen, Franzoſen und Engländern nicht nur deren gelehrten eigen bleiben, ſondern bis in die mutterſprache ſelbſt herabgefloßen', Leibniz, *Ermahnung an die Teutsche*, p. 301

24 'Daraus denn folget, daß keine Verbeßerung hierin zu hoffen, so lange wir nicht unser Sprache in den Wißenschaften und Haupt=materien selbsten üben, welches das einzige mittel, sie bei den ausländern in hohen werth zu bringen und die unteutsch gesinten Teutschen endlich beschähmt zu machen', Leibniz, *Ermahnung an die Teutsche*, p. 301

25 'so wird auch das höchste Oberhaupt samt anderen Potentaten und ständen mittel wißen, dadurch die teutsche tugend wieder zu vorigen glanz kommen möge', Leibniz, *Ermahnung an die Teutsche*, p. 305

26 'Was aber den Verſtand betrift und die Sprache, welche gleichſam als ein heller ſpiegel des Verſtandes zu achten; ſo glaub ich, dießfals habe ein ieder macht, ſeine gedancken vorzutragen; ja es iſt ſchwer, zugleich ſein vaterland lieben, dieſes unheil ſehen und nicht beclagen.' Leibniz, *Ermahnung an die Teutsche*, p. 305

27 'Es iſt bekandt, daſs die Sprach ein Spiegel des Verſtandes, und daſs die Völcker, wenn sie den Verſtand hoch ſchwingen, auch zugleich die Sprache wohl ausüben', Leibniz, *Unvorgreiffliche Gedancken betreffend die Ausübung und Verbesserung der Teutschen Sprache*, pub. in *Wissenschaftliche Beihefte zur Zeitschrift des allgemeinen deutschen Sprachvereins*, H. 30, Apr. 1908, pp. 327ff

28 'Nachdem die Wiſſenſchaft zur Stärcke kommen und die Krieges-Zucht in Teutſchland aufgerichtet worden' it is his wish that 'auch der Teutſchen Verſtand nicht weniger obſiegen und den Preiſs erhalten möge.' Leibniz, *Unvorgreiffliche Gedancken*, p. 328

29 'Gleichwohl wäre es ewig Schade und Schande, wenn unſere Haupt- und Helden-Sprache dergeſtalt durch unſere Fahrläſſigkeit zu Grunde gehen solte, ſo ſaſt nichts Gutes schwanen machen dörffte, weil die Annehmung einer fremden Sprache gemeiniglich den Verluſt der Freyheit und ein fremdes Joch mit ſich geführet.' Leibniz, *Unvorgreiffliche Gedancken*, p. 333

30 'Ich finde, daſs die Teutſchen ihre Sprache bereits hoch bracht in allen dem, ſo mit den fünff Sinnen zu begreiffen, und auch dem gemeinen Mann fürkommet; abſonderlich in leiblichen Dingen, auch Kunſt- und Handwercks-Sachen,' Leibniz, *Unvorgreiffliche Gedancken*, p. 330

31 'Am allermeiſten aber iſt unſer Mangel, wie gedacht, bey denen Worten zu ſpühren, die ſich auff das Sitten-weſen, Leidenschafften des Gemüths, gemeinlichen Wandel, Regierungs-Sachen, und allerhand bürgerliche Lebens- und Staats-Geſchäffte ziehen', Leibniz, *Unvorgreiffliche Gedancken*, pp. 331f

32 As evidenced for example in his *Briefe aus Paris zur Zeit der Revolution geschrieben*, Braunschweig, 1790

33 J. H. Campe, *Wörterbuch zur Erklärung und Verdeutschung der unserer Sprache aufgedrungenen fremden Ausdrücke. Ein Ergänzungsband zu Adelungs Wörterbuche*, Bd. 1, 2, Braunschweig, 1801. Neue stark vermehrte und durchgängig verbesserte Ausgabe, Braunschweig, 1813

34 J. H. Campe, *Ueber die Reinigung und Bereicherung der Deutschen Sprache. Dritter Versuch welcher den von dem königl. Preuß Gelehrtenverein zu Berlin ausgesetzten Preis erhalten hat*, Braunschweig, 1794

35 'daß man in allen den Urtheilen, die über Sprachreinigung und Sprachbereinigung gefällt, und in allen den Vorschriften und Verfahrungs-arten, die darüber angegeben werden, immer nur auf die Vollkommenheit der Sprache an sich oder in Bezug auf sie selbst, und nicht in Bezug auf den Nutzen, den das sie redende Volk davon haben soll, Rücksicht zu nehmen pflegt. Gleichsam, als wenn das Volk um der Sprache, nicht die Sprache um des Volkes willen da wäre!' Campe, *Wörterbuch*, 1813, p. 10

36 Campe, *Ueber die Reinigung*, p. VI

37 Campe, *Ueber die Reinigung*, p. VI

38 'Das, was ein Wort zu einem Deutschen macht, ist 1) seine Verständlichkeit für jeden Deutschen und 2) die Übereinstimmung seiner Bildung und seines Klanges mit der Bildung und dem Klange anderer Deutscher Wörter.' Campe, *Wörterbuch*, 1813, p. 8

39 'Der Deutsche hört in eben dem Maße auf, ein Deutscher, also das zu sein, wozu die Natur ihn bestimmt hat … in welchem er aus seiner Landessprache ein buntscheckiges Gemisch von ausländischen und einheimischen Lauten und Wörtern werden läßt.' Campe, *Wörterbuch*, 1813, p. 9

40 E.g., *Freistaat* as a Germanification of *Republik*, today found in the names of two of the Federal Republic of Germany's sixteen states – Bavaria and Saxony – was used by Campe in the first edition of his dictionary (although for the second edition he preferred *Gemeinstaat*)

41 'alle diejenigen Begriffe und Kenntnisse, welche allen Menschen zu wünschen sind, weil sie zu der für alle möglichen und für alle nützlichen Ausbildung gehören, (bedürfen) einer Umkleidung aus der fremdartigen Sprachhülle, worin sie bisher unter uns Umlauf hatten, in die vaterländische...' Campe, *Wörterbuch*, 1813, p. 32

42 C.G. Jochmann, *Über die Sprache*, Heidelberg, bei C. F. Winter, 1828

43 C.G. Jochmann, 'Über die Öffentlichkeit', in *Allgemeine politische Annalen*. Neueste Folge, C. v. Rotteck (ed.), Erster Band, Zweites Heft, München/Stutt-gart/Tübingen, in der J.G. Cotta'schen Buchhandlung. April 1830, pp. 105– 43

44 'Völker wie Einzelne werden wohl groß durch Gewalt, aber sie bleiben es nur durch den Geist, der eben im Worte siegt', Jochmann, *Über die Sprache*, p. 74

45 'ein Volk, um in der Tuchweberei bedeutende Fortschritte zu machen, (muß) es nothwendig auch in der Himmelskunde zu einiger Vollkommenheit gebracht haben.' Jochmann, *Über die Sprache*, p. 73

46 'eines allgemeinen Werkzeuges gesellschaftlicher Entwicklung', Joch-mann, *Über die Sprache*, p. 70

47 'Unverständlichkeit und Härte blieben in dem ganzen folgenden Zeitraum die eigenthümlichen Mängel, freilich nicht unsrer Sprache an sich, wohl aber der jedesmaligen Art ihrer Benutzung', Jochmann, *Über die Sprache*, p. 207

48 'Außer dem engen Kreise des häuslichen Bedürfnisses, und etwa noch der Kanzel mit ihrem Wechselfieber einer hitzigen Polemik oder frostigen Sittenrednerei', Jochmann, *Über die Sprache*, p. 225

49 Jochmann, *Über die Sprache*, p. 77

50 'und endlich benutzte sie der Gelehrte sogar als Lückenbüßerin zwischen den fremden Ausdrücken, auf welchen er sich, wie ein Schiffbrüchiger von Klippe zu Klippe aus dem Meere seiner Gedanken zu retten pflegt.' Jochmann, *Über die Sprache*, p. 77

51 'jeder Fortschritt ... bei uns immer nur gezeigt, und höchstens befohlen, aber desto seltner verstanden ... wurde', Jochmann, *Über die Sprache*, p. 71

52 'Das öffentliche Leben der Deutschen geht in Schreibstuben und auf Paradeplätzen vor', Jochmann, *Über die Sprache*, p. 224

53 'Herren und Knechte sind selten gute Sprecher', Jochmann, *Über die Sprache*, p. 221

54 'Auf diesem Wege vielleicht gelangen wir aus der kleinen Stadt Deutschland zu einem deutschen Volke, und haben wir erst ein Volk, so findet sich wohl auch die Sprache. Dann, aber auch nur dann', Jochmann, *Über die Sprache*, p. 246

55 By 1818 the term *Nationalliteratur* was being used by Joh. Friedr. Wachler (1767-1838) in the title of his literary history *Vorlesungen über die Geschichte der deutschen Nationalliteratur*, Frankfurt am Main,1818–19

56 'For Germans ... their national language ... was the *only* thing that made them Germans ...', E. Hobsbawm, *Nations and nationalism since 1780. Programme, myth, reality*, Cambridge 1990, pp. 102-3

57 See, for example, Ernst Moritz Arndt: *Germanien und Europa*, Altona, 1803: 'Aber nicht bloß von Fremden ist das Vaterland arg mitgenommen, und wird es bis auf den heutigen Tag; sondern der herrschsüchtige Ehrgeiz unserer Fürsten rief selbst diese Fremden gewöhnlich zum Verheeren herein', after P.Longerich (ed.), *'Was ist des Deutschen Vaterland?' Dokumente zur Frage der deutschen Einheit 1800-1990*, München, 1990, p. 42

58 Which, with true German thoroughness, was finally completed over a century after its initial inception

59 'Über eines solchen werkes antritt musz, wenn es gedeihen soll, in der höhe ein heilbringendes gestirn schweben. ich erkannte es im einklang zweier zeichen, die sonst einander abstehen, hier aber von demselben inneren grunde getrieben sich genähert hatten, in dem aufschwung einer deutschen philologie und in der empfänglichkeit des volkes für seine muttersprache, wie sie beide bewegt wurden durch erstarkte liebe zum vaterland und untilgbare begierde nach seiner festen einigung. was haben wir dann gemeinsames als unsere sprache und literatur?' Grimm, *Deutsches Wörterbuch*, Vol.1, p.iii

60 'es gibt ein lebendigeres zeugnis über die völker als knochen, waffen und gräber, und das sind ihre sprachen'

Sprache ist der volle athem menschlicher seele, wo sie erschallt oder in denkmälern geborgen ist, schwindet alle unsicherheit über die verhältnisse des volkes, das sie redete, zu seinen nachbarn.' Grimm, *Geschichte*, p. 4

61 R.H. Robins, *A Short History of Linguistics*, London, 1967, pp. 172–3

62 'auch die innern glieder eines volkes müssen nach dialect und mundart zusammentreten oder gesondert bleiben; in unserm widernatürlich gespaltenen vaterland kann dies kein fernes, nur ein nahes, keinen zwist, sondern ruhe und frieden bringendes ereignis sein, das unsere zeit, wenn irgend eine andere mit leichter hand heranzuführen berufen ist. Dann mag was unbefugte theilung der fürsten, die ihre leute gleich fahrender habe zu vererben wähnten, zersplitterte wieder verwachsen, und aus vier stücken ein neues Thüringen, aus zwei hälften ein starkes Hessen erblühen, jeder stamm aber, dessen ehre die geschichte uns vorhält, dem groszen Deutschland freudige opfer bringen.' Grimm, *Geschichte*, Widmung

63 'so könnte das Wörterbuch zum hausbedarf, und mit verlangen, oft *mit andacht* gelesen werden', Grimm, *Deutsches Wörterbuch*, Vol.1, col. xiii (my italics)

64 'ein volk ist der inbegriff von menschen, welche dieselbe sprache reden. das ist für uns Deutsche die unschuldigste und zugleich stolzeste erklärung, weil sie mit einmal über das gitter hinwegspringen und jetzt schon der blick auf eine näher oder ferner liegende, aber ich darf wol sagen einmal unausbleiblich heranrückende zukunft lenken darf, wo alle schranken fallen und das natürlich gesetz anerkannt werden wird, dasz nicht flüsse, nicht berge völkerscheide bilden, sondern dasz einem volk, das über berge und ströme gedrungen ist, seine eigne sprache allein die grenze setzen kann.' Grimm, *Kleinere Schriften* vii, p. 557

65 'Jetzt gerade beginnen in Deutschland die Früchte des Germanismus zu reifen. Bei Lichte betrachtet ist der ganze Reichstag in Frankfurt nichts Anderes, als eine Fortsetzung der früheren Germanistenversammlungen, wie man sie z.B. in Lübeck hielt, nur dass sie jetzt offen politisch und executiv sind, was sie damals verstohlen waren.' C. Hinrichsen. Die Germanisten und die Wege der Geschichte. Kopenhagen 1848 – quoted after J. Janota (ed.), *Eine Wissenschaft etabliert sich 1810-1870. Wissenschaftsgeschichte der Germanistik III*, Tübingen, 1980, p. 134

66 J. J. Müller (1974), 'Germanistik – eine Form bürgerlicher Opposition', J. J. Müller, *Germanistik und deutsche Nation 1806–1848. Zur Konstitution bürgerlichen Bewußtseins*, Stuttgart, 1974

67 Cf., for example, E. Lämmert, 'Germanistik – Eine deutsche Wissenschaft', B.v. Wiese and R. Henß (eds), *Nationalismus in Germanistik und Dichtung*, Berlin 1967, pp. 29–30: 'Schon nach der Gründung des Zweiten Reiches begann die ethische Umkehrung dieses Abhängigkeitsverhältnisses von Staatsgebilde und Nationalgeist: der Nationalgeist hatte nun der Befestigung des Reiches und der Dokumentation seiner Größe zu dienen'

68 'eine Wissenschaft ... welche ... das kühne Unternehmen wagte, ein System der nationalen Ethik aufzustellen, welches alle Ideale der Gegenwart in sich beschlösse.' W. Scherer, *Zur Geschichte der deutschen Sprache*, Berlin, 1868, pp. vi-vii

69 'staatskunst und kriegskunst und tapferkeit haben endlich dem kranken und verkümmerten baume der nation wieder spielraum und luft und licht geschaffen; die geschichtswissenschaft lehrt die werdenden und künftigen Geschlechter, wie er zu behandeln ist, dasz er nicht weiter verwachse . . . aber den saft, aus dem sein rechtes leben quillt, den hat die deutsche philologie wieder flüssig zu machen. ', Grimm, *Deutsches Wörterbuch*, Vol. 5, col. 1

70 'Wir müssen als Grundlage für das Gymnasium das Deutsche nehmen; wir sollen nationale junge Deutsche erziehen und nicht junge Griechen und Römer ... wir müssen das Deutsche zur Basis machen.', O. Lyon, 'der Kaiser über den deutschen Unterricht', *Zeitschrift für den deutschen Unterricht*, 5, 1891, p. 82f, quoted after Janota (ed.), *Eine Wissenschaft etabliert sich*, 53-4

71 'Der Deutschunterricht ist neben dem Unterricht in der Religion und in der Geschichte der erzieherisch bedeutsamste.', from: 'Lehrpläne und Lehraufgaben für die Höhere Schule in Preußen, 1901, quoted after K.-H. Roth, *'Deutsch' Prolegomena zur neueren Wortgeschichte*, Munich, 1978, p. 441

72 'Im deutschen Unterricht sollen die Schüler lernen, deutsch zu reden und zu schreiben, deutsch zu fühlen, zu denken und zu wollen'. from: 'Richtlinien für die Lehrpläne der höheren Schulen Preußens' (1925) quoted after Roth, *'Deutsch'*, 81

73 Cf. for example his *Das Urbild der deutschen Reinsprache, aus der Geschichte, dem Wesen und dem Geiste unserer Sprache dargestellt*. Heidelberg , 1847

74 Particular mention could be made of the efforts by Heinrich (von) Stephan in the Imperial Post Ministry. Some examples of the replacements made are: *eingeschrieben* for *rekommandiert, postlagernd* for *poste restante, Briefumschlag* for *Couvert, frei* for *franco, Fahrkarte* for *Billet, Bahnsteig* for *Perron, Verkehrsordnung* for *Betriebsreglement*

75 For example, in 1899, a donation of 10 marks was gratefully received from one Robert Atkinson in London

76 H. Dunger, 'Wider die Engländerei in der deutschen Sprache', *Zeitschrift des Allgemeinen Deutschen Sprachvereins*, XIV, 12 Dec. 1899, cols 241–51 reports a rise from twelve anglicisms in 1799 to 148 in 1879 with a subsequent 'massive increase' to 1899

77 'In den Kreisen der vornehmen Gesellschaft ist gegenwärtig die englische Sprache angesehener als die französische, für Kaufleute und Techniker ist die Kenntnis des Englischen unentbehrlich', Dunger, 'Wider die Engländerei ', col. 242

78 O. Streicher, 'Englisch wird Weltsprache', *Zeitschrift des Allgemeinen Deutschen Sprachvereins*, XIV, 12 Dec 1899, cols 241–55

79 Dunger, 'Wider die Engländerei ', col. 242

80 'Wir haben nicht nur mit den alten Feinden immer noch zu kämpfen, sondern müssen auch neue Eindringlinge abwehren, die keck von allen Seiten Einlaß in unsre Muttersprache begehren. Besonders auffällig ist in jüngster Zeit das Einmengen neuer Fremdwörter aus dem Englischen', Dunger, 'Wider die Engländerei ', col. 241

81 E.g., 'Schmarotzer auf dem Baum unsrer Sprache', Dunger, 'Wider die Engländerei ', col. 249; 'besonders wuchert das Unkraut der englischen Sprache ...', col. 247

82 'wo die französischen Fremdwörter in hellen Haufen ihren Einzug hielten in die ehrwürdigen Hallen unsrer Sprache', Dunger, 'Wider die Engländerei ', col. 249

83 'wir (haben) eine neue Überflutung unsrer Sprache mit Fremdwörtern zu gewärtigen', Dunger, 'Wider die Engländerei ', col. 241; 'Die neue englische Hochflut hat erst begonnen, aber sie ist auf dem besten Wege, unsre Sprache zu überschwemmen,' col. 250

84 '(Der Sprachverein) sieht die Zumutung an das`deutsche Volk, zur Herbeiführung einer allgemeinen Völkergemeinschaft das Opfer an der Muttersprache zu bringen und sich zum Dienste an der Ausbreitung der Macht und Sprache eines fremden Herrenvolkes zu erniedrigen, für eine Kränkung der deutschen Volksehre an.' Streicher, 'Englisch wird Weltsprache', col. 254

85 'abscheuliche und unwürdige Ausländerei', Streicher, 'Englisch wird Weltsprache', col. 252

86 'mannhafte Rettungsthat aus schimpflicher Selbsterniedrigung und Verirrung unsres Volksgeistes', Streicher, 'Englisch wird Weltsprache', col. 252

87 '(Diels) scheint noch nicht einmal ganz sicher darüber zu sein, ob so ein Mischmasch für ein nationales Empfinden anstößig sein würde.' Streicher, 'Englisch wird Weltsprache', col. 252

88 'die Zeit der nationalen Erneuerung ist noch nicht vorbei. Der Deutsche Sprachverein wird auf seinem begrenzten, aber wichtigen Gebiete Hand in Hand mit anderen Gemeinschaften, die es auf anderen thun, noch lange Arbeit haben', Streicher, 'Englisch wird Weltsprache', col. 255–6

89 'In unserem Volke ist die Sehnsucht nach dem Meere erwacht, der Wunsch wieder wie einst kräftig teilzunehmen an der Beherrschung der See. Im Wettbewerb der europäischen Nationen um die Aufteilung der Erde liegt auch des deutschen Volkes Zukunft auf dem Wasser', *Zeitschrift des Allgemeinen Deutschen Sprachvereins*, XIV, 11, col. 239

90 p. 94 above

91 *Zeitschrift des Allgemeinen Deutschen Sprachvereins*, 9.1906

92 *Zeitschrift des Allgemeinen Deutschen Sprachvereins*, 9.1910

93 *Zeitschrift des Allgemeinen Deutschen Sprachvereins*,1.1911

94 *Zeitschrift des Allgemeinen Deutschen Sprachvereins*, 11.1913

95 *Zeitschrift des Allgemeinen Deutschen Sprachvereins*, 7/8.1913

96 *Zeitschrift des Allgemeinen Deutschen Sprachvereins*, 1.1905

97 *Zeitschrift des Allgemeinen Deutschen Sprachvereins*, 5.1907

98 *Zeitschrift des Allgemeinen Deutschen Sprachvereins*,2.1907

99 J.Brodbeck-Arbenz, 'Ist Deutsch eine Weltsprache?', *Zeitschrift des Allgemeinen DeutschenSprachvereins*, 5.1907, 129–36

100 Brodbeck-Arbenz, 'Ist Deutsch eine Weltsprache?', 136

101 *Zeitschrift des Allgemeinen Deutschen Sprachvereins*, 5.1915

102 *Zeitschrift des Allgemeinen Deutschen Sprachvereins*, 9.1914

103 *Zeitschrift des Allgemeinen Deutschen Sprachvereins*, 4.1915

104 *Zeitschrift des Allgemeinen Deutschen Sprachvereins*, 9.1915

105 *Zeitschrift des Allgemeinen Deutschen Sprachvereins*, 6.1915

106 see p. 100 and note 78 above

107 see p. 103 and note 97 above

108 *Zeitschrift des Allgemeinen Deutschen Sprachvereins*, 1.1916, 1-4

109 'Und weil die deutsche Seele unlösbar an die deutsche Sprache geknüpft ist, so ist denn auch die höhere Entwicklung der Menschheit an ein mächtiges, sich weit über die Erde erstreckendes, das heilige Erbe seiner Sprache überall behauptendes. Deutschland gebunden.', H.S. Chamberlain, *Briefe 1882-1924*, Munich, quoted after Kauth and Palleske, 'Chamberlain über deutsche Art und Sprache' in *Zeitschrift des Allgemeinen Deutschen Sprachvereins*, 4.1932, col. 136

110 R.Palleske, 'Houston Stewart Chamberlain: Kriegsaufsätze' in: *Zeitschrift des Allgemeinen Deutschen Sprachvereins*, 9.1915, cols. 290-1

111 *Zeitschrift des Allgemeinen Deutschen Sprachvereins*, 4.1932, cols. 135–7

112 G. Schmidt-Rohr, 'Houston Stewart Chamberlain über die deutsche Sprache', *Zeitschrift des Allgemeinen Deutschen Sprachvereins*, 9.1935, cols. 301–5

113 K. Bojunga, 'Werden und Wesen der deutschen Sprache in alter Zeit. Die Fremdsprachenherrschaft und der Freiheitskampf der deutschen Sprache', Sonderdruck aus: Nollau, H. (ed.), *Germanische Wiedererstehung*, Heidelberg, n.y.p., pp. 486-546

114 'Ihr (der Akademie) sind also Zigeunerisch, Nigger-Englisch und Jiddisch-Deutsch "entwickelte Kultursprachen", vor denen sich das Indisch Kalidasas und das Griechisch Platons, die Bibel Luthers und der Zarathustra Nietzsches mit ihrer ungebildeten Sprachreinheit verstecken müssen.' Bojunga, 'Werden und Wesen', p. 543

115 for a general discussion, see F. Pasierbsky, *Krieg und Frieden in der Sprache*, Frankfurt, 1983

116 'Wir betrachten zuerst das Eindringen der militärischen Ausdrucksweise in alle Sphären sprachlicher Äußerungen. Der Begriff "militärisch" ist dabei möglichst weit zu fassen. Es genügt nicht, zu konstatieren, daß Termini, die ursprünglich aus dem Militärwesen stammen, im NS stärker als je und in wachsendem Maße auf Fernliegendes angewendet werden. Es handelt sich vielmehr darum, daß die geistige Einstellung auf militärische Ideale dauernd um Bilder der sich äußernden Kraft "bereichert". Im ns. Deutsch zeigt sich das Streben nach gewaltsamer Ausdrucksweise.' E. Seidel and I. Seidel-Slotty, *Sprachwandel im Dritten Reich. Eine kritische Untersuchung faschistischer Einflüsse*, Halle, 1961, p. 43

117 'Gewiß hat jeder Leser dieses Büchleins beobachtet, wie lebhaft der Wortschatz des soldatischen Feldes gerade in unseren Tagen sich – alter

deutscher Überlieferung treu – wieder in die Gemeinsprache eindrängt, der Wörter wie "Appell", "Parole", "Front", "Kämpfer", "Schlacht"... u.a. gang und gäbe sind auch für nicht soldatische Bereiche.' F. Panzer, *Der deutsche Wortschatz als Spiegel deutschen Wesens und Schicksals*, Cologne, 1940, p. 41

118 'Zu diesen 'nicht-soldatischen Bereichen'... gehörte auch die Germanistik im Dritten Reich. Man kann feststellen, daß Begriffe wie Kampf, Held, Einsatz, Haltung, Front, Schlacht, Krieg u.a.m. von vielen Vertretern dieses Faches offensichtlich in der Absicht verwendet wurden, einen direkten Bezug zum militärischen Bereich herzustellen; das wird besonders in den Fällen deutlich, in denen Bilder und Termini des militärischen Feldes in Zusammenhängen auftauchen, die den Gebrauch militärischer Wendungen nicht erfordern.' W. Dahle, *Der Einsatz einer Wissenschaft. Eine sprachinhaltliche Analyse militärischer Terminologie in der Germanistik 1933-1945*, Bonn, 1969, p. 29

119 'Der totale Krieg, wie wir ihn erleben, ist nicht nur eine militärische, sondern zugleich auch eine geistig-kulturelle Auseinandersetzung größten Maßes.... Vor Deutschland erhebt sich eine ungeheure Aufgabe, diesem neuen Europa auch eine neue geistige Ordnung zu geben, geistig zu durchdringen, was das Schwert erobert hat.' Fricke *et al.*, *Von deutscher Art*, p. v

120 'Militärische Sprache dient niemals bloß der Gedankenübermittlung sondern immer gleichzeitig und sogar vorweg der Hebung der menschlichen Qualitäten (Clausewitz) der Übertragung von Willenskräften.' Quoted after Dahle, *Der Einsatz einer Wissenschaft*, p. 144

121 'Ich sehe in erster Linie in der Muttersprache eines Volkes ein scharf geschliffenes Schwert zur geistigen Verteidigung der Nation.' J. Goebbels, quoted in Seidel & Seidel-Slotty, *Sprachwandel im Dritten Reich*, p.46

122 'Weltwendezeiten sind sprachliche Großkampfzeiten. Völkerringen ist nicht nur Kampf auf dem Schlachtfeld, wirtschaftliche Einkreisung, Verwüstung der Länder und rauschender Sieg oder stöhnende Niederlage: auch die Sprachen stehen gegeneinander auf, suchen ihren Geltungsraum abzugrenzen oder zu erweitern, bestreiten das Recht fremder Zungen und werfen die Kraft des sie erfüllenden Geistes in die schwankende Waagschale'. F.Thierfelder, quoted after Dahle, *Der Einsatz einer Wissenschaft*, p. 157

4 Regulation by and of language: the discourse of German fascism 1933–45

Introduction

Two major politico-linguistic topics have exercised critics of the German language since the end of the Second World War: the language of German fascism and the linguistic consequences of 'the division of Germany' after 1945. No treatment of politico-linguistic issues in twentieth-century Germany can avoid these. In this chapter and the following one, it will be argued that both the topics themselves and the ways in which they have been treated afford valuable insights into aspects of German political culture in the twentieth century.

It is not, however sufficient to discuss the significance of fascist discourse for the analysis of German fascism; our main concern is to study the political history of the German language, and it will be argued that from this standpoint, the study of German fascist discourse is important for the light it sheds on how language and discourse can be regulated and controlled, and how the regulation of language has a significant role to play in the exercise of power. For this, we shall be examining how the German fascists succeeded in establishing their own discourse and silencing opposing or alternative discourses.

If the claim is being made that linguistic and communicative analysis provides an entry-point into the understanding of political culture, then this claim must be substantiated – in the present chapter by justifying the treatment of the discourse of German fascism as a key to an understanding of German fascism as a political phenomenon.

Faced with the task of analysing and processing the fascist domination of Germany from 1933 to 1945, and then trying to learn from the experience, one could be forgiven for thinking that linguistic considerations are of minor importance. To put it more pointedly, asking how the German fascists used language, and bemoaning the 'violence' they perpetrated on the language, pale into insignificance in the face of the millions of victims of Auschwitz and Treblinka, Leningrad, Coventry and Dresden.

But what was it that made Auschwitz and Treblinka, Leningrad, Coventry and Dresden possible? Is the analysis of the discourse merely a side-issue? We argue that it is not, as it is one of the main theses of this book that language is central to the political process, and that linguistic actions are as 'real' as any other political actions – indeed, that non-linguistic political action is impossible without preceding, accompanying and subsequent linguistic action.

As we saw earlier, a growing body of literature on the relationships between language and politics bears witness to an appreciation of the role of language in the political process. Of particular relevance to the topic of language regulation is George Orwell's *Nineteen Eighty-Four*, which was written very much under the influence of events in fascist Germany, and in which Orwell displayed an understanding of the links between language, perception and potential action in his account of the state's attempt to control thought by controlling language and thus determine people's actions: 'the whole aim of Newspeak is to narrow the range of thought. In the end we shall make thoughtcrime literally impossible, because there will be no words in which to express it. ... The Revolution will be complete when the language is perfect.'[1]

In the treatment of our present topic, there has from the very beginning been a realisation of the importance of language in the process of analysing fascism; in a major study, Haug points out that the critique of fascist discourse has often played a central role in the attempt to understand German fascism. [2]

It will, however, be argued that many of the attempts to which Haug refers are deficient in a number of ways, essentially because in them language is not only the starting-point of the analysis, but also the finishing-point; the analysis of language and discourse is important, but only for what it reveals of underlying perceptions and ideologies. In far too many studies, the critique has been limited to directing moral censure towards the use (or 'abuse') of language.

A full understanding of the nature and operation of German fascism must consider the communicative environment which the German fascists managed to create, the undisputed role which their domination of public discourse played in both the assumption and maintenance of their power, the way in which many *Schreibtischtäter* committed their crimes through the medium of the word, and not least the fascists' own realisation of the power of language, as evidenced by their attempts to influence discourse and eliminate rival texts.

In the previous chapter, we considered two aspects of the German language under fascism – the militarisation of discourse in time of war, and the way in which the language became part of the war effort. Now it is time to turn to a more detailed examination of 'what happened to the German language between 1933 and 1945', and it is suggested that there are two main points at issue: the first is the analysis of language change and forms of political discourse under German fascism, and the second is the perception of these phenomena post-1945 in the process of *Vergangenheitsbewältigung* – overcoming the past. The present chapter will in the main address itself to the first of these points, while the second will form part of the broader consideration of politico-linguistic developments in post-war Germany in Chapters 5 and 6.

Methodological preliminary

Before proceeding to the main analysis of fascist discourse, it is necessary to explicate a matter of some theoretical and methodological importance.

One of the theoretical presuppositions of this book is that our discourse determines and is determined by our perceptions of reality, which can raise a number of problems when it comes to analysing language and politics. So far we have not had to confront these problems, or have chosen to avoid them; now, however, an appropriate point has been reached where we have to face them head-on.

The denial of an 'objective reality' existing outside language and independent of it necessarily precludes the possibility of an 'objective assessment' of the linguistic and social phenomena under discussion; essentially, the lack of a neutral 'meta-language' means that it is well-nigh impossible to discuss politico-linguistic phenomena without 'revealing' one's own political position. That is the one problem, which will become particularly acute in the final chapter, when the writer's own political opinions will colour not only the analysis but also the manner in which it is presented. Intellectual honesty and the need for more effective analysis both require that this should be clearly stated, a concluding point convincingly made by John Wilson, who wrote that 'The way forward in the analysis of political language is for analysts to make their own agenda clear, or as clear as it can be within a post-modernist world.'[3] The other problem, which surfaced in the preceding chapter and is particularly acute in the present one, is that of analysing a particular discourse – in our case the discourse of German fascism – without employing that discourse or adopting its presuppositions, and it is this problem which, as we shall see later, has bedevilled much writing on German fascism, as Winckler pointed out in his study of German fascist discourse.[4]

Two brief examples will serve to illustrate the point which is being made here.

The 'observant reader' will have noticed and doubtless noted that the designations 'National Socialist' and the abbreviated form 'Nazi' have so far not been deployed in this study, except in quotations, and that the term 'German fascism' has been preferred. There are two reasons for this: the first is that 'National Socialism' was the name coined for a particular German brand of fascism by its own proponents, and that the name was chosen with a specific intention; in addition, the name has been used in discussion post-1945 with a particular intention (if it has not simply been used uncritically). To avoid any hint or suspicion of association, it is deemed preferable to use a different designation (or to put the original designation in inverted commas all the time). The second reason is that, by using the term 'fascist' – which itself was of course coined to name a specific movement at a particular place and time – one is trying to point to features and similarities which German fascism shared with other movements and is denying that the dominant political views in Germany from 1933 to 1945 suddenly appeared 'out of the blue' in 1933 and just as mysteriously suddenly disappeared after 8 May 1945.

The second example[5] concerns the apparently 'innocuous' statement 'Hitler murdered (or 'was responsible for the murder of') six million Jews.' In this sentence the bone of contention rests in the word 'Jews', and that for a number of reasons. In pursuit and prosecution of their racist ideology, the German fascists chose to label certain people as 'Jews', even though only one of their grandparents might have been 'Jewish' and they themselves regarded themselves not as 'Jews' but, for example, as Germans, who, until the fascists assumed power, held German passports and all the rights of German citizens. By being labelled as 'Jews' they were progressively disenfranchised, criminalised, incarcerated, and often killed.

It is being argued here that by simply adopting the fascist categorisation one is ultimately – albeit unwittingly – accepting certain of its presuppositions – for example that some of these unfortunates were not 'proper Germans' and that there was something special about being – or being categorised as – a Jew.

The methodological problem that we shall try to face in the following pages is that of developing a discourse for talking about German fascism which is sufficiently distanced or alienated from this discourse of German fascism itself – while at the same time recognising that the discourse of analysis is not value-free either, but is predicated on a certain interpretation of history.[6] Thus the terminology of German fascism will be avoided wherever possible, and as a symbol of the attempt to achieve the maximum degree of alienation, whenever a reference to the 'leader' of the German fascists is unavoidable, it will be by the name of Adolf Schicklgruber rather than that by which he chose to be known.

The politico-linguistic significance of fascist discourse

The German fascists themselves were acutely aware of the significance of language in the political process: in *Mein Kampf*, Schicklgruber relates how, on entering the Deutsche Arbeiterpartei in 1921, he immediately assumed responsibility for propaganda, regarding this as 'the most important activity at the time',[7] and in 1922 he wrote a paper on 'The expansion of the National Socialist German Labour Party' in which he stated that 'Battles won with paper bullets do not need to be fought with ones of steel.'[8] That the 'propaganda track' could lead to high party office can be seen from the careers of Strasser, Himmler and Goebbels, all of whom at varying times held positions of responsibility in the propaganda apparatus.

The significance of fascist discourse for a political history of the German language is generally perceived to be in two main areas, the first being in the changes effected in the structure and style of the language – particularly in the lexis and the dominant metaphors – and the second in the way in which the fascists dominated and controlled the communicative environment by imposing their own public discourse and effectively silencing any competing public discourses. It will not, however, be sufficient simply to record phenomena; the analysis must also address the question of the social function of the phenomena recorded and attempt to reconstruct the political culture created through the discourse – a step omitted in a number of the 'standard' accounts of the language of German fascism.

In the course of the discussion of these two areas it will be necessary – without pre-empting the discussion in the following chapter – to consider two commonly-held views on 'National Socialist language', the first being that the German fascists drastically changed the German language – or even created their 'own language', coupled with the attendant view that, in so doing, the 'National Socialists' in some way 'abused' or 'misused' the German language, and secondly that the 'National Socialists' – particularly Schicklgruber and Goebbels – perfected the use of propaganda.

German fascism and linguistic innovation

There was a view commonly held, particularly in the first 'wave' of critique of fascist discourse post-1945, that the German fascists had in some way succeeded in 'creating' their own language which was qualitatively 'different'. Thus, for example, Sternberger *et al.* could claim that both *Menschen* (humans) and *Unmenschen* (inhumans) (by which they meant the fascists) had their own vocabulary and syntax.[9] We shall be returning later to this use of the term *Unmensch* to designate the German fascists.

An obvious way in which the German fascists effected lexical innovation[10] was firstly in the creation of designations for organisations and institutions, either because they were new or because they had been remodelled, secondly in the redefinition of extant terms, and thirdly in the 'resurrection' of older terms and/or meanings.

Thus in the first category one finds such items as *Ahnenpaß, Ariernachweis, Erbgesundheitsgericht, Eintopfsonntag, Blitzkrieg, Gauleiter, Lebensborn, Schutzstaffel, Reichsparteitag*, together with verbs such as *arisieren, entjuden* and *aufnorden*. Many of the 'new' terms are compounds, and one can observe a high frequency of certain compounding elements, for example *Volks-* and *–art-* (*arteigen, entartet*), even though instances of some of those compounds – e.g., *Volksgenosse* – are to be found prior to the fascist era. At the same time, in a sub-category we also find a 'renaming' taking place, so that the Sunday of Remembrance, which was previously known as *Totensonntag* or *Todsonntag*, and which predates the the twentieth century, has its name changed to *Heldengedenktag*, thus limiting its application to the remembrance of the military casualties of war and redefining their image.

As an illustration of the second category, Claus Mueller [11] compares definitions of selected terms from Meyers *Lexikon* of 1936 with those from the 1924 edition. Thus, *Abstammungsnachweis*, 'pedigree', changes from being a term used in animal husbandry to one used for determining the racial origins of humans, *Blutschande* is transferred from a family to a racist term, changing from denoting incest to referring to sexual intercourse between 'Aryans' and 'Non-Aryans', *Konzentrationslager* no longer primarily refers to a corral for humans used by the British in the Boer War.

In the third category we find both a reintroduction or reinstatement of 'old Germanic' terms, such as *Thingplatz* and the resuscitation of old denotations – for example, the use of *Blutvergiftung* (analagous to *Blutschande*) in a racist as opposed to a medical sense, which can be traced back to Nietzsche.

Changes were, however, not only effected in the denotations, but also in the collocations or in both. Thus, for example, the term *Bewegung* had its denotative value changed so that it only referred to one specific movement, that of German fascism, and in its associations it was quite definitely positively charged. In a similar way, words which had previously had negative associations, such as *fanatisch* and *brutal,* became positively charged as part of the fascist glorification of violence and extremism. Conversely, the term *System* (with certain derivatives, such as *Systemzeit* and – *politiker*) was used in such a way that its reference was specialised to that of the Weimar Republic, with its consequent negative associations; the German fascists saw themselves as having overcome the limitations and 'national disgrace' of Weimar. In a similar way, the word *international,* which in previous general usage was pointedly neutral in its associations, became contrasted with *national* and linked with 'international Jewry' and 'international communism', the twin bogies of the fascist ideology of racial uniqueness and purity.

The mechanisms of lexical · creation, redefinition and reassociation are ones which one can observe whenever a political system is changed, as for example in the establishment of two German states after 1949, and in themselves are no argument for the 'creation' of a 'new language'.

Not just for this reason, however, is scepticism indicated towards claims that the German fascists 'created' their own language; what one can rather observe is a collage of elements taken from a variety of sources, in the same way that there is very little that is 'original' about the ideology of German fascism. Victor Klemperer, for example, who recorded aspects of fascist discourse thoughout the twelve long years from 1933 to 1945, and whose account of 'LTI' (Lingua Tertii Imperii) was one of the first to be published, denies that the German fascists were linguistically creative; what they did was to change values and frequencies, elevated cant to general discourse, 'reserved' for party use terms which had previously been in common currency.[12]

It is indeed probably the case that very few of the characteristics of German fascist language use were in fact new or original at the systemic level; apart from anything else, it is hardly likely that far-reaching systemic changes will become established within a space of twelve years. This, however, is not to deny the existence of a specific fascist discourse, which was marked for example by the frequency with which certain lexical items, certain syntactic constructions, certain metaphors, certain stylistic figures occurred – Dahle, for example, operates with the term *Auffälligkeit*[13] – and these can then be regarded as characteristics of a certain type of discourse – but even then that is not necessarily the only form of discourse in existence.

In the following section, we shall consider certain stylistic characteristics of this discourse, before proceeding to an examination of the way in which the German fascists engineered the communicative environment in an effort to establish and maintain the supremacy of their discourse.

Characteristics of German fascist discourse

Before proceeding to an overview of some of the characteristics of fascist discourse, we must point out that it is not the intention to give a comprehensive account, for to do so would mean reproducing much of what has already been portrayed elsewhere, for example by Berning, Bork, Dahle, Klemperer, Seidel and Seidel-Slotty, Sternberger *et al.*[14] What is important for our present purposes is the functionality and dominance of the discourse.

The images and metaphors of German fascism

Individual lexical items of the type discussed above may help to establish a certain institutional and conceptual framework, but it is suggested that they do not necessarily have all that profound an effect on thought and perceptions. A far more effective and pervasive means is to be found in the use of metaphor, as Lakoff and Johnson have demonstrated: 'Metaphors are conceptual in nature. They are among our principal vehicles for understanding. And they play a central role in the construction of social and political reality.'[15] Lakoff and Johnson argue against the existence of one absolute objective truth, maintaining that 'truth is always relative to a conceptual system that is defined in large part by metaphor',[16] and 'the people who get to impose their metaphors on the culture get to define what we consider to be true – absolutely and objectively true'.[17]

The vast majority of images and metaphors of German fascist discourse are taken from clearly identifiable areas, but, as we shall indicate from time to time, they are images and metaphors which are not necessarily peculiar to that discourse.

The 'images of war' examined in the previous chapter form part of a larger set dealing with 'struggle' and 'contest', many of which are taken from competitive sport – particularly athletics and boxing. For example, in two speeches made in the aftermath of Stalingrad, Goebbels compared the German people with boxers who, in the one case, were wiping the blood from their eyes so that they could go resolutely into the next round, and in the other had been fighting one-handed, while bandaging their other fist prior to dealing devastating blows in the following round. [18]

The metaphors of sport and war are, however, often closely intertwined in Western cultures, and they also form an important part of the perception of the political process, which is predicated on notions of competition and contest.[19]

An extensive field covers anthropology and medicine in the interests of fascist racist ideas, which is often found in conjunction with strategies of self-aggrandisement and the defamation of opponents. The 'health' of the Germanic is contrasted with the 'sickness' of the Jewish and the 'non-Aryan' generally, the resultant superiority of the *Übermensch* is set off against the inferiority of the *Unmensch*. Once again, however, medical images are common in other discourses; for example, US military doctrine and strategy over the past fifteen years or so has been obsessed with notions of the 'surgical strike' to 'take out' the 'malignant growth'.

A cognate field is that of light and darkness, which in its turn is linked with images of life and death. Coupled with the images of life are those of dynamism and movement, in which the 'storm' is a powerful icon; Klemperer, for example, sees the word *Sturm* as marking both the beginning and the end of 'National socialism'.[20]

Linked with this field is that of monumentalism on the one hand and defamation on the other; the achievements (past, present and future, actual and imagined) of fascist Germany are presented as superlatives – *Jahrtausendwerk*, *Tausendjähriges Reich*, while political opponents – both within and without – are treated with scorn and derision. A cognate field here is that of 'absoluteness' and 'finality' – as evidenced in the belief in the *Endsieg* (final victory) and in the propagation of the *Endlösung* (final solution).

The images and symbols discussed so far have been built up on oppositions, and as we shall see, their adversarial nature is an important feature of the discourse. There are, however, two other fields which do not quite fit into this schema, but which are of central significance, namely the cultic-religious and the technical domains.

The use of cultic and religious imagery, with Schicklgruber cast in the role of the saviour, and *Mein Kampf* assuming the status of holy writ, pervades much of the iconography of German fascism, with widespread use being made of Christian – and particularly Catholic – imagery, with references to the Bible, particularly the New Testament.[21] Two examples will suffice to support the point: the *Völkischer Beobachter* of 15 October 1933 refers to Hitler as the 'incarnation of the thought of the race',[22] and in a speech in front of the Berlin City Hall in July 1934 Goebbels stated that they were all 'of Adolf Hitler and through Adolf Hitler',[23] in a phrase strongly reminiscent of Paul's Epistle to the Romans (11.36).

Technical images can be found in two main areas – from the vocabulary of metal-working, with images of welding, hammering, forging, with people being objects rather than subjects of the activity,[24] and in the use of the term 'material' to refer to human beings.[25] The use of technical imagery can be interpreted as a 'dehumanising', but again it is not unique; it is commonly accepted in industrial societies that 'workers' are referred to as 'Arbeitskräfte' or the 'labour force', or simply 'hands', where only those features are regarded as being of relevance or interest which are essential for the production process. In the modern vocabulary of warfare in particular, the negation of humanity is a common feature, when death becomes 'attrition' and the killing of non-combatants 'collateral damage'.

The syntax of fascist discourse as monolith and monologue – the absence of argument and dialectic

'Thus both humans and inhumans have their own peculiar grammar and syntax'.[26]

Syntactically, there are a number of features of German fascist discourse to which we need to direct our attention, and paradoxically they can be subsumed under the heading of 'statism' – we say paradoxically, because at first sight the discourse of German fascism appears to be full of movement and dynamism, but at its core it is monolithic and inert.

Let us consider some of the features. A quantitative analysis would probably reveal a preponderance of nouns and a comparative scarcity of verbs – particularly dynamic verbs. One example of this substantival style, taken from *Mein Kampf*, will illustrate the point: '(Der Staat ist) nicht eine Zusammenfassung wirtschaftlicher Kontrahenten [...] zur Erfüllung wirtschaftlicher Aufgaben, sondern die Organisation einer Gemeinschaft physisch und seelisch gleicher Lebewesen zur besseren Ermöglichung der Forterhaltung ihrer Art sowie der Erreichung des dieser von der Vorsehung vorgezeichneten Zwecks ihres Daseins.'[27]

In this extract – which is by no means unusual –, one copulative verb ('ist') 'carries' fourteen nouns, linked predominantly by genitives (nine of them).[28]

German fascist discourse is to a very large extent based on the rhetoric of the public speech; Maser, for example, sees *Mein Kampf*, which can be regarded as the basic text of German fascism, as an 'unsystematic collection of Schicklgruber speeches',[29] and as public rhetoric its appeal is mainly to the emotions. Partly for this reason, there is an absence, or at least a paucity, of logical connectors; the sentences consist very often of blocks of pre-fabricated slogans placed next to each other, phrases exist independently of a sentence structure, thus destroying the logic of the sentence.[30] Seidel and Seidel-Slotty point to the absence of logical connectors and the confusion of causal and consecutive connections. Winckler sees the 'propositions' of Schicklgruber's speeches being built up on three ritualised formulae, the conditional (wenn – dann), the modal (je – desto) and the adversative (nicht – sondern). All in all, the structure of German fascist discourse illustrates very well Marcuse's concept of 'one-dimensionality', the discourse of which he characterises as follows: 'the tension between appearance and reality, fact and factor, substance and attribute tend to disappear. The elements of autonomy, discovery, demonstration and critique recede before designation, assertion and imitation. Magical, authoritarian and ritual elements permeate speech and language. Discourse is deprived of the mediations which are the stages of the process of cognition and cognitive evaluation.'[31]

It is suggested that the 'statism' of German fascist discourse and the 'breakdown' of conventional syntax can indeed be partly explained by the fact that the appeal to the emotions is by association rather than by logic, and by the fact that Schickl-gruber, whose discourse the discourse of German fascism was, was a semi-literate dilettante, but that there are two further functional reasons. The first of these is that the ideology of German fascism itself was incapable of further development; the German fascists had a particular world-view which was absolute, final and total. It explained everything in terms of race, and race is a static category. The fascist world-view did not lend itself to further argument, it was not open to rational discussion – despite the attempts at pseudo-scientific justification – and it is this which, at least in part, explains the ultimate immobility of the discourse – and the breakdown of 'classic' sentence logic.

The second reason is that German fascist discourse was governed by an operational rationality; its aim was to produce monolithic solidarity which did not permit deviations or alternatives within its framework. The need was for a defined discourse with which people could identify, and such a need can, ultimately, only be met by standardised and static texts with clearly defined roles and rituals. Such texts assume a quasi-liturgical function in which phatic elements predominate; the content of the discourse is unimportant, new information is not being given – J. P. Stern, for example, refers to 'the party address that is really a quasi-religious ritual of mutual renewal'.[32]

The liturgical character of the texts – of which the public speech is the exemplar – requires an interaction between the individual (the speaker/priest) and the mass (the audience/congregation), with the role of the mass being restricted to giving pre-ordained 'responses' to a known stimulus. As no new information is being given, as no exercise of the intellect is required of the listeners but only assent and acclamation, there is no space for originality of discourse – indeed, originality would destroy the whole *mise-en-scène*.

A further reason for the immutability of fascist rhetoric is to be found in the 'principles' of propaganda. Fascist public discourse can be described as propagandistic in that its aim was to effect the assent of the masses. In *Mein Kampf*, Schicklgruber devotes two (highly repetitive) chapters (6, 'Kriegspropaganda' and 11, 'Propaganda und Organisation') to propaganda, the main function of which he regards as being to win support for an idea. The essence of propaganda is to be restrictive and repetitive,[33] to take a restricted repertoire of ideas or notions and to keep on hammering them home. In order to achieve maximum effect, the discourse must always be pitched at the lowest common denominator – the intellectually most limited listener – so that everyone 'gets the message'. The need for simplicity and repetitiveness requires a uniformity and predictability of discourse, thus precluding originality or creativeness.

The statism and functionality of German fascist discourse means that there is a consistency of style and language; a Schicklgruber speech typically displays a triadic structure: firstly there is the account of past deprivations and the transformation of national shame into national greatness, secondly there is the resumé of the present situation and measures to be taken, and thirdly there is the promise of future triumph, coupled with dire threats against the enemies of the German people. J. P. Stern notes a consistency in the speeches regardless of the historical context: 'The first thing to notice about Hitler's speeches on these occasions (at mass meetings) is how little difference there is between those delivered before February 1933, for the purpose of securing votes in supposedly democratic election campaigns, and those spoken after Hitler's assumption of power and designed to secure popular support for his policies. In each case much the same elements contribute to much the same effect.'[34]

As an illustration, we shall look briefly at the speech which Schicklgruber made before the Reichstag on 23 March 1933, moving the Enabling Bill (*Ermächtigungsgesetz*) which was to sweep away the last vestiges of parliamentary democracy in Germany.[35] This speech has been chosen as it comes at the caesura between the two phases which Stern mentions, and because it clearly demonstrates the features which we have identified as being typical of German fascist discourse; it also contains one of the powerful fascist myths, that of the 'revolution' which the German fascists brought about, and which was 'confirmed' by the popular vote in the elections of 1933.

According to Grünert's introduction, the session of the *Reichstag* on 23 March 1933 was held in an atmosphere of 'intimidation and latent violence', with SA and SS present in the chamber. Before Schicklgruber speaks, he is greeted with a threefold 'Heil' from members of his party (the first ritual element), and his speech is punctuated by acclamation and expressions of assent.[36]

The triadic structure of the speech is clearly distinguishable: the first phase deals with Germany's defeat in the world war and the subsequent failure of the politicians of the Weimar Republic to deal either with the consequences of Versailles or the threat posed by communism, the second relates to the new situation which has now arisen with the successful 'National Socialist Revolution', and the third announces (some of) the measures which will be taken to restore Germany's national pride and the integrity of the nation – interspersed with threats against those who endanger this integrity.

In its argument, the speech presents clear alternatives which are no alternatives; everything is either light or dark, and there is only one way forward, as typified by the closing statement in which the deputies are told that they have the choice between 'peace' and 'war'.[37] (The same technique of presenting stark 'alternatives' was also used ten years later by Goebbels in the Berlin *Sportpalast*, when he presented the 'choice' between 'total war' and 'non-total war'.)

So far, it could be argued, the structure and the argument are standard fare for political discourse; the triadic structure is one which is common, for example, to government policy statements and the election manifestos of government parties, and the presentation of stark 'alternatives' is one which is often to be found in the formulation of the 'questions' asked in referenda or plebiscites; indeed, we shall be observing an instance of it later in Chapter 5.

Schicklgruber's speech is then further characterised by its nationalism, which shades into racism, and lexically is marked by the high frequency of the type *Volk* and its derivatives and compounds such as *völkisch*, *Volkskörper*, *Volksgemeinschaft*, together with the occurrence of the terms *Blut* and *Rasse*. At the phrase level, there is an indication of the formulaic doubling which Seidel and Seidel-Slotty identify as one of the stylistic features of German fascist discourse;[38] for example there is the insistence on the role of the will,[39] but the term *willensmäßig* never appears by itself but only in the phrase *geistig und willensmäßig*.

In the imagery, we find metaphors of sickness and health: the 'political detoxication' of public life is promised, as is the 'moral healing of the national body'.[40]

The discourse is further marked by the cult of the heroic and the 'leader', and running through the whole speech is a vein of explicit violence, marked by the use of such terms as 'barbaric ruthlessness', 'cauterisation', 'exterminate', and 'eliminate'.[41]

The fascist world-view

In the same way that Schicklgruber's speech can be taken as an exemplar of a type of political speech, very few, if any, of the other features of German fascist discourse selected as ilustration and for analysis are in fact unique to that discourse; in their aggregation, however, they do open the way to a consideration of some of the elements of the world-view which is mediated and determined by this discourse.

The basic ideology can be summarised as one based on the notion of race as a natural and determining category linked with a view of human life as a 'Darwinian' struggle, with 'fascist Darwinism' being perceived as a prescriptive concept with a stated moral duty to eliminate 'inferior blood'. The world-view rests on an oppositional (or antagonistic) 'friend–foe' schema, with membership of the categories determined by genealogy; the ones have the right to supremacy, the others do not. The struggle is perceived as a violent one of 'kill or be killed', and there is ultimately no way in which the foes can escape the violence which is to be meted out to them; the brutalisation through language was a necessary prerequisite for the physical brutality which was to follow. Coupled with the notions of 'antagonism' and 'struggle' are the images of 'crisis and salvation', with the chosen people (i.e., those who enjoy natural superiority through their race) being saved from their enemies by the 'leader'. The 'leader' is another powerful image, which marks and confirms the 'elitist' elements of the ideology with its interplay of 'leader' and 'the faithful masses' – with the attendant religious imagery.

The categorial definition by 'race' and 'mass' is predicated on the negation of individuality; 'individuals' are viewed as tokens of the category to which they belong, and with this deindividualisation is linked a dehumanisation, with people being seen at best as 'material' to be 'formed' in the interests of a 'higher ideal'.

The fascist ideology is ahistorical; its world-view is a total and final one, incapable of further development. Membership of the opposing forces is determined by the static category of 'race' and the parameters are given by the 'struggle', the alternatives are either victory or nothing.[42]

The functions of the discourse

The characterisation of the discourse and its relation to the ideology remain incomplete as an analysis unless they are linked to their social and political functions, and thus it is to these that we now turn.[43] We shall then have to consider the methods and techniques which were employed to establish or impose the discourse and to disqualify or silence alternative discourses.

The immediate social and political functions of a particular discourse are often phatic, i.e., they are to generate solidarity and create a sense of 'tribal identity' by the identification of 'friend' and 'foe', and in this, German fascist discourse is no exception. This function is already inherently divisive or antagonistic, as it creates different groups, one of which is perceived as being superior to the others. Linguistically, the division into groups is achieved by processes of naming and defining (thus in our particular case there are 'Germans' and there are 'Jews') and of name-changing (e.g., by requiring all 'Jews' to bear 'Jewish' names).

In German fascist ideology, the underlying determinant for membership of the 'tribe' or exclusion from it is the 'natural category' of 'blood' or 'race'; at the same time, however, as we saw in the previous chapter, there is a strong belief in language as the marker of nationhood. In his article on H.S. Chamberlain for example, Schmidt-Rohr[44] was trying to reconcile the new ideology of 'race' with the older national metaphor of language. Using language as a marker, however, brings the German fascists up against a problem, the problem being that many of the 'enemies of the German people', the 'members of the internationalist Jewish-Bolshevik conspiracy' have German as their mother-tongue (and Germany as their fatherland). Therefore some strategy had to be developed, a 'reality' had to be constructed which would deny the apparent membership of 'Jews' in the 'German' speech-community. Partly, this was achieved by silencing them, by depriving them of their ability and the opportunity to participate in public discourse by expulsion, incarceration and – ultimately – death. At the same time, however, an attempt was made to deny that 'Jews' actually spoke or wrote German – an attempt which, paradoxically, foreshadowed the claims by some critics of 'National Socialist language' post-1945 that the language used by the the German fascists was not really German either.

The first part of the strategy was carried out ruthlessly and systematically; reading through *LTI* for example, one can follow Klemperer's gradual expulsion from articulate public life and the language community as he was refused publication for his books, removed from his teaching post, and finally even denied lending rights in public libraries or access to a radio. As far as participation in the public life of the speech community was concerned, he became a 'non-person'.

It is more difficult to establish whether there was a co-ordinated campaign to implement the second part of the strategy, although attempts were made to deny the 'Jewish' provenance of certain 'German' classics such as Heine's *Loreley* and the Mendelssohn wedding march. In the wider context, there was the crusade against *entartete Kunst* (depraved art), many of whose alleged exponents were labelled as 'Jewish', but there is less evidence in the area of language. In the previous chapter, we did observe tangentially how the Deutscher Sprachverein sought to extend its purifying activities to allegedly 'Jewish' elements in the German language, thus obviously trying to ape the efforts to preserve the 'purity' of the 'German blood'; at the same time, however, the activities of the language purists appeared to be excessive even in fascist eyes.

One further occurrence which can be cited is that of the campaign of the 'German Student Body' 'Against the Un-German Spirit' ('Wider den undeutschen Geist') which started in April 1933, the best-known manifestation of which was perhaps the infamous burning of the books on 10 May 1933. As part of their campaign, the student organisation published twelve guidelines or theses, two of which are directly relevant here. The first (no. 5) seeks to establish the principle that 'Jews' can only think 'Jewish' thoughts, and that if they write German, then they are guilty of misrepresentation, as this is in itself a lie. The second (no. 7) purports to respect the 'Jews' for what they are – 'aliens' – , but seeks to exclude them from what they 'are not' – namely 'German', and contains a specific demand that all 'Jewish' works should appear in Hebrew or, if they are published in German, they are to be marked as 'translations from the Hebrew'. In addition, there is a demand that 'German script' be reserved exclusively for 'Germans', and that draconian penalties should be imposed on those guilty of 'misusing' it.[45]

The creation of tribal solidarity is a means towards the end of regulation of language, thought and – ultimately – non-linguistic action. The identification of 'friend' and 'foe' is part of the construction of a particular view of the world which those in power seek to impose, this world-view being that which informs the ideology.

The regulation of discourse and the discourse of regulation

In a totalitarian state of the type which the German fascists sought to establish, there is no room for competing discourses or views of the world, and therefore those in power must try and control public discourse, in the hope or expectation that the one monolithic public discourse will become so pervasive that it will affect and mould general thought patterns. For the German fascists, the standardisation of discourse was to have two main functions – the first as part of a strategy which would not allow any articulate opposition to emerge, and the second to bind the whole population into the ideology and policies pursued by the rulers.

Prior to January 1933, the discourse of German fascism was only one of a number of competing discourses, and as part of the strategy of establishing a single discourse, the rival discourses had to be either disqualified or eliminated – or otherwise rendered ineffective.

The methods deployed for eliminating rival discourses ranged from persuasion to coercion, and were the standard ones that would be expected – the censorship, banning and destruction of texts, the incarceration of authors and holding out the prospects of survival through emigration[46], the control of publication outlets and distribution networks; in addition, there was voluntary self-censorship and the support and promotion of those who furthered the official discourse.

The totality of methods and policies for suppressing oppositional discourse and establishing the one discourse gave the German language a 'new' word – *Gleichschaltung* (synchronisation), one of the fascists' technical terms.

The following brief media chronicle for the first year of the German fascist regime (1933) will give an indication of some of the measures which were taken to ensure total regulation and control of the media, and thus of public discourse:

[*January 30* Schicklgruber appointed Chancellor]

February 4 Presidential decree 'Zum Schutz des deutschen Volkes' restricts freedom of press and freedom of assembly
SPD *Vorwärts* banned for a total of 11 days during the month
KPD *Rote Fahne* continually confiscated; appears for last time 26/27 February
Liberal *Tempo* banned for one week

February 28 Presidential decree 'Zum Schutz von Volk und Staat' cancels basic rights
KPD publications banned indefinitely
SPD publications banned for 14 days

March 7 *Weltbühne* appears for last time; Carl von Ossietzky had already been arrested

March 13 Creation of a new Ministry of Public Information and Propaganda (Reichsministerium für Volksaufklärung und Propaganda = RMVP) with Joseph Goebbels at its head

March 16 RMVP assumes responsibility for national radio

March/April Numerous attacks on regional and local press – approx. 200 SPD papers and 35 KPD papers 'appropriated'

May 10 SPD assets seized – including publishing facilities (over 100 printing shops)

May 23 KPD assets confiscated

May 31 *Deutsche Allgemeine Zeitung* banned for 3 months

June 28 Fascists assume control of the *Verein Deutscher Zeitungsverleger* = VDZV (Newspaper Publishers' Association) which is renamed *Reichsverband der deutschen Zeitungsverleger* = RVDZ

July 1 *Reichspressekonferenz* in Berlin 'nationalised'

July 20 Concordat with Vatican weakens Catholic press

September 23 *Reichskulturkammer* founded to exercise ideological, political, social and economic control of the media and cultural life. President: Joseph Goebbels

October 4 Schriftleitergesetz enacted to regulate journalistic practice

December 5 Foundation of a 'unified' news agency

December 13 Ban on foundation of new periodicals[47]

The steps taken during the first year effectively silenced opposition within Germany and created the structures which would ensure the greatest possible control of the media and standardisation of discourse. We shall now turn to some of the mechanics of control, and see in particular how the language of the press was to be brought into line with 'official' requirements.

The imposition of the discourse

On 15 March 1933, one day after his appointment as Minister of Popular Information and Propaganda, Goebbels appeared at the meeting of the Reichspressekonferenz in Berlin to inform the assembled journalists that 'things were going to change'.[48] One of the ways in which they were to change was that the Reichspressekonferenz was re-functioned so that it served not only as a forum for the exchange of information but also as an instrument for issuing detailed instructions to the press not only on which subjects or topics were to be treated, but also on the words and phrases to be used – or not to be used, as the case may be. Other instructions were issued by a variety of ministries and authorities, to which must be added 'internal guidelines', for example for the 'security forces'. Then, when the war was started, there were further additional instructions in the form of *Tagesparolen* (orders of the day) by the press supremo Dietrich. According to Frei/Schmitz, between 80,000 and 100,000 such instructions were issued.[49] The instructions themselves were top secret, and it was a criminal offence to reveal them – or, indeed, even to reveal that they existed.[50] Fortunately, however, a number of editors did record details of the instructions, and some reporters kept copies of internal memos laying down reporting instructions (and restrictions), and in an extended paper which stretched over several numbers of the *Zeitschrift für Deutsche Sprache*, Rolf Glunk has processed and analysed a large number of the instructions.[51]

For our purposes, a re-categorisation of a small sample of the instructions will suffice to indicate the breadth of the fields they covered and the functions they were to fulfil.

The regulation of topics to be covered (or avoided) ranged from the 'expectation' of the Propaganda Ministry that a speech delivered by Goebbels on 17 July 1933 would be reported in full[52] to 'permission' being granted on 20 November 1937 for 'favourable' articles on Greta Garbo[53] and to 'suggestions' in 1942 that articles should be published on the Baltic states (without, however, using the proscribed term *Baltikum*).[54]

Far more frequent than the regulation of topics or content, however, were the instructions regulating the terminology to be used, and here a number of different categories can be distinguished:

1. Firstly there were attempts to 'protect' key terms of the fascist ideology by eliminating them in rival contexts and by forbidding their use in non-ideological contexts. An example of the first sub-category is to be found in the use of the term *Sozialismus*. The German fascists tried 'selling' their ideology as a special national 'German' form of 'socialism' which was clearly delineated from Marxist 'socialism', and thus the term 'socialism' was only to be applied to the fascist version of it; the 'other' version was to be labelled *Marxismus*.[55]

As examples of the second sub-category, we can cite a number of instructions restricting the reference of the term *Führer* to Schicklgruber; on 17 January 1942, for example, the title *U-Bootführer* was changed to *U-Bootkommandant*.[56] Another example shows that the attempts at control even extended to newspaper advertising: on 14 January 1937, an edict went out forbidding the use of the term *Rasse* or its derivatives in advertisements.[57] Linked to this category were those instructions which proscribed the use of derogatory terms for organs of the fascist state; for example, on 8 August 1944 newspapers were requested not to use the expression *Pimpfendivision* (Kids Division) when referring to the *SS-Panzerdivision Hitler-Jugend*.[58]

2. A second, linked, category comprised terms which, although not specific to the fascist ideology, were reserved for fascist use. The term *Propaganda*, for example, which in fascist Germany was a positively loaded item, was not to be used for agitatory material put about by Germany's enemies; thus an instruction on 28 July 1937 referred to *Propaganda* as a German copyright term, and decreed that anything else was to be labelled as *Hetze* or *Agitation*, with a particular ban being placed on compounds with negatively loaded components.[59]

3. A third set related to the fascist view of historical developments, and here we do in fact find an attempt to adapt the discourse to changing perceptions. This can be illustrated using two examples, those of 'Anglo-Saxon' and *Drittes Reich*.

Glunk records six instructions issued between 1941 and 1943 prohibiting the application of the label *Angelsachsen* to the British and the Americans. In the instruction of 26 February 1943 the reason was given that previously the term *Angelsachsen* had been used in an attempt to remind the English of their German heritage, and thus to try and win them over to the German side, and that the term was no longer to be used as the policy had patently failed.

With respect to *Drittes Reich*, a number of instructions from mid-1939 laid down that the phrase *Drittes Reich* had served a programmatic function before the formation of the fascist state, and that the programme had now been realised, so that the term had outlived its usefulness and was to be replaced by *Deutsches Reich* or *Großdeutsches Reich*.[60] Previous to this, on 16 March 1939, another instruction had decreed that the label *Großdeutsches Weltreich* was 'not desired', as *its* time had not yet come![61]

4. Fourthly, there was a set of instructions – particularly during the war – which sought to regulate the defamation of the enemy; on the whole, of course, these regulations sought to exclude the application of positive terms to the enemy; thus an instruction on 11 September 1939 laid down that the adjective *tapfer* was not to be used for Poles,[62] and another one from the early days of the war instructed the Press always to refer to the Central Office of Information as Britain's *Lüge- und Reklame-Ministerium* (Ministry of Lies and Advertising) rather than using the more 'neutral' term *Informationsministerium*.[63] At the same time, however, care was taken in certain instances to *build up* the enemy, either to enhance the achievements of the German armed forces or – interestingly enough – with an eye to public opinion. An instance of this latter type of regulation is to be found under 16 December 1941, when it was decreed that the Royal Air Force was not to be accused of 'cowardice', because otherwise people might start asking why RAF pilots were still flying if they were so cowardly[64] (and the German Air Force so good).

5. A fifth category attempts to take account of the sensibilities of friendly or allied nations. Three examples that can be cited here are those of *Anti-semitisch, Asiaten* and *Madrider Regierung*.

Hostility towards the Jews was at the centre of German fascist ideology, but the term 'anti-Semitism' is not strictly speaking accurate, as there are other Semitic peoples in the Arab world towards whom the the German fascists were not only not hostile but whom they tried to recruit as allies; for this reason, a number of instructions were issued to the Press proscribing the use of the term 'Anti-semitism' and its derivatives, and trying to establish more precise denotations such as *judenfeindlich* and *Judengegnerschaft* in order to avoid alienating the Arab world.[65]

The German fascists used the image of the 'Asiatic hordes' sweeping westwards as part of their demonology, with 'Asian' or 'Asiatic' carrying clearly negative associations, and this worked 'satisfactorily' until Japan's entry into the war. At this point, the words *asiatisch*, etc., were declared non-words, as their use was offending Japanese sensibilities; Glunk quotes three instances of relevant instructions, two of which refer specifically to the imperative of not offending Germany's Japanese ally.[66]

At an earlier juncture, there was some confusion about the labels to be attached to the various factions in the Spanish Civil War, and the various instructions which went out about this made it quite clear that out of solidarity with the Spanish fascists, the term *Regierung* was only to be applied to Franco, and never to any other faction which might have formed a government.[67]

6. A sixth category seeks to regulate language use during the war years in order to present a favourable picture of the progress of the war. Under this category there is clearly the renewed use of such terms as *Frontbegradigung* ('straightening the front-line') for 're-treat', but there were also a number of instructions which seek to prohibit the use of 'unfavourable' items on the 'domestic front'- such as the replacement of the term *Evakuierte* by *Umquartierte* (rehoused), the proscription of *Luftschutzkeller* (air-raid cellar) in favour of the more positive *Luftschutzraum* (air-raid shelter) or the avoidance of the word *Katastrophe*, this last having been the subject of a special circular issued by Goebbels on 29 February 1944, in which he asked that the word be 'eradicated' from language use, as it was having a detrimental psychological and political effect.[68]

7. As a seventh category, we find a group of instructions where an attempt is made to prevent the use of terms coined by the enemy – particularly towards the end of the war. Out of these instructions too speaks the realisation that words are constitutive of reality, and that by adopting the enemy's words, one is also adopting their presuppositions and world-view. Two subsets of example will suffice to illustrate this category.

Firstly there are those instances of 'naming' where it is considered inappropriate to adopt the names which the enemy has coined either for self-reference or for reference to their enemy. Thus from 1940 onwards there was a series of instructions banning the use of *Alliierte* or *Vereinigte Nationen* for Germany's enemies, the reason given being that they were reminiscent of the First World War, which ended in Germany's defeat.[69] At the same time, positively loaded terms to designate arms of the 'allied' forces – e.g., RAF – or particular pieces of military equipment – e.g., 'Flying Fortresses' or 'Liberty Ships' – were prohibited. Then in 1944 there was an instruction that the term *Neufaschismus* or *Neofaschismus* should not be used, as it was a product of enemy agitation.[70]

Secondly, instructions were issued banning terms which constituted hostile perceptions either of elements of German fascist policy or the course of the war. As an instance of the first, we can cite an instruction issued in March 1944 proscribing such words as *Rassenhaß* or *Rassenkampf* as they evoked negative associations, whereas the Fascists were concerned to present their racist policies in as positive a light as possible.[71] Under the second sub-category, we find that in September 1943 there were 'allied' reports of the 'Battle for Berlin', and the German press was 'requested' not to adopt this term.[72] Analogous to this instruction, incidentally, was one issued in 1944 asking the press not to use the expression *Frontstadt Berlin* – a designation which was then resurrected in the post-war years to denote Berlin's position in the 'front-line against communist aggression'.

8. Finally in this categorisation we find some attempts to eliminate from external use slang terms or 'euphemisms' taken from internal texts to refer to the torture and/or murder of victims of fascist aggression such as the 'Jews'. For example, on 15 November 1941, there was an instruction condemning the use of 'slang' terms such as *liquidieren* or *in Sonderbehandlung nehmen* ('give special treatment') in the case of summary execution,[73] and in a communication of 20 April 1945, Himmler laid down that the expression *Sonderbehandlung der Juden* was to be avoided.[74]

The attempts to regulate language were not just limited to the press and other media, but on occasions apparently even extended to the linguistic disciplining of the wo/man in the street. In her memoirs, the journalist Ruth Andreas-Friedrich, for example, recounts an episode involving a woman in Berlin in 1941 who was less than complimentary about the quality of the *Magermilch* (skimmed milk) which people were being served, and as a consequence had to go to the police-station every day for three months and recite 'There isn't any skimmed milk. There's only fresh low-fat milk' ('*entrahmte Frischmilch*').[75]

It has already been suggested that the intentions behind the attempted regulation of language were clear: by seeking to impose a standardised discourse, the fascists wished to impose a standard world-view, stifle opposition and commit the population to their policies – in other words, the regulation of language serves to regulate thought and behaviour.

Even if it were possible, however, the standardisation of discourse in itself would not necessarily lead to acceptance of the discourse, for the discourse can only be imposed if there is sufficient exposure to it and there are no alternative texts. Here we have posed one question and proposed two conditions for the effective regulation of discourse, which we shall now proceed to examine. Let us turn firstly to the question of whether standardisation of the discourse is possible, and here it is suggested that two aspects need to be considered – the effectiveness of the regulatory mechanism and the willingness of the producers of text.

With between 80,000 and 100,000 instructions having been issued to the press by a variety of authorities and agencies, it would be too much to expect absolute consistency, and one can indeed find instances of contradictory instructions. Let us take the use of the term 'propaganda' as an instance, and have recourse to two examples which we quoted earlier: *Propaganda* was regarded as a protected term, and in addition to its application to enemy agitation being proscribed by a press instruction, the *Werberat* in 1937 laid down that *Propaganda* should not be used for commercial advertising either, but should be replaced by the word *Werbung*.[76] In the same year, however, another instruction had gone out forbidding the use of the word *Rasse* in advertising[77] which specifically stated that it was forbidden to use the word *Rasse* when 'making *propaganda*' for a modern hat or a particular car engine.[78] Glunk's study contains a number of such contradictions, and he also cites examples from Hitler's and Goebbels's texts where they 'offend' against the instructions which their own agencies have issued.

Effective regulation also depends on the instructions being followed and on the producers of texts being in full support of the attempted regulation, and here too some doubts may be voiced. A study of the instructions issued does suggest that they were not always followed; evidence for this is drawn from the fact firstly that at least some instructions were issued more than once – indicating that they had not always been followed previously, and secondly that some of them specifically mentioned non-observance of earlier instructions.[79] This is not to suggest that reporters or editors were being intentionally 'disobedient' or subversive; one of the problems with the instructions was that some of them attempted to reverse years of language usage – it must, for example, have been difficult always to remember that the name *Rußland* was no longer to be used.

With respect to the willingness of text-producers to carry out the will of the rulers – even assuming that this will had been unambiguously stated – there can be little doubt that, with the physical removal of 'troublesome' journalists from their jobs and the closure of the more explicitly oppositional papers, the great mass of journalistic texts did follow the 'party line'. There do, however, seem to have been exceptions, although here too it is virtually impossible to quantify non-observance – particularly as one of the sources of evidence is journalists' own statements made after the war, when they were of course concerned to place themselves in as favourable a light as possible. In their account of journalism under the fascist regime,[80] Frei and Schmitz devote a chapter (Chapter 10) to 'writing between the lines', in which they suggest that at least in some of the previously liberal 'quality press' such as the *Vossische Zeitung* and the *Frankfurter Zeitung* some journalists did attempt to show a certain independence within the very narrow bounds which were set – particularly in the less explicitly 'political' sections of their newspapers such as the cultural supplements.[81] The allusions and methods deployed, however, were of necessity subtle and indirect, and thus would probably only be understood by a section of the readership – and we must not forget that newspapers such as the *Vossische* and the *Frankfurter* only had a limited appeal among the more educated sectors of society.

As far as the exposure to the discourse is concerned, we must first of all remember that, as far as possible, all oppositional texts had been removed from the public domain, and that, as Klemperer points out, all texts produced for public consumption, whether books, periodicals or even official forms, had been trimmed to the party line,[82] so that ultimately there was no escape (except, of course, for people like Klemperer, who had been expelled from the communicative community). Exposure was also not limited to the print media; so far we have mainly discussed the standardisation of journalistic discourse, but one of the important points about fascist discourse was the use it made of the visual media (especially film) and of the 'new' medium of radio. Goebbels had set as a target that 70 per cent of all German households should be equipped with a radio by the beginning of the war, and this, together with the provision of public access to radio through loudspeakers in the workplace and in public places, made large-scale exposure to the spoken word possible.

The presence or absence of alternative texts presents a more difficult problem to assess. There can be no doubt about the existence of alternative texts under the allegedly uniform fascist regime; there was opposition and resistance, and the opposition did produce texts. For example, a Gestapo document in January 1936 not only reported on growing dissatisfaction but also specifically mentioned that on 9/10 January some 6,000 Social Democrat leaflets had been gathered in the Berlin boroughs of Köpenick and Treptow,[83] and according to Vespignani, a total of some 1,643,200 KPD and SPD leaflets were seized by the Gestapo in 1936 alone.[84] Alternative texts were also being produced outside Germany, but it was extremely difficult for them to penetrate the borders, although as the war progressed, leaflets were dropped from the air, and there was increasing coverage from foreign radio stations, even though draconian punishments were meted out to those caught listening to 'hostile broadcasts'.

The question of the existence of alternative texts does not, however, only have a synchronic dimension; there is a diachronic side to it as well. Although the fascists may well have physically destroyed large numbers of texts produced prior to 1933, they could not expunge the memory of these texts, particularly not over the short period which their 'millennium' lasted.

From what we have said, it would appear that the regulation of discourse was not total, in fact for some of the reasons suggested it is doubtful whether total control of the discourse and the communicative environment is possible, but it was probably effective enough to set the parameters for political discussion: Klemperer, for example, on more than one occasion expresses his dismay at the unthinking way in which people use offensive elements of fascist discourse, without necessarily wishing to be offensive.[85] Indeed, as we have already indicated, it was effective enough to influence post-war discussion as well, as we shall see again in the next chapter.

Although the number of alternative written texts was of necessity extremely restricted, there was also a subversive *oral* discourse typified by the political joke, which is one of the few types of oppositional text possible under a totalitarian regime. The political joke serves as an act of protest against excessive tutelage or regimentation, expressing a measure of disrespect for the 'leaders', but it also helps to present different perceptions and construct an alternative reality to the 'official' one. Two quick examples will have to suffice, both based on the 'reinterpretation' of abbreviations or acronyms, which is a powerful source of humour in German. Klemperer reports on a joke (which he does not find at all funny) about the meaning of the company abbreviation AEG (*Allgemeine Elektrizitäts-Gesellschaft*) which, in an allusion to the 'Aryan' ideology of the fascists, was reinterpreted as 'Alles echte Germanen'.[86] The second example relates to the DNB (*Deutsches Nachrichten-Büro*) referred to in the chronicle above,[87] which, as a reaction to the non-information which the agency purveyed, was said to stand for 'Darf Nichts Bringen' (May not publish anything).[88]

There were two other factors which mitigated not so much against the total regulation of discourse, but against its acceptance, and they are factors which did not only obtain under the German fascists. The first was monotony. As early as 1934, comments were being made about how boring some newspaper reporting had become, and Goebbels himself addressed the problem before the *Reichsverband der deutschen Presse* in 1934, although he suggested – cynically – that the problem lay in the reporters themselves; the basic problem, however, was probably that newspaper writers were uncertain about how far they could go, and thus erred on the side of safety.[89] The uniformity of newspaper writing probably contributed to the general decline in newspaper circulation – from 20.3 to 18.7 million during 1934, with an overall decline of some 50 per cent between 1932 and the end of 1934.[90]

Similar problems were experienced with the radio; with the transfer of the control of radio from the Interior Ministry to the Propaganda Ministry in 1933, the necessary conditions had been created for the propagandistic exploitation of this relatively new medium. The blatant propagandisation, however, made the radio programmes boring, so that in 1934 Goebbels was demanding more attractive programmes, because otherwise his plans could have been put at risk for 70 per cent of all households to have a radio by the time war began.[91]

The second factor is far more serious. One of the objects of the attempts to impose a uniform discourse was to impose a uniform world-view and set of values – a uniform ideology. By making use of the discourse, people are obliged at least to some extent to think in the categories of the ideology. Two problems remain, however: the one is the actual level of commitment to the ideology – it is not for nothing that we talk of paying 'lip-service' to a creed or ideology, i.e., we 'mouth' the words but do not necessarily accept their full implications. The other, linked to the first, is that of private discourse – it is possible to impose a discourse in public, but virtually impossible to do so in the private sphere without total surveillance – which the German fascist regime at least attempted by inducing children as members of the Hitler-Jugend to inform on any 'deviant behaviour' on the part of their parents. Thus, although the public discourse may be imposed, there will be varying degrees of commitment to the attendant ideology, ranging from fervent belief to total rejection, with a corresponding acceptance of the discourse; the majority were probably content to swim with the tide.

As we have already pointed out, the German fascist ideology was essentially static and ahistorical, incapable of further development, and the same applies essentially to the discourse. As history progressed, and the world did not behave the way it was supposed to according to the ideology, a gulf began to widen between the perceptions mediated through the discourse and those of people's everyday experience, and the greater the discrepancies became, the less willingness there was to accept the discourse – although it was still difficult for people to accept that they had been the – at times willing – victims of a massive fraud.

The 'abuse' or 'misuse' of language?

As we have already indicated, there is a suggestion in some of the literature dealing with German fascist discourse that the German fascists in some way 'misused' or 'abused' the German language, a view reflected in the titles of some works, such as Bork's *Mißbrauch der Sprache. Tendenzen nationalsozialistischer Sprachregelung* or Wulf's *Aus dem Lexikon der Mörder* and Sternberger, Storz and Süskind's *Aus dem Wörterbuch des Unmenschen*. The proposition that language can be 'misused' opens up an extremely complex field, which in some ways lies at the very centre of much of the discussion on the relationship between language and politics. In West Germany, the discussion about this relationship arose originally from the attempt to come to terms with what happened between 1933 and 1945; it is a controversial discussion, which goes to the very heart of the function and role of *Sprachkritik* (linguistic critique) and its relationship to linguistics.

The extreme positions are that on the one hand language is neutral, value-free, and that the task of linguistics is to record language use and look for underlying trends and developments: on the other hand, *Sprachkritik* argues for a link between language and speakers, and sees in linguistic surface phenomena an expression of mental states and attitudes, which are its ultimate object. Polenz sees it as an extension of *Sprachpflege*, in that it not only seeks out 'deviant' or 'reprehensible' uses of language, but also looks for the mental processes which led to them,[92] and he cites as an example Korn's *Sprache in der verwalteten Welt* .[93]

An attempt to reconcile the two approaches is to be found in Weisgerber's concept of *inhaltbezogene Grammatik* (content-related grammar), as exemplified in his paper 'Der Mensch im Akkusativ',[94] in which he argues that the increasing number of verbs in German with the transitivising prefix 'be-' replacing prepositional verbs are an indication of the growing 'dehumanisation' of modern life. An opposing position is taken up by Herbert Kolb in his reply 'Der inhumane Akkusativ'.[95]

Linked with the notion that language can be 'misused' is a further one that language itself can in some way become 'inhuman'. In our previous discussion on whether German fascist discourse was 'unique' we quoted an extract from Sternberger *et al.* who suggested that both 'humans' and 'inhumans' (by which they meant the fascists) had their own vocabulary and syntax. They lead into their proposition by claiming that 'the ruin of language is the ruin of mankind',[96] suggesting that there is a moral dimension to language. The idea of language being pervaded by a spirit of inhumanity, by *Ungeist*, is the converse of the idea of language as pervaded by a spirit of salvation (this having been the view held by Chamberlain and his ilk). Both views can be traced back to the idealistic views of language in the nineteenth century.

There can be no doubt that language can be used as a force for good or as a force for evil – however one defines these terms – but it is a bold extension then to claim that the language *per se* thus becomes good or evil, and it is even more debatable whether, within a given language, there is then a 'good' grammar and an 'evil' grammar. The argument that Klemperer and others use about language being 'sick' or 'healthy' is dubious, and this for two reasons.

The first is that it fails to recognise the social function or use of language, and the second is that it lacks the necessary historical perspective and the recognition of functionally determined language varieties.

From a methodological point of view, one must at least be allowed to doubt whether it is an effective way of dealing with the language of fascism to turn its own methods against it. To operate on a level which denotes the fascist denotation of certain phenomena as 'sick' as itself being 'sick' approaches a circular argument which takes no account of any factors outside language and a nebulous concept of *Geist* and *Ungeist*.

The historical perspective is lacking in a view which fails to recognise that very few of the characteristics of Nazi language use were in fact new or original; what was apparent was the frequency with which certain lexical items, certain syntactic constructions, certain metaphors, certain stylistic figures occurred, and these can then be regarded as characteristics of a certain type of discourse – but even then that is not the only form of discourse in existence.

Scepticism is also called for towards the view that language was abused or misused by the fascists and their followers. Such criticisms are not only levelled against German fascist language use, of course. With respect to commercial advertising, for example, one hears the complaint that language is 'manipulated' – which is only a weaker form of the misuse/abuse argument.

But what does it mean, the claim that language is 'misused'? The idea of language being used 'wrongfully' seems to include three principal categories: the first two, using language to present things in a 'false' light, and using language to 'conceal' what should be revealed, could be subsumed under the heading of 'lying'. The third, using language in such a way that people are moved to perform actions which of their own free will they would not perform, could be glossed with the term 'manipulation'.

Behind the view that language can be misused – i.e., 'wrongfully used' – there is then the implication that there is also a 'rightful' use of language.

In addition, there is a further dimension to the 'abuse' argument which operates with aesthetic categories, suggesting that certain ways in which language is used are displeasing, and attached to this aesthetic view is a further moral one, which suggests that if language were used 'properly', i.e., in a 'pleasing' way, then it could not be misused for criminal or inhuman purposes. In other words, this view sees an identity of the moral with the aesthetic.

Let us consider these points one by one.

1. Language is used to present things in a 'false' light. This can imply that there is an objectively accessible reality independent of language, and that there is only one way of denoting that reality correctly. This is a view which keeps occurring in discussions on language and politics, and which recurs for example in the perceptions of post-war language developments in the FRG and the GDR. As evidenced by testimonies from Humboldt through Whorf to Lakoff and Johnson, this view is not uncontroversial: language does not just mirror an already extant reality; it creates the reality it mediates.

2. Language is used to 'conceal' reality. Coupled with this is usually an attack on 'euphemisms' in political language. The argument is a corollary of the first, and is based on the same view of language, with the possible extension that the 'correct' denotation is assumed to incorporate the essence of the object designated. That which is to be concealed is normally 'bad' or 'evil', and the purpose of the euphemism is to conceal this evil content. This is, of course, not the original function of the euphemism; often euphemisms are used to prevent taboos being broken, but the use of the term 'euphemism' with reference to political

language is fraught with problems. Some of these problems will be demonstrated using Joseph Wulf's *Aus dem Lexikon der Mörder*. In this work, Wulf analyses a collection of official Nazi documents which use the term *Sonderbehandlung* ('special treatment') to describe one aspect of the violence perpetrated on Jews in particular. His argument is that *Sonderbehandlung* is a euphemism for *Mord*, and that the euphemism was used to conceal what was 'really happening', i.e., that Jews (and others) were being cold-bloodedly murdered, and that those who used the term used it cynically.

Without in any way wishing to detract from the enormity of the crimes committed against humanity by the German fascists, it is still possible to suggest that, from a linguistics point of view, Wulf's argument is suspect.

It is suspect on both theoretical and pragmatic grounds. Theoretically, there are problems in providing a rigorous definition of 'euphemisms' which will suit, as ultimately it is based on a view of language which is open to question. Pragmatically, there would be problems in defining the boundaries of a 'euphemism'. Wulf's argument that *Sonderbehandlung* is a 'euphemism' for *Exekution* is only a relative one, for one could argue with almost equal justification that *Exekution* is also a 'euphemism'. It could further be argued that the term *Exekution* would be inappropriate, because *Exekution*, like *Hinrichtung* presupposes some form of legal process, which is definitely lacking in the cases under consideration. Further, it could in extremis be argued that not even the term *Mord* is appropriate in the eyes of those using the term *Sonderbehandlung*, because murder is a crime directed against humans; from the viewpoint of Nazi ideology, neither of these conditions were fulfilled. It is suspect thirdly because it is questionable whether, in the documents under consideration, there was 'intent to deceive'; Wulf's argument fails to take sufficient account of the type or status of texts analysed; they were official documents, written for internal consumption, so it is to be expected that both authors and addressees were in no doubt about what was meant by the term, and in fact there was at least one press instruction prohibiting the use of the term in externally oriented texts.[97]

The third 'misuse' argument, that language is used to manipulate, is again one which should not be accepted without closer examination. This argument could be based on a very narrow view of the functions of language, on the view namely that the sole function of language is to represent and to inform. As such it would deny that other functions of language such as the persuasive, the regulative and the phatic are an important aspect of human interaction and would for this reason be deficient. Alternatively, it accepts the persuasive function, but interposes a moral filter by deeming some persuasive uses of language to be legitimate and others not.

This brings us to the implication behind the abuse/misuse argument, that if there is a 'wrongful' use of language then there is also an inherently 'rightful' use. Here one finds a confusion between the moral and the linguistic, which can presumably be traced back to the idea of language as a 'gift from God' to be used for divinely ordained purposes. But wo/man is free, and unless one pleads for a doctrine of 'linguistic original sin' (and one must not forget that the concept of original sin was linked with the acquisition of knowledge), then language can be used as a force for 'good' and a force for 'evil'. It can be used to represent, but the fact that the representation does not meet with the approval of a third party does not make the language 'bad'; it can be used to move, to persuade, but the fact that another person does not agree with the ends to which it is being put does not make the language itself 'evil' or 'immoral'. Very often too, the moral argument is linked with the aesthetic one, and an example of this is given in Betz's introduction to Berning's account of the vocabulary of German fascism,[98] when he quotes an anecdote about Carl von Ossietzky,[99] who wanted to 'sentence' the leading fascists to learn 'proper' German, the suggestion being that, if they learnt to use the German language 'properly', then they would cease to be evil – a view which Betz dismisses as wishful thinking.[100]

The suggestion thus far, using the example of German fascist discourse, has been that the approach taken by some critics can be challenged on a number of counts. Although there can be no objection in principle to a holistic approach which coalesces linguistic, aesthetic and moral judgements, it must operate from a tenable view of language functions and an appreciation of the historicity of language. More importantly, it must select the right 'targets' for its moral judgements, and not attempt to make 'language' the whipping-boy. How then should the task be approached?

The one alternative presumably would be a strictly positivist one which records, describes and orders; this is in principle the tendency behind Seidel and Seidel-Slotty's work, although here too explanations are given, and reference is made to the underlying ideology. The recording and ordering of linguistic evidence is indeed extremely important, just as it is most important to organise the evidence diachronically in order to put it into the correct historical perspective. The question is, however, whether the linguist's task finishes here.

The term 'linguistic evidence' has just been used, but evidence for what? It has already been suggested in Chapter 2 that the use of language, the way language is deployed, is itself an historical document, and this idea informs, for example, part of Berning's *Vokabular des Nationalsozialismus*,[101] which has recourse to the type of view which Jacob Grimm held.[102]

The basic tenor is clear; the language does contain information, it does say something about the processes which led to the reality it has constructed and represents. The language reveals and constitutes the ideas, the attitudes, the ideologies, the intentions.

The aim of the linguist must be to work from a firm understanding of the nature and functions of language to reveal the intentions, presuppositions and ideologies embedded in texts. Any criticism, censure or judgement must then be directed towards the intentions and the ideologies, not just towards the language. To attack the use of language as such is an unjustifiable short cut, which ultimately reveals little. A brief illustration will serve to demonstrate this.

There is no point in simply saying that using the term *Sonderbehandlung* is a euphemistic or immoral use of language, because what was really happening was murder, and then to direct the main attack against the 'misuse' of language. To start with, on the purely textual level, it would scarcely be conceivable that, in the contexts examined by Wulf, the term *Sonderbehandlung* could simply have been replaced by *Mord*.

A more promising approach would be to start off by showing that the term *Sonderbehandlung*, as a substantivisation, is stylistically significant in that it is characteristic of administrative language and points to the bureaucratisation of extermination. Further one can, by listing the selection restrictions on *Behandlung* as opposed to *Mord* demonstrate that, whereas *Mord* can only take human objects (and subjects!), *Behandlung* does not discriminate between animate and inanimate objects, let alone between human and non-human; in this way, an important inhibition is broken down. From this, deductions can then be drawn about attitudes towards the objects of the 'treatment' (in most cases Jews) and this then linked in with Nazi racist ideology, for which again other linguistic evidence can be found.

Thus, the use of the noun *Sonderbehandlung* can be shown to be an element in the creation of a reality which relegates a whole class of people to a status which potentially denies their human-ity, and which can be tied in with the whole complex of fascist pseudo-Darwinism. Then, and only then, is it possible to take up an explicit stand against the attitudes; there is no point in merely attacking what is perceived as a 'misuse' of language. The path must lead from linguistic analysis to an evaluation of the linguis-tically constituted realities, and from there to the ideological critique; these are separate steps, and cannot be treated as one. By keeping the steps separate, the criticism of the ideology can then become more direct and effective, and not obscured by linguistic red herrings.

Notes

1 G. Orwell, *Nineteen Eighty-four*, Harmondsworth, 1983, p. 49

2 'In der theoretischen Auseinandersetzung mit dem deutschen Faschismus hat schon früh die Sprache das Interesse auf sich gezogen. Karl Kraus und Victor Klemperer glaubten, durch Sprachkritik Zugang zur Analyse des Faschismus zu finden. Seither ist eine ganze Reihe von Untersuchungen erschienen, die den sprachlichen Aspekt des Faschismus zum Gegenstand nehmen.' W. Haug, *Vom hilflosen Antifaschismus zur Gnade der späten Geburt*, Hamburg, Berlin, 1987, p. 34

3 J. Wilson, *Politically Speaking. The Pragmatic Analysis of Political Language*, Oxford, 1990, p. 183

4 L. Winckler, *Studie zur gesellschaftlichen Funktion faschistischer Sprache*, Frank-furt, 1970, p. 24, 'Sprachkritik, die sich so unbefangen der Sprache ihres Gegenstands bedient, wird kaum zur Erhellung faschistischer Sprache und ihrer gesellschaftlichen Funktion beitragen'

5 For this example, as for so much else, I am very grateful to Andreas Musolff

6 It is apparent from a study of the relevant literature and the contexts in which the term 'fascist' is used that it often belongs to the province of Marxist

critique. In the present context, however, it is not necessarily being used in a manner which embraces all the Marxist presuppositions of its use (as, for example, in Winckler, *Studie zur gesellschaftlichen Funktion faschistischer Sprache*

7 A. Hitler, *Mein Kampf*, Munich 1942, 711th edn, p. 649

8 After Jäckel and Kuhn (eds), *Hitler. Sämtliche Aufzeichnungen 1905-1924*, Stuttgart, 1980, p. 705

9 'So hat der Mensch als auch der Unmensch seinen Wortschatz, seine eigentümliche Grammatik und seinen eigentümlichen Satzbau.' D. Sternberger, G. Storz and W. Süskind, *Aus dem Wörterbuch des Unmenschen*, Hamburg, Düsseldorf, 1968, 3rd edn, p. 5

10 For a full account of the 'vocabulary' of German fascism, see for example C. Berning, *Vom 'Abstammungsnachweis' zum 'Zuchtwart'. Vokabular des Nationalsozialismus*, Bern, 1964 and K.-H. Brackmann and R. Birkenhauer, *NS-Deutsch. 'Selbstverständliche' Begriffe und Schlagwörter aus der Zeit des Nationalsozialismus*, Straelen, 1988

11 C. Mueller, *The Politics of Communication*, New York, 1973

12 'Das Dritte Reich hatte die wenigsten Worte seiner Sprache selbstschöpferisch geprägt, vielleicht, wahrscheinlich sogar, überhaupt keines. Die nazistische Sprache weist in vielen auf das Ausland zurück, übernimmt das meiste andere von vorhitlerischen Deutschen. Aber sie ändert Wortwerte und Worthäufigkeiten, sie macht zum Alleingut, was früher einem einzelnen oder einer winzigen Gruppe gehörte, sie beschlagnahmt für die Partei, was früher Allgemeingut war'. V. Klemperer, *LTI. Notizbuch eines Philologen*, Leipzig, 1975, pp. 21–2

13 Dahle, *Der Einsatz einer Wissenschaft*

14 Berning, *Vom 'Abstammungsnachweis' zum 'Zuchtwart'*; S. Bork, *Mißbrauch der Sprache. Tendenzen nationalsozialistischer Sprachregelung*, Bern/Munich, 1970; Dahle, *Der Einsatz einer Wissenschaft*; Klemperer, *LTI*; Seidel and Seidel-Slotty *Sprachwandel im Dritten Reich*; Sternberger *et al.*, *Aus dem Wörterbuch des Unmenschen*, Hamburg, 1945, 1957, 1967

15 G. Lakoff and M. Johnson, *Metaphors we live by*, Chicago, 1980, p. 159

16 Lakoff and Johnson, *Metaphors*, p. 159

17 Lakoff and Johnson, *Metaphors*, p. 160

18 'Wir wischen uns das Blut aus den Augen, damit wir klar sehen können, und geht es in die nächste Runde, dann stehen wir wieder fest auf den Beinen.'
'Ein Volk, das bisher nur mit der Linken geboxt hat und eben dabei ist, seine Rechte zu bandagieren, um sie in der nächsten Runde rücksichtslos in Gebrauch zu nehmen, hat keine Veranlassung, nachgiebig zu sein.'
Both reported in Klemperer, *LTI*, p. 247

19 Just to take an instance at random, a headline in *The Guardian* of 28 March 1991 announces: 'Major fails to deal Kinnock a knockout blow'

20 'Sturm ist sozusagen sein erstes und sein letztes Wort: mit der Heranbildung der SA, der Sturmabteilungen fängt man an, mit dem Volkssturm ... steht man am Ende.' Klemperer, *LTI*, pp. 239–40

21 Cf. Klemperer in *LTI*: 'Daß die LTI auf ihren Höhepunkten eine Sprache des Glaubens sein muß, versteht sich von selber, da sie auf Fanatismus abzielt. Doch das Eigentümliche hierbei ist, daß sie als Glaubenssprache sich eng an das Christentum, genauer: an den Katholizismus lehnt', p. 117

22 'Der Führer ist nichts weiter als der Fleisch und Blut gewordene Gedanke des Volkes', quoted in Bork, *Mißbrauch der Sprache*, p. 84

23 'Wir alle, vom einfachsten SA-Mann bis zum Ministerpräsidenten, sind von Adolf Hitler und durch Adolf Hitler', quoted in Klemperer, *LTI*, p. 121

24 E.g., 'aus Menschen soll ein brauchbares Instrument für entscheidene Notwendigkeiten geschmiedet werden', *Völkischer Beobachter* , 6 January 1939

25 E.g., 'Jede Bewegung wird das von ihr gewonnene Menschenmaterial zunächst in zwei große Gruppen zu sichten haben: in Anhänger und Mitglieder', *Mein Kampf*, p.651

26 Sternberger *et al.*, *Aus dem Wörterbuch*, p. 5, cf. note 9 above

27 *Mein Kampf*, pp.164–5

28 It is, however, necessary to point out that increasing nominalisation is a common feature in the development of the German language in the twentieth century; cf. Slotty, *Sprachwandel*: p. 31 'Der nominale Stil, an sich schon ein Charakteristikum des Deutschen, wird nun in ungeheurer Übertreibung weitergeführt'

29 (*Mein Kampf* ist) 'bis zur letzten Auflage eine ausgesprochene Sammlung von Hitler-Reden in unsystematischer Folge (geblieben)'. W.Maser, *Hitlers Mein Kampf. Entstehung, Aufbau, Stil Änderungen, Quellen, Quellenwert, kommentierte Auszüge*, Rastatt, 1966, p. 50

30 Cf. Winckler, *Studie zur gesellschaftlichen Funktion*, p. 41: 'Durch Häufung solcher Formeln wird die klassische Satzlogik zerstört: anstelle syntaktischer Vermittlung von Prädikaten und Subjekten tritt die Unvermitteltheit bloßer Wörter'

31 H. Marcuse, *One Dimensional Man*, London, 1972, p. 79

32 J. P. Stern, *Hitler. The Führer and the People*, Glasgow 1975, p. 82

33 'Sie (die Propaganda) hat sich auf wenig zu beschränken und dieses ewig zu wiederholen.' *Mein Kampf*, p. 202

34 Stern, *Hitler*, p. 36

35 The text used is that in H. Grünert, *Politische Reden in Deutschland*, Frankfurt, Berlin, 1976, pp. 79–85

36 In themselves, of course, these ritual elements are ones which will be found in any parliament – manifested, for example, in the waving of order papers and the baying from the benches

37 'Mögen Sie meine Herren, nunmehr selbst die Entscheidung treffen über Frieden oder Krieg' after Grünert, *Politische Reden*, p.85

38 Cf Seidel and Seidel-Slotty, *Sprachwandel*, pp. 148-9

39 Cf. Stern, *Hitler*, Ch. 7 *passim*

40 'politische Entgiftung unseres öffentlichen Lebens', 'moralische Sanierung an unserem Volkskörper', Grünert, *Politische Reden*, p. 83

41 'Landes- und Volksverrat sollen künftig mit barbarischer Rücksichtslosigkeit ausgebrannt werden' (p. 83), 'diese Erscheinung ... in unserem Land auszurotten und zu beseitigen' (p. 81)

42 Klemperer, for example reports a 'trick' examination question set during the years of fascist domination: 'What comes after the Third Reich?' The 'correct' answer is 'Nothing. The Third Reich is the eternal empire of the Germans' ('Nichts kommt dahinter, das Dritte Reich ist das ewige Reich der Deutschen'). Klemperer, *LTI*, p. 119

43 Cf. Winckler, *Gesellschaftliche Funktion*, pp. 90–1: 'Die typischen und die allgemeinen, aber auch die individuellen und historischen Merkmale von Hitlers Sprache lassen sich nur im Zusammenhang mit der sozialen Funktion von Sprache verständlich machen'

44 Schmidt-Rohr, 'Houston Stewart Chamberlain'

45 *Leitsätze der 'Deutschen Studentenschaft' 'Wider den undeutschen Geist'*
    '5. Der Jude kann nur jüdisch denken. Schreibt er deutsch, dann lügt er.
    7. Wir wollen den Juden als Fremdling achten, und wir wollen das Volkstum ernstnehmen. Wir fordern deshalb von der Zensur: Jüdische Werke erscheinen in hebräischer Sprache. Erscheinen sie in deutsch, sind sie als Übersetzungen zu kennzeichnen. Schärfstes Einschreiten gegen den Mißbrauch der deutschen Schrift. Deutsche Schrift steht nur Deutschen zur Verfügung.' from: J.Wulf, *Literatur und Dichtung im 3. Reich. Eine Dokumentation*, Reinbek/Hamburg, 1966

46 Over 2,000 writers and journalists left Germany in the weeks and months following Schicklgruber's appointment. Cf. Frei and Schmitz, *Journalismus im Dritten Reich*, Munich, 1989, p. 17

47 after 'Medienchronik Drittes Reich' in Frei and Schmitz, *Journalismus*, pp. 208ff.

48 Cf. Frei and Schmitz *Journalismus*, p. 30

49 Frei and Schmitz *Journalismus*, p. 34

50 An obsession with secrecy which goes so far that it denies the existence of secrets was not a unique phenomenon; in the UK, for example, certain people are not only required to sign the Official Secrets Act, but are then not allowed to reveal that they have signed the Act

51 R. Glunk, 'Erfolg und Mißerfolg der nationalsozialistischen Sprachlenkung', in *Zeitschrift für Deutsche Sprache*, Vols. 22–7, 1966–71

52 After Frei and Schmitz, *Journalismus*, p. 31

53 After Frei and Schmitz, *Journalismus*, p. 31

54 Cf. Glunk, 'Erfolg und Mißerfolg', 1969, pp. 119–20

55 Cf. Glunk, 'Erfolg und Mißerfolg', 1970, pp.117–18

56 Instruction from 17 January 1942, cf. Glunk, 'Erfolg und Mißerfolg', 1966, p. 146

57 'Die Anzeigen-Abteilungen werden vom Propagandaministerium darauf aufmerksam gemacht, daß der Begriff 'Rasse' bei Anzeigen nicht verwendet werden darf' after Glunk, 'Erfolg und Mißerfolg', 1969, p.181

58 Instruction from 8 August 1944, after Glunk, 'Erfolg und Mißerfolg', 1969, p. 177

59 '28.7.37: Es wird gebeten, das Wort Propaganda nicht mehr mißbräuchlich zu verwenden. Propaganda ist im Sinne des neuen Staates gewissermaßen ein gesetzlich geschützter Begriff und soll nicht für abfällige Dinge Verwendung finden. Es gibt also keine "Greuelpropaganda", keine "bolschewistische Propaganda", sondern nur eine Greuelhetze, Greuelagitation, Greuelkampagne usw. kurzum – Propaganda nur dann, wenn für uns, Hetze, wenn gegen uns.' (Anweisung 960.) After Glunk, 'Erfolg und Mißerfolg', 1967, p.100)

60 E.g.,: 'Um die Änderungen innerer Verhältnisse innerhalb des Reiches propandistisch zum Ausdruck zu bringen, ist vor und nach der Machtübernahme der Ausdruck "Drittes Reich" für das nationalsozialistische Reich geprägt und gebraucht worden. Der tiefgreifenden Entwicklung, die seitdem stattgefunden hat, wird diese historisch abgeleitete Bezeichnung nicht mehr gerecht.' After Glunk, 'Erfolg und Mißerfolg', 1966, p. 67

61 'Die Verwendung des Begriffs "Großdeutsches Weltreich" ist unerwünscht. Letzteres Wort ist für spätere Gelegenheiten vorbehalten.' after Glunk, 'Erfolg und Mißerfolg' 1969, p. 183

62 'Das Wort 'tapfer' soll auf Polen überhaupt nicht mehr angewandt werden. Die Ereignisse der letzten Tage haben gezeigt, daß diese Armee diesen Ehrentitel nicht verdient.' After Glunk, 'Erfolg und Mißerfolg', 1971, p. 120

63 Inst. no. 992, 9 September 1939 after Glunk, 'Erfolg und Mißerfolg', 1970, p. 85

64 '… wir wollen den englischen Flieger, der sich als beachtlicher Gegner der deutschen Luftwaffe herausgestellt hat, nicht verächtlich machen und nicht der Feigheit zeihen, weil sonst das deutsche Volk zu der Frage käme: "Ja, wenn sie so feige sind, warum sind sie dann überhaupt noch vorhanden?"' After Glunk,'Erfolg und Mißerfolg', 1969, p. 127

65 E.g., Instruction no. 1578 on 22 August 1935: 'Das Propagandaministerium bittet in der Judenfrage das` Wort: antisemitisch oder Antisemitismus zu vermeiden, weil die deutsche Politik sich nur gegen die Juden, nicht aber gegen die Semiten schlechthin richtet. Es soll stattdessen das Wort: antijüdisch gebraucht werden.' After Glunk, 'Erfolg und Mißerfolg', 1966, p. 64

66 E.g., 9 February 1943 'Die Verwendung des Wortes "Asiaten" für die Sowjetrussen und des Wortes "Mongolen" in absprechendem Sinne in Zusammenhang mit dem Vorgehen der Sowjets verletzt unseren japanischen Bundesgenossen,' after Glunk , 'Erfolg und Mißerfolg', 1969, p. 119

67 E.g., Inst. 84 on 16 January 1937: 'Die Franco-Regierung ist zu nennen "spanische Nationalregierung", die anderen dürfen niemals mit dem Wort "Regierung" in Verbindung gebracht werden. Sie heißen schlechthin "Die Bolschewisten".' After Glunk, 'Erfolg und Mißerfolg', 1970, p. 93

68 'Ich bitte, dafür zu sorgen, daß aus allen Organisationsplänen, Erlassen und Verordnungen und aus dem gesamten Sprachgebrauch das Wort "Katastrophe" ausgemerzt wird, da es sich psychologisch und politisch unerfreulich auswirkt.' Runderlaß des Reichssicherheitshauptamtes vom 29.2.1944, Ref. –I Org. Nr. 710/43 – 151 –, quoted after Glunk, 'Erfolg und Mißerfolg', 1970, p. 86

69 Cf. Glunk, 'Erfolg und Mißerfolg', 1969, p.117 and 1971, p.122

70 23 April 1944 'Die Bezeichnung 'Neufaschismus' oder 'Neofaschismus', die in der Feindagitation wieder auftaucht, soll von den deutschen Zeitschriften nicht aufgegriffen werden.' After Glunk, 'Erfolg und Mißerfolg', 1970, p. 95

71 Unter 'Vermeiden': 'Die Ausdrücke Rassenkampf, Rassenkrieg, Rassenhaß, da sie Erfindungen der Gegner des Rassengedankens und dem Wortschatz positiver Behandlung des Rassengedankens fremd sind.' After Glunk, 'Erfolg und Mißerfolg', 1970, p. 181

72 Cf. Glunk,'Erfolg und Mißerfolg', 1971, p. 115

73 'Naßforsche Ausdrücke, wie "liquidieren" oder "in Sonderbehandlung nehmen" ... sind höchst unangebracht. 'After Glunk, 'Erfolg und Mißerfolg', 1967, p. 83

74 'Er wünscht, daß an keiner Stelle von "Sonderbehandlung der Juden" gesprochen wird'. After Poliakov and Wulf, *Das Dritte Reich und die Juden, Dokumente*, Berlin-Grünewald 1955, 2nd edn, p. 241

75 '"Magermilch?" schimpfte kürzlich eine Frau. "Den Dreck können Sie selber trinken," und muß nun drei Monate lang täglich auf der Polizei das Sprüchlein herbeten: "Es gibt keine Magermilch. Es gibt nur entrahmte Frischmilch."' R. Andreas-Frisch, *Der Schattenmann*, Berlin 1947, p. 84

76 '(es muß) als grundsätzlich unerwünscht angesehen werden, daß das Wort "Propaganda" zu Zwecken der Wirtschaftswerbung Verwendung findet'. After Glunk, 'Erfolg und Mißerfolg', 1967, p. 201

77 Cf. p. 141 above

78 'Es ist unzulässig, mit dem Stichwort "Rasse" Propaganda für einen modernen Hut oder für einen bestimmten Motor der Auto-Industrie zu machen.' Glunk, 'Erfolg und Mißerfolg', 1967, p. 201

79 E.g., *Zeitschriftendienst* 5341 (12 September 1941), 'Trotz eindeutiger Sprachregelung und zahlreicher weiterer Hinweise in der Pressekonferenz werden die genannten Anweisungen von einem großen Teil der Presse in den Wind geschlagen'

80 Frei and Schmitz, *Journalismus*

81 Cf. Frei and Schmitz, *Journalismus*, pp.121–35 *passim*

82 'alles, was in Deutschland gedruckt und geredet wurde, war ja durchaus parteiamtlich genormt; was irgendwie von der einen zugelassenen Form abwich, drang nicht an die Öffentlichkeit; Buch und Zeitung und Behörden- zuschrift und Formulare einer Dienststelle – alles schwamm in derselben braunen Soße.' Klemperer, *LTI* , pp. 17–18

83 After R.Vespignani, *Nach den zwanziger Jahren: Faschismus*, Berlin/Ham- burg, 1976, p. 130

84 Vespignani, *Faschismus*, p. 131

85 E.g., in Klemperer, *LTI*, Chap XVI pp. 101-4 *passim*

86 Klemperer, *LTI*, p.48

87 Cf. p. 139 above

88 Cf. Frei and Schmitz, *Journalismus*, p. 33

89 Cf Frei and Schmitz, *Journalismus*, p. 34

90 Frei and Schmitz, *Journalismus*

91 Frei and Schmitz, *Journalismus*, p. 36

92 'Sprachkritik... die hinter den "Sprachvergehen" über den jeweiligen Sprach- oder Schreibakt hinaus geistige Ursachen und Zusammenhänge sucht'. P. v. Polenz, 'Sprachkritik und Sprachwissenschaft', *Neue Rundschau*, 74, 1963, p. 6

93 K. Korn, *Sprache in der verwalteten Welt*, Frankfurt, 1958

94 L. Weisgerber, 'Der Mensch im Akkusativ', *Wirkendes Wort*, viii, 4, 1958

95 H. Kolb, 'Der inhumane Akkusativ', *Zeitschrift für deutsche Wortforschung*, 14, 1960, pp. 168–77

96 'Der Verderb der Sprache ist der Verderb der Menschen', Sternberger *et al.*, *Aus dem Wörterbuch*, p. 5.

97 Cf. p. 144 above

98 Berning, *Vom 'Abstammungsnachweis' zum 'Zuchtwart'*

99 Carl von Ossietzky, journalist and editor of *Die Weltbühne*, had already been imprisoned before the Fascists' assumption of power. Under the Fascists, he was thrown into concentration camp, and died in 1938

100 'Dolf Sternberger bringt in seiner Rede über "Maßstäbe der Sprachkritik" vor der deutschen Akademie für Sprache und Dichtung in Darmstadt als Beispiel für Sprachwirkung und Nationalsozialismus eine Ossietzky-Anekdote: "Die Strafe, die sich Ossietzky (wie die Anekdote will) für die Naziführer ausgedacht hatte – 'Deutsch müssen sie lernen!' gewinnt ja gerade dadurch ihre Pointe, daß sie, die Nazis, lernten sie wirklich Deutsch, nämlich korrektes, gutes Deutsch, in demselben Augenblick aufhörten, das zu sein, was sie waren. Es wäre das Ende des Nationalsozialismus und das Ende der Diktatur." Es wäre schön, aber es ist wohl zu schön, um wahr zu sein. Ein schlechter Mensch kann kein gutes Deutsch schreiben, denn durch das gute Deutsch würde er notwendig auch zum guten Menschen werden?' Berning, *Vom 'Abstammungsnachweis' zum 'Zuchtwart'*, p. v

101 'Kein Element ist so wie die Sprache geeignet, Spuren geistiger Bewegungen aufzunehmen und in sich zu bewahren.' Berning, *Vom Abstammungsnachweis zum Zuchtwart*, p. 1

102 Cf. Chap. 3, p. 93 above

5 A question of identity

Introduction

This chapter and the final one will be devoted to an overview of the main politico-linguistic concerns in Germany since 1945. The main emphasis will be on developments in the West, and where East German issues are addressed, they will mainly be those which are of relevance to East Germany's relationship to its Western neighbour. We shall endeavour to show some of the ways in which the regulative, persuasive and phatic functions of language have been realised, which are seen as forming the foundation of politico-language usage, and we shall also be continuing to observe some of the perceptions of the role that language plays in the political process.

The years since 1945 have witnessed a high level of politico-linguistic activity and discussion in Germany. Examples are to be found in the attempts to come to terms with German fascist discourse between 1933 and 1945 as part of the general process of *Vergangenheitsbewältigung*, in the research into the possible divergences in the German language between East and West, some of which at least was funded by the West German government, in research in the GDR on language and politics, in the setting up of a language advisory group by the West German CDU in the 1970s, in the establishment of *ad hoc* political groupings by linguists,[1] in the number of academy sessions and conferences devoted to the topic – in 1983, for instance, the West German *Germanistenverband* invited the Secretaries-General of the SPD and CDU to address their annual conference, and in the growing number of research projects and university courses devoted to politico-linguistic themes. An indication of the amount of interest generated in politico-linguistics is given by a bibliography which Walter Dieckmann and his associates produced in Berlin in 1986, which contains some 1,500 titles produced between 1975 and 1984,[2] and in the bibliography of some 1,000 titles appended to a study by Erich Strassner on the relationships between language and ideology[3], by ongoing research work at Germany's leading language research institute, the Institut für Deutsche Sprache in Mannheim[4] and by the fact that theses on politico-linguistic topics at both doctoral and professorial level are an accepted part of the German linguistics scene.

This upsurge of interest and activity has been motivated by a number of factors from both within and without the linguistic disciplines. The external factors are ones which will concern us later, but internally what we can observe is a growing occupation of academic linguists with what is known as *Sprachkritik* – linguistic critique.[5] The development of a tradition of *Sprachkritik* can originally be traced back to the concerns of the language purists, and there is still a strong strand which is preoccupied with matters of 'correctness' and 'purity' - which, as we have seen, have had strong political and nationalist connotations. In the Federal Republic of Germany, however, we can observe a shift in the concerns of *Sprachkritik* towards an analysis of political discourses. As late as 1980, an article on *Sprachkritik* in a standard reference work[6] could link it with language regulation and linguistic purism, which have traditionally been its primary focus. In 1982, however, Hans Jürgen Heringer was producing what has become one of the key texts on *Sprachkritik*,[7] which he opened with a paper entitled 'Sprachkritik – die Fortsetzung der Politik mit besseren Mitteln', and when Rainer Wimmer attempted to define the new aims and tasks of *Sprachkritik*[8] in 1985, the political aspect was firmly established in the forefront.

Within linguistics, the increased interest of academic linguists in *Sprachkritik*, which it is hoped will lead to a more rigorous analysis of political texts and trends in political discourse, has been aided by such developments within the linguistic sciences as discourse analysis, speech act theory, 'practical semantics' and pragmatics, together with work in sociolinguistics. In addition, there has been a willingness on the part of linguists to widen the range of texts which they treat and to see 'political' texts as fruitful objects of investigation.[9]

Although linguists have been involved in *Sprachkritik*, and are perhaps becoming more involved, it is still useful to make a distinction between *Sprachkritik* and linguistics. The former often does not meet the demands of scientific rigour which should apply to the latter – or, to put it another way, linguistics has not yet succeeded in fully developing theories, methods and techniques which will allow it to meet many of the demands of *Sprachkritik*. Also, one can still argue that the main concern of linguistics is with language-as-system and with speakers as exemplars and that as a discipline it is essentially non-judgemental, whereas *Sprachkritik* is concerned with language use, with language-as-text and with speakers as individuals, and does involve an evaluation or judgement both of text and speaker. In addition, the linguist subordinates herself to the analysis, whereas the linguistic critic is exposed, and many of the products of *Sprachkritik* perhaps sometimes reveal more about the critic than about the object of her criticism.

External factors which help to explain the increased involvement of linguists in political *Sprachkritik* can be sought in general developments in West German political culture and in particular in the experiences of the student movement of the late 1960s which had definite consequences for West German linguistic culture. Political *Sprachkritik* often demonstrates an awareness of language and a sensitivity to its political implications, and as an idealist, one could argue that a concern with and for political discourse is a sign of democracy and political maturity. As a cynic, one could maintain that the lack of a strong political linguistic culture in Britain is evidence of the converse, although there are now some indications – at least for a reader of *The Guardian*! - that care for the language is spreading beyond ill-informed – though doubtless well-meaning – readers' letters to the Editor of *The Times* on 'the decline of the English language' and allied topics and that a concern with the way that political realities are linguistically constituted is beginning to emerge.

The main concerns

For present purposes, we shall find it useful to distinguish two main foci of politico-linguistic interest in West Germany. The first, which can be related to the first two decades of the post-war era – i.e., up to the late 1960s – has an external orientation, i.e., it is concerned with developments outside West Germany, while the second is internally oriented, concentrating on politico-linguistic developments within the Federal Republic.

As we have already seen in Chapter 3, the awareness of the phatic function of language as a political factor in Germany is closely linked with the 'national question'; the unity of the German language has often been regarded as a symbol of the unity of the German nation, and the struggle against foreign political domination has been reflected in the various attempts to eradicate 'foreign influences' from the German language.

If we now view the post-war language scene in West Germany, we find that in the two decades from 1945 to 1965 the two over-riding political concerns which determined the main topics of *Sprachkritik* can be linked with the role of language as a 'national' identifier. The first was the attempt to process and deal with the era of German fascism from 1933 to 1945, and the second was the determination to establish the legitimacy of the new state in the West as the true representative of the German nation and to defend this claim against opposing claims emanating from the new German state in the East.

Both these endeavours reflect the attempts of the new West German state to establish its own identity and represent instances of what the German social psychologist Peter Brückner calls *Abgrenzung* – demarcation – the attempt to set the West German state off ideologically against hostile or conflicting ideologies.[10] The attempt runs along two dimensions, those of time and space. On the one hand, the new West German state had to set itself off clearly against the preceding fascist regime – while at the same time establishing itself as the legitimate successor of the *Reich*, and in the spatial dimension the Federal Republic had to set itself off against the German Democratic Republic in its claim to be the sole representative of the German nation. The two dimensions were linked in that the fascist era was presented as being – for the West

– a temporary aberration, the totalitarian aspects of which were, however, allegedly being continued in the East.

Over the first one and a half decades of the Federal Republic's history, interest was focused on linguistic developments in German beyond West Germany's borders in time and space. Despite a few tentative approaches, there appeared to be little inclination on the part of West German linguists and linguistic critics to examine their own ideological presuppositions, or to examine the nature and role of ideology in West German public language. What investigations there were either concerned themselves with the allegedly increasing technocratisation and bureaucratisation of language or, if they did examine persuasive uses of language in the West, tended to concentrate on the language of commercial advertising.[11]

That *Sprachkritik* did not initially concern itself with politico-linguistic developments within West Germany is in its turn a reflection of the ideology which regarded the Federal Republic as a *nivellierte Mittelstandsgesellschaft* (levelled middle-class society) in which social barriers had been removed and social class was no longer regarded as a significant political factor.

It was not until the mid-1960s in West Germany that a body of literature began to develop on language and politics which, firstly, approached the topic from a more systematic and rigorous point of view and, secondly, started looking at ideological manifestations in the public language of the Federal Republic; at least some of the impetus for this second development came from outside the field of linguistics, and was linked to the ideological critique of the Frankfurt School. This second development took place as part of an intellectual reorientation in the West German state against the background of the decline of the CDU as a political force and the radical questioning of 'traditional' values which culminated in the student movement of the late 1960s and found its institutional reflection in the formation of the first SPD-led government in the history of the Federal Republic.

Vergangenheitsbewältigung – Overcoming the past

As with any political upheaval, political developments in the territory of the former German Reich following the unconditional

surrender of the German fascist regime in 1945 necessitated innovations and changes in the vocabulary of German. One small
group of neologisms is marked by the common prefix *ent-*, the
best-known being *Entnazifizierung* (denazification), the attempt to
'undo' not only the apparatus of the fascist regime, but also the
mind-set which it had engendered. Institutional frameworks were
established (e.g., the *Spruchkammern* or tribunals) and certificates
of clearance (known familiarly as *Persilscheine*) were issued. The
processes of denazification (and demilitarisation, decentralisation
and the deconcentration of industry) formed part of a wider
process known as *Vergangenheitsbewältigung* – overcoming the
past. This term itself is not without its problems; with its root –
walt- as in *Gewalt* (violence) it suggests forceful submission rather
than 'coming to terms' or 'learning to live with' the past, but be
that as it may, part of this process was connected with language,
with the attempt to understand and process German fascist discourse and evaluate the role it had played.

The reception and evaluation of German fascism and its discourse after 1945 is one important aspect of the role played by
attitudes towards German fascist discourse, but it is not the only
one. Although the early critics of the discourse (such as Klemperer)
were concerned as far as possible to expunge the use of 'fascist
words' from German, we do in fact find that the discourse of
German fascism – or at least certain of its terms – continues to play
a significant role in the political discourse of the new West German state, for example in the instrumentalisation of the fascist era
in the campaign against the new East German state.

While accepting that *Vergangenheitsbewältigung* is an ongoing
process, it is still possible to distinguish three main phases of
Vergangenheitsbewältigung in West Germany. The first is approximately synchronous with the period of denazification, and can be
regarded as ending with the original restitution (*Wieder-
gutmachung*) paid to the state of Israel under the Treaty of Luxem-
bourg (September 1952); it was followed by over a decade of
collective repression during which the twelve years of the fascist
regime do not play a significant role in the West German political
consciousness.

The second phase, initiated in part by the Auschwitz trials of
the early 1960s, can be located in the latter half of the 1960s,
which witnessed the first serious generation conflict in West

Germany, when a student generation made up of young people who had no direct experience of life under fascism started asking questions of their parents who had.

The beginning of the 1980s saw the onset of the third main phase, which was preceded by the cathartic experience of the (US American) TV series *Holocaust* in 1979, which appeared to provoke a heartfelt response from large sectors of the population. In the third phase, an attempt was made to 'draw a line' under the fascist past. Politically, it was marked by the claim that a generation had now assumed political power in West Germany which was 'untainted' by the fascist past (Chancellor Kohl could claim for himself 'Die Gnade der späten Geburt' - the grace of having been born later in time) and by the controversy surrounding the symbolic meeting between Kohl and Reagan over SS graves in the cemetery at Bitburg. Intellectually, it was characterised by the so-called *Historikerstreit*, in which neo-conservative publicists and historians attempted to 'normalise' Germans' relationship to their 'recent' (i.e., fascist) past, and by the debates surrounding the speeches delivered by the Federal President Richard von Weizsäcker in 1985 and the Speaker of the West German Parliament, Philip Jenninger, in 1989.

When we come to consider the instrumentalisation of fascist discourse in West German political discourse, we find there are two main elements, one with an external, and one with an internal orientation. Externally, we note above all attempts to brand the new East German state with the mark of fascism by applying fascist terminology to it, and internally we note tendencies to try and use terms from fascist discourse to discredit political opponents within the West German state.

One of the strategies for 'overcoming' the past was founded in the view that the 'National Socialist era' had been a unique aberration which 'could only have happened in Germany' (if one was not a German), or which 'could never (be allowed to) happen again' (if one was a German). It was felt that if the trappings and outward manifestations of German fascism could be banned or otherwise eradicated, then the phenomenon itself could never recur. Thus, legislation was enacted prohibiting the public display of fascist emblems and the dissemination and/or glorification of 'National Socialist ideas'. The first treatments of German fascist discourse have to be seen as part of this general tendency. By recording the 'vocabulary of National Socialism', authors such as Klemperer and Sternberger hoped to alert their fellow-citizens to dangers inherent in this vocabulary and thus either to prevent the words being used, or at least to stop them being used uncritically.

The language-theoretical position behind the efforts of Klemperer and others derives from the view that language incorporates a certain 'spirit' or – in the case of fascist vocabulary – a 'demon', and that by adopting the words one is also adopting the 'spirit' (or 'demon') and running the risk of being 'possessed' by it.[12] Klemperer sees in language a controlling factor not only of creativity and thought but also of feeling and the whole affective self, and the control is all the stronger the less one is aware of it; for this reason he sees his task as a pedagogical one to heighten the level of awareness of language.[13] If words have become so 'tainted', then they should be withdrawn from circulation altogether until they have been 'purified' - and here Klemperer draws parallels with the orthodox Jewish ritual of burying eating vessels which have become 'impure'. He believes that many of the terms of German fascist discourse should be withdrawn from circulation – 'buried' - for a long time, and some for ever.[14]

Evidence of the effects of this attitude represented by Klemperer is to be seen in the way in which words which had been central to the fascist ideology and regime became stigmatised after 1945. Thus, there was a reluctance to use the word *Führer*; instead of a phrase such as *politische Führer*, *führende Politiker* was preferred, and Stötzel sees in the replacement of *Führerschein* by *Fahrerlaubnis* in the GDR a deliberate attempt to take the word *Führer* out of circulation.[15]

If the first phase of linguistic *Vergangenheitsbewältigung* was concerned to record and identify the elements and characteristics of German fascist discourse in order to 'warn' against their (un-critical) use, the second phase raises the question of how one does talk about German fascism. This is a question which we first raised in the previous chapter,[16] and to which we shall now return.

The question is bounded by two extreme positions; the one, represented by Steiner's argument that 'The world of Auschwitz lies outside speech as it lies outside reason'[17] asserts that a 'discussion' of German fascism is rendered impossible by the barbaric enormity of the phenomenon itself. At the other extreme, one finds the orthodox Marxist position – represented for example by

Haug[18] – which derives a theory of fascism based on the analysis of fascism as a logical and necessary development of capitalism, to which 'standard' economic and political terminology can be applied.

The line which we are following is that German fascism was an historical phenomenon which might have been unique at a certain phenomenological level, manifestations of which however can and do recur, so that a discussion must take place. Such a discussion requires a high level of linguistic awareness and reflection, and this brings us to the 'corpus' for our examination of the discourse of the second phase of *Vergangenheitsbewältigung*.

This second phase represented a serious attempt to 'come to terms' with the past rather than to 'overcome' it,[19] and in an attempt to answer the question of 'how does one talk about fascism?' we shall take as our starting point Haug's criticism of a series of university lectures delivered in the mid-1960s at the universities of Tübingen, Berlin and Munich on the German fascist era.[20]

Without wishing to duplicate the findings of Haug's analysis (and the political analysis advanced by Winckler, for example[21]), attention will be paid to two aspects of the terminology used, the denotative and the evaluative.

In his analysis of university public lectures delivered on the topic of Germany's fascist past up to 1945, which, it is suggested, are typical of much of the discourse of *Vergangenheitsbewältigung*, Haug found among other things that the critics had a tendency to use the terminology of the object of their criticism.

An important question facing any political critique is that of the extent to which it is necessary to adopt and deploy the terminology and discourse of the object under scrutiny, for adopting this terminology and discourse could make it difficult for the critic to establish the requisite distance from the object.

Within the terminology of the German fascist party and regime up to 1945, it is useful to distinguish between denotations for real institutions (i.e., 'proper names') and official or quasi-official epithets. The first category would include such terms as *SS*, *SA*, *Gauleiter*, etc, while terms such as *Endlösung*, *Arisierung* and probably *Führer* would fall into the second category. *National-sozialistisch* and *Nazi* form a special intermediate category to which we shall return.

There is no way of avoiding the use of terms in the first category – neither is there any 'need' to avoid them; they denote institutions, and if one is to deal with the institutions, then the proper names must be used. Without wishing to reopen the debate on 'euphemisms' in political discourse, it is, however, suggested that the terms of the second category are of a different kind. Official terms they may well be, but they are ideologically charged in a way that the terms in the first category are not, and using them makes it extremely difficult to establish the necessary distance from them. Very often, of course, terms such as these are placed in inverted commas, which are supposed to indicate that the original use of the term was either illegitimate or inappropriate. If this is the case, then one might well be justified in enquiring why the critic still finds it necessary to use illegitimate or inappropriate terms, unless the critique is a linguistic one with the aim of demonstrating in what way the terms are either illegitimate or inappropriate.

A special case of the borrowing of fascist terminology is provided by the term *Nationalsozialismus* and its derivatives. It is suggested here that the continuing use of the term beyond 1945 to refer to the German fascist movement, although superficially justified by the argument of 'well, that was the name of the movement', tends to reflect the view that 'National Socialism' was a unique aberration, and fails to recognise underlying causes and common features of German fascism with political developments elsewhere. A further reason, however, is to be found in the link that can be created between '*National* Socialism' as a totalitarian regime up to 1945 and that form of 'Socialism' which was imposed on East Germany after 1945; the negative connotation of the former proved very useful in the instrumentalisation of fascist terminology to discredit the new East German state.

If the indiscriminate borrowing of fascist terminology betrays a lack of critical distance, it is the evaluative terminology which really displays the 'helplessness' of much of the anti-fascist critique. Here we shall examine four phenomena, namely the turning of fascist evaluative terminology against fascism itself, the use of general terms of horror and of moral disapprobation, the use of terms which propagate and reinforce certain myths concerning fascist domination, and the ultimate recourse to speechlessness.

Using the example of 'sick', reference has already been made above to the way in which critics of fascism have used fascist terms of abuse against fascism; it is suggested that this type of 'name-calling' is not helpful, as it puts the criticism on the same plane as that criticised, and thus again fails to establish the necessary critical distance.

It would indeed be wrong not to express horror and disgust at the deeds perpetrated by the German fascists, but the critique, the coming to terms with the past cannot stop at the expression of disgust. Unfortunately, however, this is far too often what happens; to take one example more or less at random, Rudolf Buchner's 'Bilanz der Regierung Hitler'[22] (an interesting heading, as it immediately individualises and personalises the epoch, relieving the author of the need to search for systemic causes) is marked by terms such as *erschütternd, vernichtend, ungeheuerlich, Schandfleck für die deutsche Geschichte* .

Haug labels the terms of horror and disgust in his corpus *Phrasen* (emotive words); in his analysis, they are the end rather than the beginning, and all too often take the place which should be occupied by critical terms.[23]

As an example of the way that evaluative terminology is used in a way that perpetuates certain myths about the rise of German fascism and its assumption of power, let us briefly consider the widespread use of the term *Machtergreifung* – or the more restrictive *Machtergreifung Hitlers* to denote the installation of a German fascist *Reichskanzler* and the assumption of state power by the fascists. The term was originally used by the fascists themselves, as it fitted in with their ideology of revolution, but in usage post 1945, *Machtergreifung* has overtones of an illegitimate seizure of power, a putsch or a coup; it suggests the imposition of a minority will, circumventing the legitimate procedures of the state for the transfer of power.

It is not necessary here to rehearse the historical events leading up to Hitler's installation as Chancellor, but we need to remind ourselves that Hitler did not stand alone, that he was at least tolerated, if not actively supported, across a broad band of the political spectrum: as Schieder put it, the conservative and liberal parties were prepared to enter into a coalition with a partner that could counter the Socialists and Communists.[24]

The support – covert or overt – lent to the NSDAP by other bourgeois parties leads Haug[25] to the conclusion that the term

Machtergreifung in fact conceals what was really a *Machteinsetzung*, an installation rather than a seizure.

A term such as *Machtergreifung* incorporates a whole mythology, and a similar – equally illustrative – case can be found at the end of the German fascist regime, when one comes to describe what happened on 8 May 1945, for here too a mythology arises around the labels used – and, as is so often the case, the labels used often tell us a great deal about the users' attitudes. As an illustration, we shall take short extracts from three texts. The first two are from linguistic articles about post-war developments in the German language, and the third is from the German Federal President's speech on 8 May 1985:

1. Der *Zusammenbruch des Deutschen Reiches*, 1945, hat einen qualitativ und quantitativ tiefgreifenden Einschnitt in der institutionellen Kommunikation, der Alltagskommunikation und der religiösen Kommunikation in Deutschland gebracht.[26] (The *collapse of the German Reich* in 1945 effected a qualitatively and quantitatively profound caesura in institutional, everyday and religious communication in Germany.)

2. Historische Untersuchungen zur Lage nach der *bedingungslosen Kapitulation 1945* haben verdeutlicht, welche Faktoren dafür zuständig waren, daß eine intensive Auseinandersetzung mit der jüngsten Vergangenheit nicht zustande kam,...[27] (Historical studies of the situation obtaining after the *unconditional surrender of 1945* have revealed the reasons why an intensive debate on the recent past did not take place.)

3. Und dennoch wurde von Tag zu Tag klarer, was es heute zu sagen gilt: *der 8. Mai war ein Tag der Befreiung*.[28] (What we must say today nevertheless became clearer from day to day: the *8th of May was a day of liberation*.)

In each text there is a reference to 8 May 1945, and all three deploy a nominalisation, 'collapse of the German Empire', 'unconditional capitulation', 'day of liberation'. Only one text (1) specifies a subject ('Deutsches Reich'); in the second, we are not told explicitly who capitulated (or to whom), and in the third text, which is the only one to use a transitive, we can only assume that 'liberation' is passive, but neither subject nor agent (instrument?) are mentioned. There is a strong contrast and tension between the three phrases, with each one working from different perceptions and presuppositions. The first, although specifying a subject, uses the 'official title' 'Deutsches Reich', and by using the intransitive verb 'collapse' denies any outside intervention and conceals the 'fact' that the 'collapse' came about as the result of a military defeat: the second, by using the verb 'capitulate' presupposes war and defeat, however by concealing the subject does not take up any position on the controversy about whether it was the 'Reich' which surrendered or 'just' the armed forces: the third, although concealing the war and the actors, presupposes enslavement or illegal imprisonment.

In terms of political position, the second text reveals a more 'progressive' attitude than the first. The third text must be regarded separately; the use of the term 'liberation' unleashed a storm of conservative protest in West Germany, and that for two reasons: for many years, the use of the term *Befreiung* to denote the end of the war in Europe was a characteristic of official East German texts – with the 'heroic Red Army' cast in the role of liberators. If *Befreiung* was used in West German texts, it was – at least in conservative eyes – restricted to denote the liberation of the inmates of the concentration camps. The first two texts can be abstracted from their authors; for the third text, the authorship is highly significant, for in this text we have a Federal President, whom conservative forces would probably like to regard as 'one of their own', deliberately using a phrase which up to that point would have been inconceivable in the discourse of his office. Within the wider context, Weizsäcker's text, with its final admission that the Germans had been liberated from without, opens a new phase in the processing of Germany's fascist past, and as such stands in stark contrast to the Bitburg spectacle, in which the Federal Chancellor tried to close the history books.

And so to the final point, the final recourse to speechlessness. We have already quoted Steiner's remark that Auschwitz was 'beyond language', and there can be no doubt that the sheer horror of the crimes perpetrated under German fascism often leaves one struggling for words. The 'speechlessness' takes different forms; in its most extreme form, it is silence, the refusal to confront, the denial. Alleged speechlessness can also be used as a rhetorical device to express horror – *das Unaussprechliche* – as in a quotation from Dahrendorf in Haug's corpus 'Kaum wagt man zu sprechen, was es möglich machte',[29] where the 'speechlessness' in fact becomes one of the expressions of horror referred to above. Then, in a slightly weaker form, there is an unwillingness or an inability actually to articulate words such as 'Hitler', *Drittes Reich*, which become taboo words, to be replaced by abstractions such as *damals, jene Zeit*, 'das was in unserem Vaterland möglich war'.[30]

Speechlessness is, however, a less than adequate response, even less adequate than expressions of horror or attempting to come to terms with German fascism using German fascism's own terms. The political process is essentially mediated through language, and the political analysis can only take place linguistically. Any attempt to avoid or compromise the lingusitic confrontation is an attempt to avoid or compromise the political confrontation; history repeats itself if we fail to learn from it, if we fail to confront it. The language we use is a measure of the sophistication and power of this confrontation.

The demarcation from the East and the linguistic *Alleinvertretungsanspruch*

As we have already observed, much linguistic discussion and *Sprachkritik* in Germany forms part of a wider political debate, and the treatment of language development in the two German states after 1945 is no exception.

Ideally, developments in the German language after 1945 have presented linguists with a golden opportunity to observe and analyse what happens as a language develops along the same time axis in two differing, indeed opposing, socio-economic systems; this point was made by the Swedish linguist Andersson, who used the metaphor of the laboratory to describe the situation, likening it to a scientific experiment.[31]

However, the observation and analysis of the 'experiment' have not always satisfied normal scientific criteria, partly at least because many of the experimenters have themselves been part of the experiment. This in its turn, however, gives us an ideal opportunity to observe some of the problems of the 'participant observer', and provides us with an insight into linguistic attitudes and perceptions. As Hellmann quite rightly points out, the discussion of language change in Germany East and West has frequently been influenced by extra-linguistic concerns,[32] and thus the political context of West German preoccupation with language in the German Democratic Republic reflects trends in West German political attitudes towards the GDR, in the same way that East German perceptions of language developments in the GDR reflect the GDR's self-perception of its status and development.

We shall consider the topic of German East and West from four different perspectives. To start with, we shall consider the early Western reception accorded to linguistic change in East Germany after the defeat of German Fascism and the instrumentalisation of fascist discourse to devalorise political developments in the new East German state. After viewing the perceptions of linguistic developments, we shall look at some of the linguistic evidence and examine changes in the German language in both East and West to show the interaction of linguistic change and socio-economic change and discuss some of the ways in which linguistic polarisation functions. This will then lead us to a consideration of the processes of continuity and innovation in language development, before we question the view commonly held in West Germany that the 'division of Germany' was mirrored by a 'division of the German language'.

Hellmann[33] distinguishes three periods of concern with linguistic developments in the two German states – the first stage up to the *Aueler Tagung* of 1962, and the publication of the proceedings as *Das Aueler Protokoll*[34] in 1964, from then to a Mannheim Symposium in 1970 and the publication of the proceedings as *Öffentlicher Sprachgebrauch in der Bundesrepublik Deutschland und in der DDR*[35], and from 1970 up to 1989, at which time the discussion came to an end for all practical purposes as far as 'differences' were concerned.

Much of the early West German work on language developments in West and East Germany runs parallel to the efforts to come to terms with what happened to the German language under Fascism. There is a clear tendency here to regard the German language as used in East Germany as the natural successor to the language of Fascism, this being a linguistic extension of the – politically very useful – view that the political system in the East German state shared the characteristics of National Socialism – a very useful argument, because it absolved West Germans of the need to reflect on the true origins of German Fascism. This could partly perhaps be explained by the fact that much of this early work was not carried out by linguists. Winckler suggests that the 'Cold War' and the forces of social restoration in the West promoted the view that both 'East German socialism' and 'National Socialism' were manifestations of an underlying 'totalitarianism'; in this way, the West Germans were absolved of the necessity of critically examining the role of bourgeois forces in the rise of German fascism.[36]

The view of the GDR as the heir to National Socialism – and it is a view reflected in some of the titles of the works which appeared, for example 'Die Sprache des vierten Reiches' - regards the FRG as the guardian of 'true German values' - presumably from a mythical past before the unfortunate 'derailing' of German society in 1933 – and as such also sees the FRG as the true home of the German language, while in the GDR the language is 'misused', 'manipulated', indeed one even finds – what an unfortunate *lapsus linguae* – a reference to 'Die Sprachentartung in der Sowjetzone'.[37] German as used in the GDR (with the reference usually being to 'public language') is presented as being in the service of a totalitarian ideology, and just as fears were expressed for the 'unity of the German nation', so too fears are voiced about the 'division of the German language.' German in the GDR is seen as being defaced, deformed, as being subject to excessive Russian influence – the term *Sowjetdeutsch* is coined. A particularly crass example of the type of study being referred to was produced by Riemenschneider in 1963 under the title *Veränderungen der deutschen Sprache in der sowjetisch besetzten Zone Deutschlands seit 1945*, but even in a seemingly respectable publication edited by a Nestor of German Studies in 1964, the *Aueler Protokoll*, a distinction can seriously be postulated between the 'organic' development of the German language in the West and the 'manipulation' and 'misuse' of the language in the East. [38]

The equation of the GDR with 'National Socialism' and the parallels drawn between alleged language 'misuse' under Fascism pre-1945 and Socialism post-1945 is then further aggravated by East German socialism being regarded as an 'alien' ideology imposed from outside; thus the anti-socialism is compounded by xenophobia.

Linguistically, the confrontation with the new East German state is marked not only by the attempt to draw parallels between

East German discourse and fascist discourse, but also by the use of terms taken from fascist discourse by critics in the West to refer to the East, and these terms fall into two categories. Firstly, as one would expect, there is the denotation of East Germany or its institutions with the names of fascist institutions: thus the establishment of a separate administration for East Berlin on 30 November 1948 was labelled as a *Machtergreifung* in the Western press,[39] and on various occasions the whole of the GDR was called a 'concentration camp'.[40] Secondly, however, one finds occasions on which Western critics – who perhaps were not too mindful of the concerns expressed by Klemperer – use defamatory terms which the fascists had applied to their opponents; an example has already been given above with the reference to *Sprach*entartung.[41]

Many of the attacks on linguistic developments in the German Democratic Republic reveal the same deficiencies – both in theory and methodology – shown by the analyses of language under Fascism, which is perhaps not surprising, as many of them were being written concurrently with each other, sometimes even by the same people. In the same way, for example, that there is a failure to place language phenomena under Fascism in an historical context, so too phenomena which are common under fascism and in the German Democratic Republic are seen as a manifestation of 'totalitarianism' rather than as underlying linguistic trends; one could for example point here to developments in the language of administration, such as the increase in the use of the verbal prefix be-, which led to Weisgerber's critique of 'Der inhumane Akkusativ' to which we have already referred. And in the same way that many language phenomena under fascism are criticised because they do not fit in with an idealised bourgeois-humanist conception of the German language, so too are linguistic phenomena from one register in the German Democratic Republic criticised for departing from an ideal of language which is probably based on literary models. As Polenz points out in a slightly different context, complaints about the 'decline' of language in certain types of text apply the wrong standards; utilitarian texts cannot be measured by the aesthetic ideal of classical literature.[42]

On the whole, then, up to the mid-sixties, the predominant view in the West is of a 'divided' language, on the one hand corrupt and loaded with ideological bias, on the other free of any ideological pollution. Despite a few tentative approaches, there appears to be little inclination on the part of West German linguists to examine their own ideological presuppositions, or to examine the role and nature of ideology in West German public language. What is developed over the first twenty years after 1945 is a linguistic *Alleinvertretungsanspruch*.

Then, from the mid-sixties onwards, there was on the one hand some sign of a decline in interest in the subject, and at the same time, particularly after the publication of Dieckmann's seminal paper 'Kritische Bemerkungen zum sprachlichen Ost–West-Problem',[43] a turn towards more scientific and less overtly ideological approaches, with much of the effort being directed towards lexicological studies. The changing emphases in linguistic work around this time mirrored both a change in attitudes towards the German Democratic Republic – culminating politically in the *Grundlagenvertrag* between the Federal Republic of Germany and the German Democratic Republic in 1973 – and the development of a more critical perception of language development and language use in the FRG. What happened was that, whereas until the mid-sixties language was used as an instrument of *Abgrenzung* between the Federal Republic and the German Democratic Republic, from the turn of the decade there is an indication that language in West Germany was being used as an instrument of internal demarcation – *Ausgrenzung* – from certain elements within West German society.

After considering some ways in which linguistic reflection and political perceptions can become linked, we shall now turn to some of the linguistic evidence and consider some of the ways in which the German language did possibly proceed along different paths in the FRG and the GDR. Much of the work carried out has, as we indicated before, dealt mainly with public language – particularly in the political and ideological domain – and has concerned itself principally with lexical analyses (partly at least because these are clearly definable and relatively simple), although some work has been done on ideological diction and some on youth language.

The important point to bear in mind in any kind of comparative analysis involving the FRG and the GDR is that, despite the stronger restorative tendencies in the Federal Republic, it is by no means the case that the German language has stood still in the Federal Republic. This point sounds so obvious that it should not need mentioning, but it is not obvious from some of the papers that one reads. On the lexical level, one could point to the introduction of new terms such as *Staatsrat, Volkskammer, Kombinat, Kollektiv, Plansoll, Produktionsgenossenschaft, Agronom, Aktivist, VEB (Volkseigener Betrieb), HO (Handelsorganisation)* in the GDR, and possibly point to some Russian influence, but these are 'matched' in the FRG by such expressions as *Bundesebene, Bundeswehr, Konfessionsproporz, soziale Marktwirtschaft, Lastenausgleich, Zonenrandgebiete, Weiße Kreise, Splitting-Verfahren, Hearing, Team, konzertierte Aktion, WRK (Westdeutsche Rektorenkonferenz)*, and one can point to the increasing Anglo-American influence on the German language in the West.

If one looked beyond the level of the individual lexical item at phrases in the GDR such as *entwickeltes gesellschaftliches System, historisch objektiv notwendig,* one could easily find counterparts such as *Wiedervereinigung in Frieden und Freiheit* in the West. In short, the divergent socio-economic developments in East and West were reflected in linguistic developments, particularly in the area of lexis.

In the FRG and the GDR we were, according to the ideology of both states, dealing with mutually antagonistic systems, and the antagonism was obviously constituted and mediated by language use in both states; thus before proceeding to a closer investigation into the linguistic manifestations of the antagonism, let us consider some of the linguistic mechanisms of polarisation, of which we can perhaps distinguish five.

In the first, different denotations can be applied to the 'same' *signifiant*; thus one person's *Arbeitswilliger* is the other's *Streikbrecher*, and the same relationship applies between *Unternehmer* and *Kapitalist, Freisetzung von Arbeitskräften* and *Massenentlassungen*.

In the second, connotations are reversed; thus, in one ideology *Kommunist* carries positive connotations, in the other negative, and the same applies to terms such as *Streik, Arbeiter* and *Genosse*.

Thirdly, certain terms can become taboo under one ideology, and be replaced by an alternative: thus in the FRG the dominant ideology would not admit the term *Klassenkampf,* but speaks of *Sozialpartnerschaft*; rather than talking about *Profit,* the phrase

Einkommen aus Unternehmertätigkeit is preferred, while the *sozialistische Staatengemeinschaft* 'became' the *Ostblock*, and rather than accept the name *Rat für gegenseitige Wirtschaftshilfe*, the Anglo-American abbreviation *Comecon* was preferred.

Fourthly, one finds the 'same' term being used differently – the prime example here being the sign *Demokratie*, and fifthly there are terms which have either positive or negative connotations and are therefore restricted in their collocations. An example here is the negatively connotated *Elemente*, which in the GDR could be used with the epithet *faschistisch* but not *kommunistisch* whereas in the FRG it can be (and is) used with the modifier *kommunistisch*.

If we try and apply a comprehensive contrastive scheme to the analysis of West and East German lexis, we need to distinguish between differences in the *signifiant* and the *signifié* in order to allow firstly for items which only appear in the one set and denote something for which the other set does not require a sign, secondly for different denotations for the 'same' *signifié*, and finally for the 'same' signs with different denotations. Here we shall follow the system set up by G.D.Schmidt.[44]

1. There are in the German language today 'old' lexemes – i.e., ones which pre-date 1945 – which after 1945 were specific to one system, e.g., *Beamter*, which was only used with reference to the FRG, and *Arbeitsbuch*, which was only used with reference to the German Democratic Republic.

2. There were neologisms which were specific to one system, for example *Sex-Shop* (FRG), *Intershop* (GDR).

3. There were 'old' lexemes which were only used in one system – thus *Personalabteilung* is FRG-specific (GDR: *Kaderabteilung*).

4. There were new signs for which there was an exact correspondence in the other system, e.g., GDR *Broiler* (FRG: *Brathähnchen*),

5. New signs were developed in each system with the 'same' reference to denote new phenomena – e.g., GDR: *Republikflüchtige(r)*, FRG: *DDR-Flüchtling*.

6. Identical signs were developed in both systems which possess different reference, e.g., *APO* = *außerparlamentarische Opposition* (FRG), *Abteilungsparteiorganisation* (GDR), *Kulturraum* = culturally homogenous region (FRG), large public room for cultural events (GDR), *Brigade* = army unit (FRG), smallest organisational unit in a factory (GDR).

7. Signs which were present in both systems but had evolved further in their meaning in one system, becoming either more general or more specialised, e.g., *Kollege* = co-worker at a place of work (FRG), member of the wider community of labour (GDR), *Neuerer* = innovator (FRG), workers who concern themselves with modernising obsolete working practices (GDR). Alternatively there was a shift of reference, e.g., the title *Oberstudienrat* was common to both German states, but whereas in the FRG it is a grade, a rank, in the GDR it was an honorary title.

8. Finally there are what Schmidt calls the *ideologische Lexeme*, which existed in both systems and were marked for positive or negative connotations. Thus, in both systems *Demokratie, Freiheit, Humanismus* bore positive connotations, while *Ausbeutung, Imperialismus, Unterdrückung* had negative connotations, whereas *Klassenkampf, Kommunismus, Revolution* bore negative connotations in the West and positive ones in the East, with the positions being reversed for *Pluralismus, soziale Marktwirtschaft*.

As society evolves, technology progresses, and world-pictures change, we are obliged to develop new signs to match the new meanings or adapt the old signs. Thus, although the term *Bundesrat* dates back to the nineteenth century, it has become endowed with new meaning in the present FRG. The most apparent and far-reaching changes in any language are in the lexis and it is probably for this reason that much of the Western research on language developments in the German Democratic Republic concentrated on the vocabulary. At the same time, however, there is a danger, when one looks at the vocabulary, of perceiving the problem to be greater than it really is. Hellmann[45] postulates a range of lexical differentiation between the FRG and the GDR from a maximum of 10 per cent in newspaper texts down to around 1 per cent in some literary texts. A comparison of dictionaries between the *Wörterbuch der deutschen Gegenwartssprache* from the GDR and Duden. *Das große Wörterbuch* and Wahrig-Brockhaus from the FRG reveals a differentiation of between 1.8 per cent and 3 per cent. Kinne/Stube-Edelmann's *Kleines Wörterbuch des DDR-Wortschatzes*[46] contains some 1,000 entries, and Hellmann estimated that an equivalent *Kleines Wörterbuch des BRD-Wortschatzes* would contain some 1,500– 2,000 entries – not all that many compared with the richness of the total vocabulary.

Although there were differences in vocabulary between Germany West and Germany East, they must be seen in perspective; in some ways, for example, they were not as extensive as those between, say, German in the FRG and German in Austria. If we take the headwords under the letter 'B' in the 1980 edition of the Duden *Rechtschreibung* and compare them with the headwords in the 35th edition of the *Österreichisches Wörterbuch* (1979), we find that 20 of the first 50 headwords in the *Duden* are not listed in the *Österreichisches Wörterbuch*, and 8 of the first 28 headwords in the *Österreichisches Wörterbuch* are not listed in the *Duden*; in other words there is quite some variance between the 'Austrian language' as recorded in the one and the 'West German language' as recorded in the other. Even allowing for the fact that the first 50 headwords under 'B' are a very small random sample, the percentages concerned are high, higher than those which we would find in a comparison of dictionaries from the FRG and the GDR. By comparison, if we take the corresponding headwords from the *Duden* and compare them with the headwords from the GDR *Handwörterbuch der deutschen Gegenwartssprache*, we find that 13 of the headwords in the Duden are not in the *Handwörterbuch*, while none of those in the *Handwörterbuch* are not contained in the *Duden*, and the discrepancies can at least partly be explained by the fact that 3 of the *Duden* headwords are proper names – and the GDR dictionary does not list proper names in the same way – and 5 of them are English terms – including 'Bad Trip', which is not a spa, but the result of an over-indulgence in narcotics.

Simple word-counts and dictionary definitions do not, however, necessarily reveal the extent of the problem – if indeed one is justified in talking about a 'problem' at all. Dictionaries deal in types, not tokens, and purely quantitative comparisons do not reveal the extent to which the differing items assume central significance. Thus, for example, although the term *Generalsekretär* occurred in 'both' German vocabularies, and could indeed be given the same definition in each, so that it would not feature at all in a contrastive lexical study, the status of a *Generalsekretär* of a political party in a Marxist-Leninist or Stalinist socialist state was vastly different from that in a pluralist Western state, with the result that one would expect different frequencies and collocations for the term in West German texts compared with East German texts.

Thus, although there are compelling reasons for engaging in comparative lexical studies, such studies will not give the whole picture, and can possibly divert attention from developments in other areas of language which are equally worthy of consideration. One could for example draw attention here to some of the phonological changes occurring in German in the territory of the German Democratic Republic, and to the shifts in the status being accorded to dialect.

Much of the attention in the West concentrated on 'public language', and in the earlier years in particular on the 'systemic' language of the new ideology and on propagandistic uses of language – partly at least because this type of study easily lent itself to the kind of 'moralising critique' which the dominant ideology in the West required. At least, however, an attempt was made here to lift the discussion above the level of the individual lexeme, even though it did often get stuck with the *ruhmreiche Sowjetarmee* and formulaic phrases of that ilk, of which 'official' GDR discourse offers enough examples – as too does official FRG discourse, but this, for obvious reasons, does not appear as alien to us.

To concentrate on public language, however, does not do full justice to the phenomenon under discussion, to the synchronous development of the German language under differing socio-economic systems. Citizens of the German Democratic Republic did not speak the way that *Neues Deutschland* wrote, neither did they speak in private interaction in the public discourse of party functionaries. There is evidence to suggest that citizens of the German Democratic Republic were highly sensitive to differences in discourse types, and could move freely and consciously between them. In support, one could quote a passage from Erich Loest's *Es geht seinen Gang*, where we find the following passage:

Die Probleme der sozialistischen Integration erwähnte Hupperl in seiner Antrittsrede und die unermeßliche Weite des Bruderlandes. 'Der Staat Lenins' formulierte er ernsthaft. Wir rührten in unseren Kaffeetassen, das Gute war nur, daß jeder wußte; Nach einer Viertelstunde redeten wieder alle, wie ihnen der Schnabel gewachsen war. (In his inaugural speech, Hupperl mentioned the problems of socialist integration and the vast expanses of the brother land. 'Lenin's state', he declared seriously. We stirred our coffee, knowing that the only good thing was that in quarter of an hour everybody would be talking perfectly normally again.)

In a paper of central importance for the insight it gives into changing linguistic perceptions in the GDR, into the move away from the *Abgrenzungsideologie* of the early 1970s towards a perception of the underlying unity of the German language, Wolfgang Fleischer points out that even if one only considers the standard written language, it is a mistake only to take account of media and official discourse.[47]

Hellmann[48] points to the need to examine GDR discourse at all levels, and also to undertake comparative and diachronic studies of developments in lexis.

The question of whether the German language had been 'divided', of whether there was 'one language or two' was basically an ideological one; there was very little linguistic evidence to suggest that the German language was 'growing apart' or 'divided'. What we found in both German states were certain underlying trends which were common to both. Obviously the official German language as used in the GDR seemed alien to many in the West, because it was a reflection of an ideology which itself was alien to them. An important point to remember, however, is that there was not a 'big bang', a linguistic *Stunde Null* in 1945 in the territory of what was to become the GDR: the ideology of the GDR, which formed the basis of much of the official language, was in fact an ideology which goes back into the nineteenth century, an ideology which was substantially formulated in the German language. What we found in the GDR was that an ideology which had been formulated in the German language since its inception in the nineteenth century then assumed the role of a dominant ideology; this did not, however, mean that its linguistic expression was radically new or revolutionary.

Another factor that needs to be taken into account when comparing 'East German' with 'West German' is that in the official discourse of the GDR the ideology was often made more apparent, which is not to say that West German official discourse was not ideologically loaded as well. One could perhaps propose as a hypothesis that in the GDR the ideology was carried more by the denotations, whereas in the FRG it is carried more by the connotations. If, for example, one takes a pair of signs with a 'common' reference such as *antifaschistischer Schutzwall* and *Berliner Mauer*, one finds a certain ideological openness about the GDR term, whereas the West German term, while appearing neutral, in fact carried a whole connotative field which was far from neutral.

Even before November 1989, the growing consensus among linguists East and West was that the German language was developing in both the GDR and the FRG, admittedly along slightly differing paths, but at the same time following certain underlying long-term trends which were common to language use in both states. The official German language as used in the GDR was not something radically new which started in 1945; it could trace its ideological roots back to the working-class movements of the nineteenth century. The significant change was that the ideology underlying official discourse, which before 1945 had been pushed to the sidelines, then became a dominant ideology, and thus more visible.

To a certain extent, in fact, the question represented a non-problem. The so-called 'problem' arose as a result of political preoccupations rather than of linguistic insight. Events since November 1989 seem to have vindicated the view that the underlying unity of the German language was not a fiction; public discourse in the territory of the ex-GDR was transformed practically overnight, but the problems encountered by the citizens of the ex-GDR are not principally linguistic ones, although they are of course having to 'learn' a new discourse in certain areas. The prior examples of writers who moved from East to West, such as Becker and Loest, had already provided ample evidence of the ability of Germans to move between the two communicative communities.

What's in a name?

Naming plays an important role in the process of political identification, and a number of political controversies in and between the German states since 1945 have revolved around names. Nowhere has this been more apparent than in the names given to the German states by and to each other, and in the claims which have been laid to the name *Deutschland*. At times, the issue has verged on the farcical, with names and abbreviations being the subject of official – and at times contradictory – terminological guidelines.

On occasions, an almost obsessive importance has been attached to the 'correct' use of names and abbreviations, and in his attempt to answer the question 'Was ist des Deutschen Vaterland?', Peter Brückner concluded that the question had been reduced to that of the right *name*.[49]

In the West (and not only in West Germany), there was a strong tendency to equate the Federal Republic of Germany with 'Germany', illustrating the effectiveness of the official regulation of usage in this area. The equation went right back to the beginnings of the Federal Republic of Germany and the debate about the name of the new West German state.

From the enactment of its constitution on 24 May 1949, the Federal Republic of Germany regarded itself as the legitimate representative of the German Reich and assumed the right to speak for all 'Germans', whether or not they resided within its territory. The name which the new West German state gave itself was from the beginning a symbol for this assumption. The *Parlamentarischer Rat*, which had been empowered with formulating the constitution, also concerned itself with the name of the new state, for which there were two main contenders: *Bund Deutscher Länder* and *Bundesrepublik Deutschland*.

A conference of Ministers-President of the West German Länder held at Herrenchiemsee in August 1948 had proposed the name *Bund Deutscher Länder*, in order to stress the federal structure of the proposed new state. The name *Bundesrepublik Deutschland* had been put forward by an FDP deputy to the Parlamentarischer Rat, Theodor Heuss, who was later to become the first Federal President, and was accepted in order to stress the unity of the nation and the special status of the Federal Republic of Germany as the representative of the *Reich*.[50] Thus the Federal Republic of Germany became the first state in German history with a title which actually contained the word 'Deutschland', and – paradoxically – it was the smallest state which had ever claimed to represent the German 'nation'.

With the constitution of the German Democratic Republic in October 1949, a rival state with a competing terminology and discourse was established, and in the relationships between the two states, titles had an important role to play.

In contrast to the *Grundgesetz*, which remained basically unchanged (with the important addition of the Emergency Powers Acts in June 1968), the constitution of the German Democratic Republic underwent two major revisions, which reflected both the state's self-image and its perception of the relationship between the two German states.

Article 1 of the GDR Constitution of 7 October 1949 proclaimed the unity of Germany and a single German nationality,[51] a view reflected in the choice of Johannes R. Becher's text for the national anthem, with its opening lines 'Auferstanden aus Ruinen/ Deutschland, einig Vaterland.' In its external relations, the GDR maintained the existence of a 'Germany' - for example in the Warsaw declaration of 6 June 1950 and the Görlitz Treaty of 6 July 1950, it explicitly recognised the Oder-Neisse-Line as the 'state border' between 'Germany' and Poland.

By the mid-1950s, with West Germany's accession to NATO and the formation of the Warsaw Treaty Organisation with the GDR as one of its founder-members, East Germany moved away from its perception of a single Germany, and developed a theory that there were two German states, but still one German nation; this change was registered in a new constitution enacted in 1968, in which the German Democratic Republic declared itself to be 'ein sozialistischer Staat deutscher Nation'. A further constitutional revision in 1974 denied the existence of one German nation,[52] and the change in the constitution of the GDR was accompanied by a whole wave of renamings designed to expunge the notion of 'Germanness': thus, for example, the radio station *Deutschlandsender* became *Stimme der DDR*, the *Deutsche Akademie der Wissenschaften* became the *Akademie der Wissenschaften der DDR*, the *Hotel Deutschland* in Leipzig was renamed *Interhotel am Ring*, and the 'dictionary definition' of 'Deutschland' was revised in the 1974 edition of the *Wörterbuch der deutschen Gegenwartssprache* to turn it into an historical term.[53] The renaming was, however, not consistent, and the name *Deutschland* remained in such key institutions as the *Sozialistische Einheitspartei Deutschlands* (Socialist Unity Party of Germany) and its main press organ *Neues Deutschland*.

In the relationships between the two German states, the West German state for virtually two decades refused to acknowledge the existence of the East German state, and under the Hallstein doctrine imposed sanctions on third states which recognised the GDR.[54] There was very little direct contact between the two states, and in the contacts which did take place, the West German state was at pains to avoid any formulation which could possibly be construed as acknowledging the existence of a second state on 'German soil'. Two examples will serve to illustrate this.

On 20 September 1951, the 'Berlin Agreement' was signed which regulated trading and financial transactions between the two German states. The agreement, however, was declared to be one governing 'Trade between the currency areas of the German Mark of the *Deutsche Notenbank* (DM-East) and the currency areas of the German Mark (DM-West)',[55] and the contracting parties are not explicitly identified. In this case, both parties were content for the names of the territories not to be mentioned as political entities.

The second case documents an attempt by the East German state to establish its political identity, and by the West German state to deny this identity. In 1966, three West German gliders had landed in the GDR, and an East German aircraft had made a forced landing on the territory of the Federal Republic of Germany; in consequence, a correspondence was conducted between the two civil aviation authorities to arrange for the return of the aircraft. On 5 December 1966, the Head of the Administration of Civil Aviation Paul Wilpert (GDR) wrote to the Director of the Federal Aviation Authority Friedrich Möhlmann (FRG). The letter was headed 'Council of Ministers of the German Democratic Republic, Ministry of Transport' with an address in the centre of Berlin. There are various references to the German Democratic Republic and the GDR in the letter, which is signed by Wilpert as 'Deputy of the Minister'. The letter clarifies the procedures which will be followed for the aircraft to be returned from the German Democratic Republic to the Federal Republic and vice versa. Möhlmann's reply is much shorter. It is addressed simply to the 'Head of the Main Civil Aviation Authority', and the address is given as 'Berlin Schönefeld' (i.e., the East Berlin airport). There is not a single reference to a 'German Democratic Republic' or a 'GDR', and the letter confirms the procedures for 'the return' of the aircraft without any mention of state territory involved.[56]

Formal acknowledgement by the Federal Republic of Germany of the existence of the German Democratic Republic had to wait upon the election of Willy Brandt as Chancellor[57] and the implementation of his new *Ostpolitik*, which resulted in a series of agreements, including the *Grundlagenvertrag* of 21 December 1972 that governed the 'bases of the relations between the German

Democratic Republic and the Federal Republic of Germany'.[58]

If the name *Deutsche Democratische Republik* or the abbreviation *DDR* was officially taboo until 1969, how was the territory 'East of the Elbe' to be named by the West? According to 'official' terminology up to 1971, a 'German Democratic Republic' simply did not exist; a 'Terminology Guideline' of 1965 lays down that 'The German territory west of the Oder-Neisse-Line occupied by the Soviet Union in 1945, with the exception of Berlin, is known politically as the *Soviet Occupation Zone of Germany*, abbreviated *SOZ*, or in its shortened form *Soviet Zone*. There are no objections to the term 'Central Germany' being used as well.'[59] 'Unofficially' the title was often further abbreviated to *Zone*, a term which remained in currency in such compounds as *Zonengrenze*, *Interzonenzug* and *Zonenrandgebiet*. If the abbreviation *DDR* was used (the full name *Deutsche Demokratische Republik* hardly ever occurred in West German texts), it was for many years *de rigueur* either to place it in inverted commas and/or to preface it with the epithet *sogenannt* (so-called) to make the point absolutely clear. There were also tendencies to avoid any name, so that in the same way that the period of fascist dictatorship was referred to as *damals*, the Stalinist state was called *drüben*. The most famous example of 'namelessness' was perhaps provided by Federal Chancellor Kiesinger, who in a parliamentary debate on 13 October 1967 reluctantly admitted that there was 'something over there', with which he had even entered into correspondence, but rather than admit that it might be a state of some kind, he preferred to refer to it as 'ein Phänomen'.[60]

In keeping with the doctrine that the Federal Republic of Germany is the continuation of the *Reich*, the same Guideline lays down that, wherever possible, the short form *Deutschland* should be used if the full name *Bundesrepublik Deutschland* is not explicitly required. The use of a short form *Bundesrepublik* or the abbreviation *BRD* is proscribed, and as the adjectival form, *deutsch* is laid down.[61]

The usage proposed by the Guideline for reference to the Federal Republic became firmly established in the West – and the usage and its attendant policy were of course finally vindicated by the collapse of the German Democratic Republic and the incorporation of its territory into an extended Federal Republic. *Deutschland* as synonymous with the *Bundesrepublik Deutschland* was to be found in areas as disparate as political reports in newspapers, cultural reviews, sports reports, election posters and surveys on sexual habits and practices.

By the 1970s, the 'proscribed' abbreviation *BRD* became something of a shibboleth within West Germany, and was the subject of a further ministerial ban in 1974; it was the abbreviation commonly used in official East German texts, and thus by association became regarded as a 'communist' phrase by the authorities, so that those who used it were suspected of having 'communist sympathies'. For those who regarded themselves as being politically on the left, the use of the abbreviation became a code-word which revealed their political position. Paradoxically, however, the abbreviation had previously been admitted as official usage in a terminology guideline issued by the Federal Ministry of Defence in 1958 (when a staunch anti-communist, Franz-Josef Strauß, was the Minister responsible).[62]

With the end of the GDR, the proscription of the abbreviation *BRD* has now been lifted. In an attempt to regulate official nomenclature in accordance with the 'new political realities', a working group in the German Interior Ministry has produced guidelines which, among other things, lay down that there is no longer any need to ban the abbreviation *BRD* (and *FRG* and *FRA*) as 'with the demise of the GDR as a state and the unification of Germany they are no longer liable to transmit an ideological message and put the continued existence of Germany in question.'[63] The officials do, however, point out, that 'good taste' would continue to suggest that the abbreviation should still not be used.

The use of a particular word or phrase as a political ID is one which, though of course not restricted to German,[64] is highly developed there, and this now brings us to a consideration of some of the internal linguistic conflicts within the West German state.

From the enemy without to the opponent within

The mid-1960s saw an intellectual reorientation in the West German state against the background of the decline of the CDU as a political force and the radical questioning of 'traditional' values which culminated in the student movement of the late 1960s and found its institutional reflection in the formation of the first SPD-led government in the history of the Federal Republic.

The election of Willy Brandt as Federal Chancellor in 1969 marked the end of an era in a Federal Republic which for the first sixteen years of its existence had been dominated by one party, the Christian Democratic Union, and by one man, Konrad Adenauer. The CDU had become institutionalised as the ruling party, and perceived itself as such. Conservative in essence, and anti-communist in orientation, the party embodied those restorative tendencies which determined the political path of the Bonn Republic. The departure of Adenauer, the absence of a strong successor, and the ossification of the party, whose watchword was summed up in the slogan 'Keine Experimente' – 'No experiments' – made it difficult if not impossible for the party to respond to the changing intellectual climate of the mid-1960s and to take the initiatives which were required if it were to remain in power.

The accession of the Brandt administration in 1969 after the interregnum of the 'Grand Coalition' of SPD and CDU ushered in a new era of internal political confrontation in West Germany.

The Brandt administration was sustained by a reform ideology which at least potentially extended to most areas of political life. Linguistically, the reform movement manifested itself in a number of different ways, for example, in an interest in socio-linguistics, particularly in the discovery and reception of Bernstein's work on linguistic deprivation[65], and in a rejection of unreflected bourgeois views of language, with their emphasis on the language of literature. Perhaps the best-known manifestations of the 'new' approach to language were to be found in the development of new language curricula for schools in the state of Hesse, as laid down in the *Hessenplan* (1969) and the *Hessische Rahmen-richtlinien* (1973), with their concentration on the communicative needs of advanced industrial society rather than on bourgeois humanitarian ideals.

Our concern is not, however, with these developments, but with the politico-linguistic reaction (using the term 'reaction' advisedly) which was set in train at the beginning of the 1970s and which heralded an era of 'semantische Kämpfe' – 'semantic battles'. A typical product was a book published in 1979 by publicist and journalist Wolfgang Bergsdorf, a CDU supporter, with the title *Wörter als Waffen. Sprache als Mittel der Politik* – Words as Weapons. Language as a Political Instrument.[66]

Regardless of any inherent merits this work may or may not have, its publication was significant for three reasons:

Firstly, it marked a stage in an intellectual and political development within the CDU which had been initiated by the election of Helmut Kohl as Party Chairman in 1973 and by a keynote speech from the new CDU Secretary-General, Kurt Biedenkopf, at the Party Conference in the same year. This conference was historically significant, as it marked the public beginning of a strategy aimed at regaining power after the traumatic unseating of the CDU as the 'party of government' for the first time in the history of the Federal Republic.

Secondly, the title points to one important aspect of the role language plays in politics, the fact that language mediates policies and politics. Thus the work, or at least its title, possesses a functional significance.

Thirdly, by using the image of 'words as weapons' it demonstrates an antagonistic view of politics and a militarisation of language. Thus the title also has a metaphorical significance.

The reaction initiated by the CDU in the 1970s is interesting for a number of reasons. On one plane it demonstrates how the CDU, having lost the political initiative in the mid-1960s and with it a great deal of intellectual support, tried to regain the initiative on an intellectual level. On a second plane it shows how, for the first time in the Federal Republic, a political party consciously discovers the importance of language in the political process and is forced, as part of the general reflection on strategy and tactics, to reconsider its own linguistic position. On a third plane it illustrates how concrete language planning was approached and provides an insight into the views of language which underlay the planning.

At about the same time that radical students were preaching the strategy of 'the long march through the institutions', the new CDU Secretary-General Kurt Biedenkopf in his keynote speech to the 1973 party conference saw the danger approaching from a different quarter – from control of language: the modern revolutionary no longer needs to occupy government buildings, but instead takes possession of the terms by which the government rules.[67]

This view was echoed by another of the CDU's supporters, Gerd-Klaus Kaltenbrunner, in the Preface to his book *Sprache und Herrschaft* (Language and Power), when he wrote that the decisive battle would be won without bloodshed if one's opponents could be forced to use a language which prevented them from articulating their own interests and an independent intellectual and political position.[68]

The CDU's thesis, as advanced for example by Biedenkopf in his 1973 CDU conference speech, was that the SPD had managed to gain the political initiative through its use of language, and this in two ways: firstly the SPD had launched a number of key terms which were marked as 'its' property, and secondly the SPD had established a claim to certain central terms by 'occupying' them with its 'meanings'.

To combat the SPD's perceived dominance in the mastery of political language, the CDU pursued a dual strategy: on the one hand it developed its own language-critical analysis in an attempt to regain the upper hand intellectually, and on the other it tried to establish the dominance of its own political terms and to gain (or regain) possession of those on which the SPD had staked its claim.

Its efforts on the first level resulted in a spate of publications from the mid-1970s on language and politics which, although addressing themselves to some fundamental issues, were mainly concerned with attacking the way the Left had 'changed the meanings' of key political terms – thus Kaltenbrunner's *Sprache und Herrschaft* bears the subtitle *Die umfunktionierten Wörter* – The Re-functioned Words. Most of these publications, which in the secondary literature are usually classified under the heading *konservative Sprachkritik*, were written not by linguisticians but by journalists and by academics from disciplines such as political science, sociology and philosophy. They range from the scurrilous 'Despotie der Wörter'[69] or 'Rote Semantik'[70] which implicitly equates the 'New Left' with National Socialism, to historical accounts of political language ('Aktuelle Tendenzen der politischen Sprache')[71] and philosophical tracts on 'Being and Naming'.[72]

Many of the products of conservative 'Sprachkritik' remind one of the products of the 'moralisierende Sprachkritik' of the 1950s and 1960s, which attempted to establish the moral ascendancy of the German language in the Federal Republic over the 'debased' version peddled in the Democratic Republic, only now the target is not to be found in the past or in another regime, but within the Federal Republic, thus mirroring a significant shift from *Abgrenzung* to *Ausgrenzung*, from the attempt at delimitation from the Democratic Republic to the linguistic disqualification of groups or movements within the Federal Republic. In some ways, the standard of argument is lower than that of the earlier epoch, as if the conflict between *Sprachkritik* and *Sprachwissenschaft* had never taken place. Behrens, Dieckmann and Kehl[73] have undertaken a profound critical analysis of many of the issues involved in the CDU's 'Sprachkritik', but there are three issues which we shall take up again here as significant for the whole field of political uses of language, and these are, firstly, the functions of language in general and of language in politics in particular, secondly, the relationships between linguistic signs and meanings in political language, and thirdly the question of the extent to which politics is 'merely' a matter of words.

As we have already suggested, what is happening in linguistic criticism is that, whereas until the mid-1960s language was used as an instrument of 'Abgrenzung' to consolidate the existence and legitimacy of the Federal Republic, from the turn of the decade there is an indication in West Germany that language is starting to be used as an instrument of *Ausgrenzung*, of internal legitimation and ideological demarcation.

Before proceeding to this, however, let us turn first to the second strand of the CDU's language strategy in the 1970s, to its attempt to establish its terminology within the political agenda.

Organisationally this was done when the party set up an *Arbeitsgruppe Semantik* attached to the Secretary-General's office; the function of the *Semantik-AG* was to advise on the use of language and to develop a practical language strategy for the party. The objective was a uniform discourse which would encourage feelings of solidarity within the CDU and would be identified with the CDU within the public at large.

In order to achieve this, it was *inter alia* necessary for the CDU to re-establish its claim to positively-charged key terms, and if possible to deny the SPD access to those terms. One such term for example was *Solidarität*, which had traditionally been linked with socialism or social democracy in the sense of working class solidarity. The CDU attempted to appropriate this term and turn it from a key word of the class struggle to a more general slogan of

'democratic solidarity', i.e., the solidarity of all those who sub-
scribed to the basic constitutional order of the Federal Republic.

The important point was, however, not just to secure identification with individual terms such as *Solidarität*, *Freiheit* but to set up
terminological networks. Behrens pointed out that terms in political discourse had to be co-ordinated, firstly by using them in a
uniform manner in all party proclamations, so that they could be
identified as CDU terms by constant repetition, and secondly by
combining them with each other and placing them in a systematic context.[74]

In the same vein, Biedenkopf had stated at the twenty-third
party conference that terms such as liberty, justice and solidarity,
responsibility, social duty and achievement would remain isolated
unless the connections between them could be exploited for
political purposes.[75]

It was not, however, just a question of creating networks of
mutually supportive terms; what was also important beyond this
was to set up oppositions, so that the CDU could not only establish its own image, but could also set itself off against the SPD;
these considerations gave rise to what was probably the most
controversial campaign slogan in the history of the Federal Republic: *Freiheit oder Sozialismus* – Freedom or Socialism.

In this slogan, three basic mechanisms were at work which are
of significance for the study of political uses of language. This
particular example is an election slogan, the purpose of which is
not just to solicit support, but to move people (in this case the
electorate) to a particular course of action, namely, firstly to go to
the polls and secondly to cast a vote for the CDU/CSU.

The slogan is striking for its simplicity; potentially complex
issues are reduced to a simple formula which presents the voter
with a straightforward binary choice between two allegedly mutually exclusive alternatives. The voter must of course accept the
presuppositions of the discourse (i.e., must accept that she only
has one choice, and that this choice is correctly reflected); normally this is not too difficult, because in language interaction the
initiative participant is usually at an advantage – she who asks the
questions to a large extent determines the answers. In the case of
election slogans, however, there are competing texts, namely the
slogans of the other parties.

The slogan *Freiheit oder Sozialismus* not only appeals through its

simplicity and the way it requires the voter to make a clear
decision, it also supports a particular view of the political process
as an antagonistic one, which reflects a friend/foe, us/them
schema.

Of the two terms, *Freiheit* is without a doubt positively charged;
it is also extremely vague, as indeed are many central political
terms (e.g., 'democracy', 'equality', 'justice'). No attempt is made
to define what is meant by *Freiheit* – it is not even clear which
preposition it is meant to govern, whether it is freedom 'to' or
freedom 'from'; all that the voter needs to know is that the
antonym of this positive term is *Sozialismus*, which must then
logically be *unfrei* – socialism as the negation of liberty. Here the
authors of the slogan have recourse to a long tradition of anti-
socialism in German politics, stretching back to Bismarck's
Sozialistengesetze. The inference is then clear: *Sozialismus* is presented as an undefined bundle which can draw on deep-seated
antipathies, and it is set up in opposition to the positively associ-
ated *Freiheit*.

The next step is then to associate the negative term with the
political opponent, and the positive term with one's own party;
this first half is achieved partly by phonetic similarity
(*Sozial*ismus: *Sozial*demokratisch) and partly by latent association,
the second half by explicit identification on the election posters of
the CDU/CSU as author of the slogan.

In discourse terms, the slogan can be regarded as highly successful: it dominated the agenda, and the SPD found little to set
against it, in fact the only tactics were either those of ridicule, for
example by deploying an 'alternative' slogan 'Freiheit statt
Apfelmus' – Freedom, not stewed apples[76] – or crying 'foul', which
involves stepping outside the discursive framework and thus tac-
itly admitting defeat. In perlocutionary and political terms, however, the slogan did not immediately persuade enough electors to
cast their votes for the CDU/CSU, and the SPD/FDP coalition
emerged as victors from both the 1975 and 1979 elections.

After this brief excursion, let us now return to the theoretical
writings of the pro-CDU circles and to the three topics of particular interest for our present purposes, namely the functions of
language, the relationship between *signifiant* and *signifié* in political language, and finally the extent to which politics is 'merely' a
matter of words.

In their writings Maier and Kuhn assume that the primary function of language is to reflect or portray an underlying 'reality'; 'Despotie der Wörter' opens with the thesis that the function of words was to signify. that they should present things as they were, and that if they did that, they were telling the truth.[77] Maier implies a 'natural relationship' between 'words' and 'things' when he observes that in the political discourse of the Federal Republic key terms in the political order have been unseated .[78]

The notion of there being an independent 'truth', that there is a reality apart from language which is mediated by language, impinges on the second of our three interlinked topics, but let us suspend the discussion of this second question and remain with the first. Even if one assumes that words exist to denote 'things' – whatever 'things' may be – this still does not explain to what ends language is used in personal or social interaction, for the presentation of 'reality' would only be a means to an end, not an end in itself.

This is not to suggest, however, that the conservative critics disregard the social and political functions of language; Lübbe, for example, reveals an understanding of a most important function of political language when he writes that one of the functions of politics is to generate acceptance in the public mind.[79]

Bergsdorf, in his introduction to *Wörter als Waffen*, refers to Karl Bühler's linguistic theory when he postulates description, expression and appeal as three basic functions of political language which enable the politician to to inform, to interpret, to direct, to convince and to indoctrinate.[80]

But even this list is not exhaustive, although Bergsdorf does acknowledge a link between 'language' and 'action' in politics.

As the relationship between language and action has already been dealt with at some length in Chapter 1, it is not necessary to pursue this line of thought further here. It is sufficient to make the point that the conservative language critics operate from a restricted view of the functions which language has in political action. However, the restriction arises perhaps not just from their view of language, but also from a view of politics which is mainly limited to a consideration of *Ordnungspolitik* (the state order) and to the concept of *Staat* rather than being concerned with the whole ramification of economic and social interaction within the body politic. Politics is seen as being essentially an activity for state organisations and constitutional bodies, with the ordinary citizen cast in a passive role – and here we can cite Lübbe's view that the role of politics is to generate 'public acceptance' rather than to encourage active and intelligent participation.

That conservative language critics tend to regard the *signifiant–signifié* relation in a simple and idealised fashion has already been indicated; there is, however, a danger in postulating a heterogeneous body of *konservative Sprachkritik* with a uniform approach. Beside Kuhn's idea of 'language as truth' must be set Bergsdorf's awareness firstly that certain key terms undergo a process of diachronic change, secondly that they are of necessity vague and thirdly that they contain an emotive element.[81]

It is central terms such as *Demokratie* and *Freiheit* which show that the extreme form of the position taken up by Kuhn is not tenable with regard to political vocabulary, as otherwise it would deny the processes of historical change and reduce political key words to the unidimensionality of technical terms.

The weaker (i.e., less extreme) position that is actually taken up by conservative critics is to bemoan the fact that languages have changed their meanings, that they are no longer used in their 'traditional' sense, and that confusion is the result. 'Begriffe haben sich aus ihrer Normallage gelöst' ('key terms in our political order have been unseated'), as Maier puts it, the meanings of terms were established by tradition, by consensus, and now everything is in flux and confusion: 'Im Schaufenster von Worten und Werten läßt man Hüllen und Füllungen der Begriffe durcheinandergeraten.' – 'In the shop window display of words and values, packages and their contents have become all jumbled up'.[82] The fiction is still maintained that the traditional 'meanings' were the correct ones: 'neue Legierungen verfälschen (bewußt oder unbewußt) den Kurs der Begriffe' (new alloys falsify the exchange value of words (either consciously or unconsciously))' – in true conservative style, any change is seen as being necessarily a change for the worse.

It is, however, not sufficient simply to brand the conservative critics as being 'anti-change'; it is also necessary to examine what it is about the change that evokes their censure. The first question that must be asked is about the reference point: if words are no longer used in their 'traditional' sense, to which 'tradition' is it that recourse is had? In the post-1945 discussion of language under German fascism, critics appealed to a mythical state of the German language which they could not actually place in space or time. Their heirs in the 1970s also appeal to a myth, but to a myth from the recent past, a myth which can be located in time and space, and which is extremely powerful in conservative ideology: the myth of social solidarity, of a homogeneous community, the myth of the *nivellierte Gesellschaft*. The social levelling which is supposed to have taken place after 1945, or 1948, is, it is claimed, also reflected in the language; thus Maier writes that post-1945, the development of the German language – at least in the Federal Republic – was marked by a progressive dismantling of role-specific and class-specific varieties, of individual and regional idioms, in short, of regional and social language barriers. Thus, he claimed, language reflected, albeit with some delay, developments in society, which were marked by a social levelling on the one hand, and a social revaluing of previously low-status activities and positions on the other.[83]

Thus, as a result of the social and linguistic levelling process, barriers were broken down, with the result, it is claimed, that everybody spoke 'the same language' – or at least knew what everyone else meant. There was, Bergsdorf asserts, a common understanding of key terms; even though the political parties disagreed over policies, the meanings of key political terms remained relatively stable over a fairly long period of time. All those engaged in political dispute used the same words and understood them in more or less the same way.[84]

The appeal, then, is to the 'democratic consensus' in political discourse, and the charge levelled against the 'New Left' is that it has broken with this consensus, that key political terms are no longer universally recognised tokens of exchange; Dietz can accuse the Left of 'forgery' – thus he draws on the image of finance, claiming that the metal composition of the coinage has been changed and the currency debased – 'Neue Legierungen verfälschen den Kurs der Begriffe'.

It is not, however, only the change *per se* that is attacked, but the qualitative nature of the change, which is perceived as a change from reality to irreality. Kuhn, whose writing is a peculiar mixture of the pseudo-philosophical and the defamatory, attacks what he calls *Neusprache* (shades of Orwell!), where the 'new words' do not denote things – at least, not things as they are – but denote that which is not, but which should be – and that is their novelty.[85]

Maier argues in a similar manner, seeing the change as a two-fold shift of aspect and modality: from the static to the dynamic, and from the actual to the potential.[86] He sees a destabilisation of key political terms, which have shifted from denoting the present order into promises of things to come.

This, then, is what the conservative critics cannot accept; they cannot accept the refusal to regard terms describing the body politic as incorporating absolute values; they cannot accept that political language is not only used to describe present or past states, but is also used to articulate ideals and wishes for the future. In the Federal Republic, politics is regarded as the monopoly of the political establishment, it is essentially mediated by the state. In the latter half of the 1960s there was a movement against the tutelage of the political establishment, against a monopolist inter-pretation of key political terms, there was an attempt to attach different denotations to terms whose main value lay in their connotations and which hitherto had been regarded as absolutes legitimising the status quo.

The reaction of the Right was a twofold one: on the metalevel it contested the Left's claim to key terms, partly by accusing the Left of 'ignoring reality', by attacking the discourse of the Left for its 'loss of reality', and by attempting to disqualify the discourse of the Left by putting it 'beyond the pale' through equating it indiscriminately with official discourse in the German Democratic Republic and with the language of German fascism; on the practi-cal level a strategy was developed for regaining control of the central terms and restoring them to their 'rightful owners'.

Having examined the nature of the conservative objection to the 'New Left's' use of certain key terms, let us now conclude by drawing together some of the relevant characteristics of these terms and examining their role in political discourse.

In 'normal' political use, linguistic signs such as *Demokratie, Freiheit, Diktatur*, often do not have sharply defined denotations; notwithstanding this, they can also form the subject of theoretical or philosophical treatises and refer to actual political systems or phenomena. Thus they can cover a wide spectrum of possible reference, which makes them extremely difficult to handle in political discussion. As Mario Cattaneo put it, one of the particularly astonishing things about political discussions is the confusion and lack of clarity in the terms used.[87]

Terms such as *Freiheit, Gerechtigkeit, Demokratie* illustrate in particularly graphic form a statement by Murray Edelmann: 'Language is always an intrinsic part of some particular social situation, it is never an independent instrument or simply a tool for description.'[88]

The function of these terms is not to *denote* but to *connote*; they appeal not to reason, but to emotion. The passage from Cattaneo quoted above continues as follows: 'The very words liberty, justice and democracy, all very emotive terms which create a favourable atmosphere, are used by the exponents of diametrically opposed political movements to denote completely different things and to allude to widely differing values. This is done to gain support and loyalty towards those who use the terms. Our political life is dominated by irrationality and myth.'[89]

Key words form an important part of a power strategy; they are used to persuade, to gain and maintain support, to control. Although it would probably be wrong to regard them as completely devoid of denotative meaning, this meaning is not of prime importance – indeed, the 'actual' references are interchangeable, and ultimately it is not possible to state whether a term is used 'correctly' or 'incorrectly' with reference to a given or imagined political construct. For political statements which use such key words and are neither verifiable nor falsifiable, Ernst Topitsch uses the term *Leerformel* – empty formula.[90] This reflects a common and current metaphor which regards linguistic signs (or 'words') as cases or containers which have to be 'filled' with meaning; it is to be found when one talks about the 'contents' of a word, or when terms such as *Worthülle* or *Worthülse* – wordcase – are used. A good example for this is contained in the earlier quotation from Dietz. Topitsch's use of the term *Leerformel* reflects this metaphor, but also gives it an added dimension: the terms, the 'formulae', are not empty, but their denotative core is irrelevant. Their effect is achieved by connotation, which is promoted from a secondary to a primary characteristic.

The terms appeal to hopes, dreams, aspirations, and here there is a clear link with another type of emotive or persuasive language, the language of advertising. As one commentator put it, 'Politik ist Käse – beides sind Markenartikel' ('Politics is like cheese. Both rely on brand names').[91] Advertising makes its appeal to the irrational;

it propagates not a product *qua* product, but the image of a product, it suggests that the use of a product will result in health, enhanced status, prestige, happiness. To achieve its effect it uses slogans to a persuasive end. What is being sold, in politics and in commercial advertising, is not the product but the effect; to stay with the casing/contents metaphor, not the policy or the product is important, but the packaging. And all the elements of advertising, commercial or political, are but means to an end, the end being power and control. Mackensen for example sees the acquisition of power as one of the functions of language.[92]

In the 1970s, then, much of the discussion on political uses of language in the Federal Republic was dominated by the CDU's 'discovery' of the significance of language in political action, and by their attempts to develop a strategy to counter what they perceived as the 'linguistic dominance' of the SPD in order to regain the political control in West Germany.

With the shift from external to internal demarcation ('Abgrenzung' to 'Ausgrenzung'), a new era of political debate came to the fore which was marked by a conflict of discourses within the West German state. It is this internal conflict which will provide the material for our final chapter.

Notes

1 The term 'linguist' is being used here more in the sense of the German 'Linguist', one who describes and analyses language, rather than in its traditional English sense of one who has a practical command of languages. This is to avoid having to use such phrases as 'linguistic scientist' or the neologism 'linguistician'

2 W.Dieckmann and P.Held, *Sprache und Kommunikation in politischen Institutionen. Interdisziplinäre Bibliographie zur politischen Sprache in der Bundesrepublik Deutschland 1975-1984 (1986)*, Berlin, 1986

3 E. Strassner, *Ideologie – Sprache – Politik: Grundfragen ihres Zusammenhangs*, Tübingen, 1987

4 Apart from its well-established work on German East and West (e.g., by Hellmann, Kinne), the IDS has also produced a number of theoretical papers on language and politics (e.g., by Strauß) and the monographic dictionary on German 'hard words', many of them taken from the political sphere, Strauß, Haß and Harras *Brisante Wörter von Agitation bis Zeitgeist*

5 This is not to be confused with *Sprachkritik* as a strand of philosophical enquiry pioneered for example by Wittgenstein

6 H-P. Althaus, H. Henne and H-E. Wiegand (eds), *Lexikon der Germanistischen Linguistik*, Tübingen, 1980 2nd edn, pp. 508–15

7 H. Heringer (ed.) *Holzfeuer im hölzernen Ofen. Aufsätze zur politischen Sprachkritik*, Tübingen, 1982

8 R. Wimmer, 'Neue Ziele und Aufgaben der Sprachkritik' in *Kontroversen, alte und neue. Akten des VII Internationalen Germanisten-Kongresses Göttingen 1985*, Vol. 4, Tübingen, 1986, pp. 146–58

9 Thus, for example, P. v. Polenz bases the analyses in his *Deutsche Satzsemantik. Grundbegriffe des Zwischen-den-Zeilen-Lesens*, Berlin, 1985, on ten texts, six of which can be classified as 'political'

10 Brückner, *Versuch, uns und anderen die Bundesrepublik zu erklären*

11 E.g., R. Römer, *Die Sprache der Anzeigenwerbung*, Düsseldorf, 1971 2nd edn

12 A variation on this is to be observed in the position adopted in the present work, where it is being argued that terms carry certain associations and presuppositions which are necessarily adopted when one uses the terms

13 'Aber Sprache dichtet und denkt nicht nur für mich, sie lenkt auch mein Gefühl, sie steuert mein ganzes seelisches Wesen, je selbstverständlicher, je unbewußter ich mich ihr überlasse.' Klemperer, *LTI*, p. 21

14 'Wenn den rechtsgläubigen Juden ein Eßgerät kultisch unrein geworden ist, dann reinigen sie es, indem sie es in der Erde vergraben. Man sollte viele Worte des nazistischen Sprachgebrauchs für lange Zeit, und einige für immer, ins Massengrab legen.' Klemperer, *LTI*, p. 22. (The use of the term *Massengrab* here is somewhat problematic, given the other mass graves which are part of the legacy of German fascism)

15 G. Stötzel, 'Nazi-Verbrechen und öffentliche Sprachsensibilität', *Sprache und Literatur in Wissenschaft und Unterricht*, 63, 1989, p.43

16 Cf. p. 122-4 above

17 G. Steiner, *Language and Silence*, London, 1985, p. 122

18 E.g., in such statements as 'Wenn die kapitalistischen Besitz- und Verfügungsverhältnisse formaldemokratisch nicht mehr zu sichern sind oder wenn es dem formaldemokratischen System nicht mehr möglich ist, die sozialen und politischen Bedingungen den Erfordernissen des kapitalistischen Verwertungsprozesses anzupassen, dann besteht ein systemimmanenter Faschismusbedarf.', in W.Haug, *Vom hilflosen Antifaschismus zur Gnade der späten Geburt*, Hamburg/Berlin, 1987, p. 149

19 See, for example, W. Paterson, '*Vergangenheitsbewältigung* to the *Historikerstreit*', R. Woods (ed.), *Vergangenheitsbewältigung West und Ost*, Birmingham, 1989, pp. 27–37, esp. pp. 29–31

20 W. Haug, *Vom hilflosen Antifaschismus zur Gnade der späten Geburt*, Hamburg, Berlin, 1987

21 Winckler, *Gesellschaftliche Funktion*

22 R. Buchner, *Deutsche Geschichte im europäischen Rahmen*, Darmstadt, 1975, pp. 451–7

23 'In der Auseinandersetzung mit dem Faschismus okkupieren sie den Platz, für den sonst kritische Begriffe gefunden werden müßten. ... Häufig ersetzen Reizwörter ... analytische Begriffe der faschistischen Herrschaft.' Haug, *Vom hilflosen Antifaschismus*, p. 36

24 'Schließlich waren die konservativen und liberalen Parteien sowohl in Italien wie auch in Deutschland bereit, es mit dem Faschismus zu versuchen. Die eigene Unfähigkeit, sich auf die Bedingungen der Massendemokratie einzulassen, ließ sie nach einem Partner Ausschau halten, der es mit den Sozialisten und Kommunisten aufnehmen konnte.' W. Schieder, 'Am Anfang war die Bewegung. Die faschistischen Regime in Italien und Deutschland', *Frankfurter Allgemeine Zeitung*, 28 September 1985

25 Haug, *Vom hilflosen Antifaschismus*, pp. 175ff

26 H. Steger, 'Sprache im Wandel', quoted from *Sprache und Literatur in Wissenschaft und Unterricht* 63, 1989, p.3 (italics added)

27 Stötzel, 'Nazi-Verbrechen', 1989, p. 32 (italics added)

28 R. v. Weizsäcker, 'Zum 40. Jahrestag der Beendigung des Krieges in Europa und der nationalsozialistischen Gewaltherrschaft', Ansprache am 8. Mai in der Gedenkstunde im Plenarsaal des Deutschen Bundestages Bonn (italics added)

29 R. Dahrendorf, 'Soziologie und Nationalsozialismus', A. Flitner (ed.), *Deutsches Geistesleben und Nationalsozialismus*, Tübingen, 1965, quoted from Haug, *Vom hilflosen Antifaschismus*, 1987, p. 35

30 Cf. Haug, *Vom hilflosen Antifaschismus*, 1987, pp. 43ff

31 'Es ist fast wie ein Experiment: ein Land, Deutschland, wird in zwei Staaten aufgeteilt, die an zwei verschiedene Gesellschafts- und Wirtschaftssysteme angeschlossen werden und in gewisser Hinsicht als zwei voneinander getrennte Kommunikationsgemeinschaften funktionieren. Was geschieht dabei mit der Sprache der früher ungeteilten Kommunikationsgemeinschaft?' S.-G. Andersson, 'Deutsche Standardsprache – drei oder vier Varianten?', *Muttersprache* 93, 1983, p. 259

32 'Es ist eine erwiesene und mehrfach diskutierte Tatsache, daß die Beschäftigung mit unserem Arbeitsthema von außerfachlichen Bedingungen u.a. auch politischer Art beeinflußt worden ist und wohl auch immer be- einflußt werden wird.' M. Hellmann, 'Bemerkungen zur Entwicklung und zur gegenwärtigen Lage des Arbeitsgebietes "Ost-West-Sprachdifferenzierung"', *Mitteilungen des Instituts für Deutsche Sprache*, 11, 1985, pp. 76–7

33 Hellmann, 'Bemerkungen zur Entwicklung ', pp. 76-92

34 H. Moser (ed.), *Das Aueler Protokoll. Deutsche Sprache im Spannungsfeld zwischen West und Ost*, Düsseldorf, 1964

35 M. Hellmann (ed.), *Öffentlicher Sprachgebrauch in der Bundesrepublik Deutschland und in der DDR*, Düsseldorf, 1973

36 '... der Ost–West-Konflikt und die gesellschaftliche Restauration in West- europa konservierten politische Verhaltensweisen und Vorurteile des Bürger- tums aus der Zeit des Faschismus bis weit in die Nachkriegszeit hinein. Anstelle einer selbstkritischen Faschismustheorie entstand die apologetische

Totalitarismuskonzeption. Mit ihrer Hilfe konnte das eigene Versagen auf den kommunistischen "Erzfeind" projiziert werden. Mit dem Hinweis auf letztlich formale Übereinstimmungen zwischen faschistischem Herrschafts- und sozialistischen Planungsapparat verdeckte man die weitgehende Kontinuität der gesellschaftlich-ökonomischen Struktur und Zielsetzung von Faschismus und Kapitalismus.' Winckler, *Gesellschaftliche Funktion*, p.12

37 K-F. Borée, 'Die Sprachentartung in der Sowjetzone', *PZ-Archiv*, 2, 3, 1952, pp. 23–4

38 'Lange Zeit war die Sprachwissenschaft der Meinung, Sprache entwickele sich natürlich. Heute muß man die Erscheinung der gelenkten Sprache stärker beachten... Im Osten Deutschlands nehmen die maßgebenden Männer an, daß, wie viele andere Lebensbereiche, auch die Sprache beliebig manipulierbar sei.

Es handelt sich bei den von uns beobachteten Erscheinungen also in erster Linie um einen Sprachmißbrauch, nicht um einen Strukturwandel der Sprachgemeinschaft.' Moser, *Das Aueler Protokoll*, 1964, p. 139

39 E.g., by the *Rheinische Post* on 1 December 1948 (cf. Stötzel, 'Nazi-Verbrechen' 1989, p. 44)

40 Cf. Stötzel, 'Nazi-Verbrechen' 1989, pp. 45f

41 See p. 178 above

42 'Die Klagen über den "Sprachverfall" in der Gebrauchsprosa messen meist mit falschen Maßstäben. Man entdeckt Neuerungen gegenüber dem traditionellen Sprachgebrauch und Abweichungen von dem sprachästhetischen Ideal, das vom Kunststil der Dichter (vor allem der klassischen) abgeleitet ist, und verwirft all das als "Sprachverderb" oder "Verarmung".' P. v. Polenz, 'Sprachkritik und Sprachwissenschaft', *Neue Rundschau*, 74, 1963

43 W. Dieckmann, 'Kritische Bemerkungen zum sprachlichen Ost–West-Problem', *Zeitschrift für deutsche Sprache*, 23, 1967, pp. 136–65

44 G. D. Schmidt, 'Die deutschen Varianten des Deutschen. Zum Einfluß der Politik auf Interpretation, Bewertung und Verlauf der Sprachentwicklung in der DDR', *Muttersprache*, xciii, 1983, pp. 284–9

45 M. Hellmann, 'Deutsche Sprache Ost und West', *Mitteilungen des Instituts für Deutsche Sprache*, 11, 1985, pp. 63–8

46 M. Kinne and B. Strube-Edelmann, *Kleines Wörterbuch des DDR-Wortschatzes*, Düsseldorf, 1980 2nd edn

47 'Auch wenn man zunächst von der Differenzierung der Existenzformen absieht und zunächst nur die Literatursprache berücksichtigt . . . ist die "deutsche Sprache in der DDR" nicht zu reduzieren auf den Sprachgebrauch in Presse, Publizistik und Amtsverkehr. Es muß vielmehr die ganze funktional-stilistische Vielfalt einer modernen Literatursprache gesehen werden: Wissenschaft und Populärwissenschaft, Alltagsverkehr und künstlerische Kommunikation.' W. Fleischer, 'Die deutsche Sprache in der DDR. Grundsätzliche Überlegungen zur Sprachsituation' in D. Nerius (ed.), *Entwicklungstendenzen der deutschen Sprache seit dem 18. Jahrhundert*, Berlin, 1983, p. 265. The passage continues: 'Wie eingangs bereits angedeutet, ist unter der "deutschen Sprache in der DDR" aber nicht nur die Literatursprache in ihrer historischen Tiefe und ihrer funktionalstilistischen Differenziertheit zu verstehen, sondern das ganze Gefüge der Existenzformen. Die seit den 60er Jahren in der DDR intensivierten soziolinguistischen Untersuchungen haben unsere Erkenntnis in dieser Hinsicht außerordentlich gefördert' (p.266)

48 Hellmann, 'Bemerkungen zur Entwicklung', p. 86

49 'Die Frage, "Was ist des Deutschen Vaterland?" lautet heute: wie *heißt* es?' Brückner, *Versuch*, p. 7

50 Cf. Mangoldt and Klein, *Das Bonner Grundgesetz (Kommentar)*, Vol.1, Berlin, 1957, p. 27: '(die Hinzufügung dieses Wortes [*Deutschland*]) … soll ein Bekenntnis zur Einheit Deutschlands sein. Sie soll aber auch […] zum Ausdruck bringen, […] daß die neue Bundesrepublik mit dem alten Reich identisch ist'

51 'Deutschland ist eine unteilbare demokratische Republik' and 'Es gibt nur eine deutsche Staatsangehörigkeit'

52 In Article 1 of the 1974 Constitution, the GDR is described as follows: 'Die Deutsche Demokratische Republik ist ein sozialistischer Staat der Arbeiter und Bauern'

53 'Deutschland: Ländername für das Territorium der deutschen Nation, besonders des ehemaligen deutschen Staates bis zur Herausbildung der zwei deutschen Staaten DDR und BRD nach 1945'. Klappenbach and Steinitz (eds), *Wörterbuch der deutschen Gegenwartssprache*, Vol. 2, Berlin, 1974, p. 801

54 Thus, for example, diplomatic relations were broken off with Yugoslavia (19 October 1957) and Cuba (14 January 1963)

55 'Abkommen über den Handel zwischen den Währungsgebieten der Deutschen Mark der Deutschen Notenbank (DM-Ost) und den Währungs-gebieten der Deutschen Mark (DM-West)', quoted from: Ministerium für Auswärtige Angelegenheiten der Deutschen Demokratischen Republik (ed.), *Beziehungen der Deutschen Demokratischen Republik zur Bundesrepublik Deutschland und zu Berlin (West)*, Berlin, 1990, p. 160

56 *Beziehungen der Deutschen Demokratischen Republik zur Bundesrepublik Deutschland*, pp. 163/4

57 In his policy statement ('Regierungserklärung') Brandt used the term 'DDR' no fewer than six times.

58 However, in its verdict on the treaty, the Federal Constitutional Court still maintained the unity of the German nation

59 'Das 1945 von der Sowjetunion besetzte Gebiet Deutschlands westlich der Oder–Neiße-Linie mit Ausnahme Berlins wird im politischen Sprachgebrauch als *Sowjetische Besatzungszone Deutschlands*, abgekürzt als *SBZ*, in Kurzform auch als *Sowjetzone* bezeichnet. Es ist nichts dagegen einzuwenden, daß auch die Bezeichnung *Mitteldeutschland* verwendet wird.' In *Gemeinsames Ministerialblatt*, 1965, p. 227, quoted after H. Berschin, *Deutschland – ein Name im Wandel*, Munich/Vienna, 1979, p. 23

60 'wir erkennen natürlich, daß sich da drüben etwas gebildet hat, ein Phänomen, mit dem wir es zu tun haben, ein Phänomen, mit dessen

Vertretern ich in einen Briefwechsel eingetreten bin ...' In *Verhandlungen des Deutschen Bundestages, 5. Wahlperiode, Stenographische Berichte*, Bd. 65, S. 6360

61 'Statt der ausdrücklichen Bezeichnung *Bundesrepublik Deutschland*, die das Grundgesetz festgelegt hat, sollte daher die Kurzform *Deutschland* immer dann gebraucht werden, wenn die Führung des vollständigen Namens nicht erforderlich ist. [...] Die Abkürzung *BRD* oder die Bezeichnung *Bundesrepublik* ohne den Zusatz *Deutschland* sollten nicht benutzt werden. [...] Als adjektivische Form sollte nur die Bezeichnung *deutsch* verwendet werden.' *Gemeinsames Ministerialblatt*, 1965

62 Cf. Brückner, *Versuch*, p.7

63 'da sie nach dem Untergang der DDR als Staat und der Herstellung der Einheit Deutschlands ideologische Gehalte nicht mehr transportieren und den Fortbestand Deutschlands in Frage zu stellen nicht mehr geeignet sind.' Quoted in 'Spuren deutscher Sprache', *Die Zeit*, 27, 28 June 91

64 Examples which by now are familiar in Britain and Ireland are those such as 'Londonderry' *v*. 'Derry', and 'poll tax' *v*. 'community charge'.

65 E.g., B. Bernstein, *Class, Codes and Control*, London, 1971, and its reception by U. Ammon, *Probleme der Soziolinguistik*, Tübingen, 1971

66 W. Bergsdorf (ed.), *Wörter als Waffen. Sprache als Mittel der Politik*, Stuttgart, 1979

67 'Die gewaltsame Besetzung der Zitadellen staatlicher Macht ist nicht länger Voraussetzung für eine revolutionäre Umwälzung der staatlichen Ordnung. Revolutionen finden heute auf andere Weise statt. Statt der Gebäude der Regierungen werden die Begriffe besetzt, mit denen sie regiert.' K. Biedenkopf, 'Bericht des Generalsekretärs auf dem 22. Bundesparteitag der CDU, Hamburg 18 – 20 November 1973, quoted from *Protokolle des 22. Parteitages*, p. 61

68 'Die entscheidende Schlacht ist völlig unblutig gewonnen, wenn es gelingt, dem Gegner eine Sprache aufzuzwingen, die ihn daran hindert, seine Interessen und eine eigene geistig-politische Position zu artikulieren', G.-K. Kaltenbrunner (ed.), *Sprache und Herrschaft*, Munich, 1975, p. 8

69 H. Kuhn, 'Despotie der Wörter. Wie man mit der Sprache die Freiheit überwältigen kann', Kaltenbrunner, *Sprache und Herrschaft*, pp. 11–19

70 H. Dietz, 'Rote Semantik', Kaltenbrunner, *Sprache und Herrschaft*, pp. 20–43

71 H. Maier, 'Aktuelle Tendenzen der politischen Sprache', Bergsdorf, *Wörter als Waffen*, pp. 30–43

72 H. Lübbe, 'Sein und Heißen – Bedeutungsgeschichte als politisches Sprachhandlungsfeld', Bergsdorf, *Wörter als Waffen*, pp. 71–84

73 M.Behrens, W.Dieckmann and E. Kehl, 'Politik als Sprachkampf. Zur konservativen Sprachkritik und Sprachpolitik seit 1972', J. H. Heringer (ed.), *Holzfeuer im hölzernen Ofen. Aufsätze zur politischen Sprachkritik*, Tübingen, 1982

74 'Die betonte Notwendigkeit der "Koordinierung der Begriffe" hat also zwei verschiedene Aspekte: Ihr Gebrauch muß im Sinne einheitlicher Anwendung in allen Verlautbarungen der Partei koordiniert werden, damit sie sich durch Wiederholung als CDU-Wörter einprägen können; sie müssen aber auch untereinander koordiniert und in einen systematischen Zusammenhang gebracht werden.' Behrens *et al.*, 'Politik als Sprachkampf', pp. 226–7

75 'Freiheit, Gerechtigkeit und Solidarität, Verantwortung, Sozialpflichtigkeit und Leistung stehen als politische Begriffe beziehungslos nebeneinander, wenn es nicht gelingt, den Zusammenhang zwischen ihnen für die praktische politische Arbeit deutlich zu machen'. K. Biedenkopf, 'Bericht des General-sekretärs auf dem 23. Parteitag der CDU, Mannheim, 23–25 Juni 1975, quoted from *Protokolle des 23. Parteitages*, p. 172

76 The linguistic joke here rests on a deliberate confusion of the part-suffix –mus from 'Sozialismus' with the compound element 'Mus' (pulp)

77 'Worte sind dazu da, Dinge zu bezeichnen. Sie sollen sagen, was ist; und sofern ihnen das gelingt, sagen sie die Wahrheit.' Kuhn, *Despotie der Wörter*, p. 11

78 'zentrale Begriffe unserer politischen Ordnung . . . (sind) aus ihrer Normallage gelöst . . . worden .' Maier, 'Aktuelle Tendenzen', p. 35

79 'Politik ist nicht zuletzt die Kunst, im Medium der Öffentlichkeit Zustimmungsbereitschaften zu erzeugen.' Lübbe, 'Sein und Heißen', p. 8

80 'Für die Politik sind Darstellung, Ausdruck und Appell als Leistungen der Sprache in gleicher Weise wichtig und unverzichtbar. Die Sprache bietet der Politik das Mittel zu informieren, zu interpretieren, anzuweisen, zu überzeugen und zu indoktrinieren.' Bergsdorf, *Wörter als Waffen*, p. 8

81 'Diese zentralen Begriffe, ohne die Geschichte nicht geschrieben und Politik nicht durchgesetzt werden kann, sind mit Werten befrachtet, sie müssen, um sich ein möglichst breites Verständnispotential zu erschließen, vage sein und sind deshalb anfällig für inhaltliche Veränderungen.' Bergsdorf, *Wörter als Waffen*, p. 9

82 Dietz, 'Rote Semantik', p. 21

83 'Die Sprachentwicklung nach 1945 stand – zumindest in der Bundes-republik – im Zeichen eines fortschreitenden Abbaus von rollen- und schicht-spezifischen Sondersprachen, individuellen und landschafts-gebundenen Idiomen, kurz räumlichen und sozialen Sprachabgrenzungen. Sie spiegelte hierin, wenn auch mit Verzögerungen, die sozialgeschichtliche Entwicklung wider, die einerseits durch soziale Nivellierung, andererseits durch Rangerhöhung bisher sozial zurückstehender Tätigkeiten und Positionen in der Gesellschaft gekennzeichnet war.' Meyer, 'Aktuelle Tendenzen', p. 30

84 '. . . in der Gründungs- und Aufbauphase der Bundesrepublik . . . wurde zwar häufig z. B. die Einfachheit und Schlichtheit des Adenauer-Vokabulars kritisiert, aber der Sinn der zentralen Begriffe der Politik war ziemlich scharf umrissen . . .
Natürlich wurde auch damals um die Inhalte der Politik zwischen den Parteien gerungen. Aber die Bedeutungen der politischen Schlüsselbegriffe waren über einen längeren Zeitraum relativ stabil. Alle an der politischen Auseinander-setzung Beteiligten benutzten die gleichen Wörter und verstanden darunter Vergleichbares.' Bergsdorf, *Wörter als Waffen*, p. 7

85 'aber diese neuen Worte bezeichnen nicht eigentlich Dinge, jedenfalls

nicht Seiendes, sondern – und das macht ihre Neuartigkeit aus – sie benennen Nichtseiendes, das sein soll.' Kuhn, 'Sein und Heißen', p. 12

86 '. . . zentrale Begriffe unserer politischen Ordnung (sind) in den letzten Jahren aus ihrer Normallage gelöst, dynamisiert, ja eschatologisch aufgeladen worden: Das gilt für Verfassung, Demokratie, Sozialstaat so gut wie für Rechtsstaat und Grundrecht. Aus Ordnungsbegriffen sind Verheißungen geworden.' Maier, *Aktuelle Tendenzen*, p.35

87 'Eine der Tatsachen, die bei der politischen Diskussion in besonderem Maße Erstaunen erregen, ist die Verwirrung, die geringe Klarheit der dort gebrauchten Begriffe .' M. Cattaneo, 'Sprachanalyse und Politologie', in R. Schmidt (ed.), *Methoden der Politologie*, Darmstadt,1967, p. 330

88 M. Edelmann, *Political Language. Words that Succeed and Politics that Fail*, New York, 1977, p. 58

89 'Schon die Wörter Freiheit, Gerechtigkeit und Demokratie, die – stark emotional aufgeladen – eine günstige Stimmung erzeugen, werden von Exponenten entgegengesetzter politischer Strömungen zur Bezeichnung ganz verschiedener Dinge benutzt und um auf Werte anzuspielen, mit denen es eine ganz unterschiedliche Bewandtnis hat. Das geschieht, um Sympathien und Treue im Lager dessen zu gewinnen, der sie ausspricht und vertritt. Die Mythen und der Irrationalismus beherrschen unser politisches Leben.' Cattaneo, 'Sprachanalyse und Politologie', 1967, p. 330

90 E. Topitsch, 'Über Leerformeln. Zur Pragmatik des Sprachgebrauchs in der Philosophie und politischen Theorie', E. Topitsch (ed.), *Probleme der Wissenschaftstheorie. Festschrift für V. Kraft*, Vienna, 1960, pp. 233–64

91 L. Schmidt, 'Politik ist Käse – beides sind Markenartikel', *Blick durch die Wirtschaft*, Supplement to the *Frankfurter Allgemeine Zeitung*, 23 June 1980. The German word 'Käse' is familiarly used to mean 'rubbish'

92 'Sprache birgt jedenfalls die Möglichkeit, mit ihrer Hilfe Macht über andere zu gewinnen: das ist eine ihrer Funktionen.' L. Mackensen, *Verführung durch Sprache*, Munich, 1973, p. 208

6 Constructions of reality

Introduction

It is one of the theoretical contentions of the present study that language has a Janus-like quality, in that it not only mediates perception but is also constitutive of it. In this final chapter, we shall be examining three case studies which illustrate the productive relationship between language and 'reality'. They will demonstrate how language is used to 'constitute realities', and the third will in addition show how attempts have been made to develop a language strategy to uncover a suppressed 'reality'. In all three cases, the linguistic constitution of reality will be shown to be of eminent political significance in that it is part of a strategy for influencing perception in order to affect attitudes and justify further action, which may be linguistic or non-linguistic.

The three case studies have been chosen not only for their intrinsic linguistic interest, but also because they incorporate three key political concerns of the late 1970s and 1980s in West Germany – the nuclear arms race, the protection of the environment and the bounds of legitimate protest, and the status of women.

1—The NATO 'dual-track decision', the use of 'Nachrüstung', and who is the peace movement?

The background

From the end of the Second World War until the beginning of the 1990s, geopolitics were characterised by a struggle for supremacy between the two so-called 'super-powers' of the USA and the USSR. The competition took a variety of forms, including the waging of armed combat through intermediary 'client states', but one of the most overt manifestations was the nuclear arms race, which has led to a massive build-up of means of mass destruction capable of wiping out the world's human population several times over. The perverted 'rationale' behind the arms race is that every arms step by one side is interpreted as a 'threat' by the other, the 'threat' then having to be countered by a further arms increase in the interests of 'defence' against potential 'aggression'. In this 'arms race' the two German states and Berlin were continually at the interface, and most of the 'war scenarios' would have led to their devastation.

From the mid-1970s onwards, the Soviet Union had started replacing its SS-4 and SS-5 land-based intermediate-range nuclear missiles with the more advanced multi-warhead SS-20. NATO perceived this modernisation programme as a new 'threat' which, in keeping with the automatism of the nuclear arms race, could only be countered with the stationing of 'equivalent' (or, preferably, superior) forces on the Western side. In consequence, on 12 December 1979, a meeting of NATO Foreign and Defence Ministers in Brussels passed what became known as the 'dual- (or twin) track decision', under which intermediate-range land-based American Pershing II and Tomahawk Cruise Missiles equipped with thermonuclear warheads would be stationed in 'selected' Western European countries from the end of 1983 unless the Soviets had agreed to withdraw their SS-20s by that time.

Given that NATO's self-image was that of a defensive alliance, the perceived 'rationale' of which was to counter the 'threat' emanating from the Soviet Union, any stationing of new weapons by NATO had to be perceived as a counter to this threat; thus, the proposed installation of LRINF[1] with a first-strike capacity was presented as a programme of 'modernisation' to counter the Soviet arms build-up – in other words, the 'new' weapons were not deemed to be qualitatively different from their predecessors, in contrast to the Soviet SS-20s which, according to the 1979 West German Defence White Paper, represented a 'radical innovation' and not just a 'modernisation'.[2]

In Western Europe, the proposed arms build-up was the subject of a far-reaching public debate, which took place from the late 1970s onwards, and in Germany was widely known as 'Die Nachrüstungsdebatte'. Linguistically, the debate demonstrates a myriad of fascinating aspects of politico-linguistic use,[3] but in the present study we shall concentrate on two aspects – on the term *Nachrüstung* itself, and on competing claims to the title of *Friedensbewegung* ('peace movement').

The terminology – *Nachrüstung*

With English as the main NATO language, there is a tendency for German defence documents to use either English terminology or loan-translations until terms become more firmly established and German equivalents are found.[4] In the case under discussion, the terms *modernisieren* and *Modernisierung* are first used – for example in the official German communiqué issued after the Brussels meeting in December 1979.[5]

A 'native' German term was, however, also available from the technical domain, and what we can observe in the discursive strategies deployed is the increasing dominance of the German term, coupled with a shift in its semantics which strengthens the official view being purveyed.

The 'native' term was *nachrüsten*, with its derived noun *Nachrüstung*; as stated, it is a technical term meaning 'modernise' or, to use a morphologically closer equivalent, 'retro-fit'.

For purposes of linguistic analysis, one can postulate two sets of lexical items with the root '-rüst-', $RÜST_1$ and $RÜST_2$. $RÜST_1$ is the more general, and has the core meaning 'equip' or 'prepare', while

RÜST$_2$ is more specific, with the core meaning 'arm' (i.e., 'equip with weapons'). The postulation of two sets of items is justified *inter alia* by restrictions on the compounds which can be formed: thus, for example, *Ausrüstung* (equipment) is a compound based on RÜST$_1$, while *aufrüsten* (increase armaments), *abrüsten* (disarm), *Wettrüsten* (arms race) are based on RÜST$_2$. Originally, *nachrüsten* was classifiable as a RÜST$_1$ compound, and in the 1983 Defence White Paper there is sufficient evidence to suggest that on many occasions *Nachrüstung* is being used synonymously with *Modernisierung*: thus the Index contains ten references to *Nachrüstung*, but in five of them, the term 'Nachrüstung' does not appear in the text, but *Modernisierung* does.[6]

It is perhaps inevitable that, given the outward identity and semantic similarity of RÜST$_1$ and RÜST$_2$ and the military context of the NATO 'modernisation', this particular use of *Nachrüstung* should drift from RÜST$_1$ to RÜST$_2$; it is suggested, however, that this 'drift' was in fact actively encouraged by the proponents of the NATO strategy, and that in the course of the shift a semantic change was effected which not only affected the core (RÜST$_1$ => RÜST$_2$) but also the reference of the prefix 'nach-', and that this then allowed a new opposition to be set up which supported the contention that the increase in the level of NATO nuclear arms in Europe was a direct response to a new 'Soviet threat'.

As a preposition, *nach* has three basic applications. To start with, it has both a directional and a temporal signification; directionally, it carries the meaning 'in the direction of', 'towards', 'to', and stands in opposition to *aus*, *von*. Temporally, it means 'after', and stands in opposition to *vor*. A third meaning is that of 'according to'/'in accordance with' or 'in the style/manner of'.

In its function as a verbal/nominal prefix, the directional/temporal signification is maintained in such verbs as *nachschicken* (to forward, 'send after') and *nachfolgen* (succeed, in the sense of 'be the successor'), where it stands in contrast to 'vor-', 'voraus-'; thus oppositions can be set up such as *vorausschicken* (send in advance') – *nachschicken* or *Vorgängerin* (predecessor) – *Nachfolgerin* (successor). In addition, following from its temporal signification, it can carry the meaning of 're-' (as in *nachladen* – reload) or 'subsequent' (as in our example *nachrüsten* – retrofit), where it has no contrasting item, but is part of a sequence as in *laden* – *nachladen* or *Ausrüstung* (original equipment) – *Nach-*

rüstung. Finally – and crucially – as a prefix 'nach-' carries the meaning of 'following or responding to the example', where again it stands in contrast to 'vor' in such pairs as *vormachen* (demonstrate as a model for imitation) and *nachmachen* (follow the example set).

What happened with this particular change in the usage of *Nachrüstung* was that there was a double shift – firstly in the core from $RÜST_1$ to $RÜST_2$, and secondly in the prefix from the second to the third of the above uses, to give an overall shift from 'modernise' or 'retro-fit' – which can be seen as a response to technical progress – to 'counter-arm', i.e., matching a prior armament initiated 'on the other side'. In this way, the prevailing view could be maintained that any increase in the destructive capacity of NATO armaments was justified as a response to a prior Soviet threat. This view, and the semantic shift in *Nachrüstung* was then further strengthened by the setting up of an opposition with the terms *Nachrüstung – Vorrüstung*[7] – prior arming.

This opposition *Vorrüstung – Nachrüstung* fulfilled an important role in official government and CDU/CSU discourse up to and including the debate which was conducted in Germany prior to the actual stationing of Pershing II missiles in December 1983,[8] and it is proposed to use two texts as an illustration of this. The first text is that of the *Weißbuch 1983*, to which reference has already been made, and the second is the complex text of what became known as the *Nachrüstungsdebatte* in the German Bundestag on 21 and 22 November 1983.

The *Weißbücher* are occasional statements of West German defence policy, the first of which appeared in 1969. The *Weißbuch 1983* appeared in October 1983, and was the first to be presented by a CDU/CSU/FDP coalition government; the significance of its date of appearance lay in the fact that it was published a year after Helmut Kohl's first election as Federal Chancellor on 1 October 1982 and seven months after the CDU/CSU/FDP election victory of 6 March 1983, and thus provided an early opportunity for a statement of the new government's defence policy. Of greater significance, however, was the fact that it appeared less than two months before the scheduled stationing of American Pershing II missiles on German soil, and thus constitutes an important element in the *Nachrüstungsdebatte*; that it was 'rushed out' is evidenced by the fact that, in contrast to its predecessors, it did not contain a section on the structure of the Bundeswehr, but that this appeared as a separate *Weißbuch* in 1985.[9]

Given the controversy surrounding the proposed stationing of Cruise and Pershing, the West German government decided to procure the agreement of the Bundestag to its prior decision to proceed with the stationing, and thus initiated a formal debate on 21 and 22 November 1983. (The first Pershings were then flown in on 25 November 1983.)

As already stated, the term *Nachrüstung* appears a number of times in the *Weißbuch 1983*, and on most occasions it is used synonymously with *Modernisierung*. In section 422, however, it appears for the first time in this text in its 'revised' meaning and in conjunction with *Vorrüstung*, when it is argued that the 'dual track decision' represents the first attempt to break the chain of arma- ment and counter-armament ('Vorrüstung und Nachrüstung') and to encourage an agreement on disarmament.[10]

The text of the parliamentary debate is a complex one, consist- ing of a number of sub-texts (in particular, the written texts of the motions presented to the Bundestag, the set speeches, the inter- ventions and the written account of the proceedings). For our present purposes, we shall restrict ourselves to an examination of those parts of the motions and the set speeches as recorded in the official transcript[11] which provide evidence of the shift of meaning in *Nachrüstung* and the setting up of an opposition with *Vorrüstung*.

Whereas the *Weißbuch 1983* introduces the link 'Vorrüstung und Nachrüstung' only in a general manner where it could prob- ably be replaced by a term such as *Rüstungswettlauf* (arms race – if this term were not negatively connotated), the motion presented to the Bundestag by the CDU/CSU/FDP coalition is far more specific, referring to the 'massive Soviet arms build-up' (*Vorrüstung*) and recalling that for four years the NATO alliance had refrained from counter-armaments (*Nachrüstung*) in the hope of achieving a negotiated settlement.[12]

In the set speeches, the link *Vorrüstung – Nachrüstung* appears a number of times, for example in the contribution by Federal Minister of Defence Wörner[13] and – significantly enough – by ex- Chancellor Schmidt[14]. The tenor of Wörner's remarks is that the Soviets are subjecting Western Europe to an additional and unac- ceptable threat through their policy of *Vorrüstung* and must not be allowed to 'get away with it'.

In the texts by the proponents of *Nachrüstung*, we find that this term is not only linked with the 'new meaning' of *Vorrüstung* but that *Vorrüstung* also forms part of a larger field which includes such terms as *Aufrüstung*, *Überrüstung* (excessive arms) and *Hochrüstung*, and as we saw in the extract from the CDU/CSU/FDP motion, these terms can be qualified by such epithets as *massiv*.

The significance of the use of the *Vorrüstung – Nachrüstung* link by Helmut Schmidt lies in the fact that – with the exception of Egon Bahr, who uses the term *Nachrüstung* – his is the only reported speech by a member of the SPD parliamentary party which accepts the terminology,[15] and this brings us to another important aspect of the question.

In the discussion on the designation for the West German state, we saw one example of how a particular sign can act as a shibboleth, an identifier of political position, and in German political culture it is often important to use the ideologically 'correct' term. The term *Nachrüstung* affords a further example: it is definitely not a neutral term, and by using it one subscribes to a particular view of the balance of nuclear terror. Thus, with the exception of the two SPD speakers referred to above, those using the term support NATO military policy (or that of the West German government – there is no difference), and if opponents of the policy find it necessary to refer to the term, then it is common to preface it with the epithet 'sogenannt'.

At the same time, however, opponents of the policy do try to 'turn' or re-function such terms or slogans (we have already observed one example in the case of 'Freiheit statt Sozialismus – Freiheit statt Apfelmus'), and here we can just pause briefly with two examples for the 'turning' of *Nachrüstung – Vorrüstung*:

In the so-called *Nachrüstungsdebatte*, Minister of Defence Wörner detailed all the disarmament steps 'the West' had already undertaken, including the withdrawal of 1,000 nuclear weapons from Europe in 1981 and the announcement that a further 1,400 weapons would be withdrawn; in response to this, the Green MdB Otto Schily interjected 'Da scheinen wir vorgerüstet zu haben!' ('We seem to have been the ones doing the first arming!'),[16] turning the whole scenario on its head by using the verb *vorrüsten* with a first person subject and thus breaking the (unspoken) selection restriction that the verb *vorrüsten* could only be used with 'the Soviets' as a subject.

The second example concerns *Nachrüstung*, and is taken from a banner reproduced on the cover of Pasierbsky's *Krieg und Frieden in der Sprache* and variously spotted as a graffito[17] (for example on a wall of Mannheim University): 'Nach Rüstung kommt Tod'. Here, the sign *Nachrüstung*, consisting of root plus prefix, has been 'deconstructed' into an adverbial phrase made up of a preposition plus noun to give the meaning 'After armaments comes death', i.e., *nach* has been 'restored' to its temporal significance – although the causal is often inherent in the temporal.

As a postscript to this part of the discussion, it is worth noting that not long after the debate, the term *Nachrüstung* reappeared in the public domain in a completely different context, and re-endowed with its (original) technical meaning of 'retro-fit', when car owners were encouraged to retro-fit (*nachrüsten*) their vehicles with catalytic converters in an effort to reduce the pollution from internal combustion engines.

Die Friedensbewegung

In Chapter 5, we observed how a linguistic strategy was identified (and then pursued) of attempting to 'occupy' certain key terms in the political debate; during the *Nachrüstungsdebatte*, one could watch this strategy in action with reference to the terms 'peace' and 'peace movement'. As we have already noted, the stockpiling of weapons of mass destruction is always presented as being in the interests of defence, and we are expected to believe that the only reason for the maintenance of a war-machine is the preservation of peace – thus, within this view, it is, for example, only logical that the United States Air Force Strategic Air Command should have as its motto 'Peace is our profession'.

In the *Nachrüstungsdebatte*, the CDU/CSU/FDP government is clearly concerned to present itself as the party of peace – although, significantly enough, their commitment to 'peace' is not an absolute one, for the interests of 'peace' are subordinated to those of 'freedom'. The government – and Chancellor Kohl in particular – operate with the formula of 'Frieden in Freiheit' in a way that implies the 'better dead than red' argument.[18]

The actual debate in the Bundestag on 21 and 22 November 1983 took place against the background of expressions of public protest outside the parliament building against the stationing of further American nuclear missiles, and a number of speakers referred to the protests. Their strategies obviously varied depending on their party allegiances, and here we shall concentrate on two linked aspects, the 'right' to bear the title of 'peace movement', and the use of 'force'.

The application of the label 'peace movement' to extra-parliamentary groupings opposed to 'official "defence" policy' is generally accepted usage. During the Bundestag debate, government speakers pursued a dual strategy of trying to dispute the 'right' of the 'peace movement' to the title and of claiming it for themselves. Two main arguments are deployed, which we can categorise under the headings of 'appropriateness' and 'exclusiveness'.

The 'appropriateness' argument seeks to deny that 'peace' is a defining characteristic of the 'peace movement', and here two different definitions of 'peace' are deployed. The first is the conventional one of 'non-violent', and here the – far from non-violent – demonstrations outside the parliament building are used as evidence to deny the demonstrators' peacefulness; thus in his speech, the Foreign Minister Hans-Dietrich Genscher refers explicitly to the *Gewalttäter* (violent criminals) outside who are attacking the 'freedom' of 'our German parliament' to exercise its sovereign rights.[19] In a similar manner, Alfred Dregger, who consistently refers to 'die sogenannte Friedensbewegung' ('the so-called peace movement') accuses them of 'violence and deception'.[20] The second definition of peace is the more specialised 'government-specific' one of the peace for which 'freedom' is a condition, and here the argument runs that the 'peace movement' is opposed to the values of freedom and democracy and is prepared to sacrifice freedom: thus Dregger can refer to 'diese sogenannte Friedensbewegung, die ... objektiv eine Unterwerfungsbewegung ist' ('this so-called peace movement, which ... in fact is a submission movement'[21]). Linked to this last argument is the 'treason' argument, which sees the 'peace movement' as accomplices to the expansionist designs of the Soviet Union: thus Dregger can claim that there is no incentive for the Soviets to disarm as long as they can rely on the help of the peace movement and the SPD.[22]

The 'exclusiveness' argument, while maybe admitting that 'the peace movement' is sincere in its desire for peace, seeks to deny that the members of the peace movement are alone in this desire. In his opening speech of the debate, Chancellor Kohl makes an appeal to consensus by claiming that 'everybody' wants peace ('Wir alle sind für den Frieden').[23] Hans-Dietrich Genscher picks up the argument, and thematises the reference of the term 'peace movement' by attacking the SPD Parliamentary Leader for using the term in an 'undifferentiated manner', then to claim that 'the whole German people is one great peace movement' in its rejection of radicalism and its commitment to peace both within and without.[24] He develops this line further by specifically including in his 'peace movement' 'the young policemen defending the sovereignty of our German Parliament' and the 'soldiers of the Federal Armed Forces who defend the free parliamentary system',[25] a point echoed later by Theo Waigel, who expresses his thanks to the five million young men who have performed their military service and thus form 'a peace movement of our democracy'.[26]

We have already seen how government speakers attempted to disqualify the 'peace movement' by accusing it of violence; an analogous argument is used by representatives of the Greens to demonstrate how 'unpeaceful' the government's policy is. As an illustration, we shall take two short extracts from the debate.

After the Chancellor's opening speech, the Greens intervened to move an adjournment of the debate in order that Members could go outside and witness the violence being perpetrated by the police on the 'concerned citizens' assembled outside the building. The argument runs that while the Government is paying lip service to the cause of peace inside the building, its agents are demonstrating what the government really means outside.[27] With this, the Greens attempt to show their perceived illogicality of a government policy which attempts to secure 'peace' through force and thus creates 'unpeaceful' conditions within the state.[28] Thus the first argument is that 'peace' cannot be maintained with violence.

The second strand of the Greens' argument then picks up the prioritising of 'freedom' over 'peace'. In her speech, Marieluise Beck-Oberdorf attacks the Government for this priority and seeks to deny that in the atomic age, 'freedom' can be guaranteed with nuclear weapons.[29] The second argument, then, is that the

Government, by pursuing a policy based ultimately on the threat or exercise of force is not only prepared to sacrifice its subordinate goal of 'peace', but also places its primary goal of 'freedom' at risk.

In summary, this brief illustration shows how a key term, 'peace', has positive values ascribed to it, and how both 'sides' in the parliamentary debate attempt to claim proprietary rights over the term, partly by actively denying these 'rights' to their 'opponents'.

2—Loaded 'weapons'

Nachrüstung presented us with one example of a shift of meaning for a particular purpose; the next example represents a far more blatant case of 'semantic engineering', and concerns the restoration of an archaic term.

For many years now,[30] West German political culture has been marked by a high level of environmental awareness;[31] the issues around which the environmental debate has concentrated are many and various, but one topic which has been present from the start of the 'green movement' was that of atomic power, which again presents us with a shibboleth – what does one call it? In English, there are two terms – 'nuclear' and 'atomic'; German has three – *Atom-*, *Kern-* and *Nuklear-*, of which *Nuklear-* appears to be the most specialised, being found in official and technical military texts and in such specialised compounds as *Nuklearmedizin*. An antagonistic relationship exists between *Atom-* and *Kern-*, in which *Atom-* carries negative and *Kern-* positive connotations. This can partly be explained by the fact that *Atom-* is an 'alien' which is prejudiced by its link with 'atomic' weapons – *Atombombe*, while *Kern-* is a 'native' element which is positively connotated through the association with such words as *kernig* ('robust'), *kerngesund* ('fit as a fiddle') and *Kernholz* ('heartwood'). In the deployment of these two elements, there is a clear split between the proponents of nuclear energy, who clearly prefer compounding with *Kern-* and the opponents of atomic power, whose predilection is equally clearly for *Atom-*. A simple example can be seen in the polyglot sticker which in English carries the slogan 'Nuclear power – no thanks', while in German the text is 'Atomkraft – nein danke' (and presumably, if the nuclear lobby produced a counter-sticker, it would be 'Kernenergie – ja bitte').

The campaign against atomic power has been marked by a series of issues, most of which – like battles – have been linked with place-names such as Gorleben (the proposed site for the disposal of toxic nuclear waste), Wyhl (an atomic power plant near the Kaiserstuhl in Baden), Brokdorf (an atomic power plant near Hamburg) and Wackersdorf (Bavaria), which was to be the site of West Germany's nuclear reprocessing plant, until public protest and the realisation that sending spent fuel for reprocessing to Windscale (aka Sellafield) was cheaper led to the abandonment of the project. It is with the protests surrounding Wackersdorf that this second case of semantic engineering is concerned.

The protests and demonstrations against Wackersdorf were at times more reminiscent of pitched battles, with serried ranks of armed men, their faces obscured and without visible marks of identification, confronting a colourful collection of concerned women, men and children (that is, until the authorities declared the vicinity of Wackersdorf a 'no-go area' for all those aged under twelve on the grounds that it was 'too dangerous'[32]).

The 'right to demonstrate'[33] is derived from Article 8 of the (West) German constitution which, under the heading 'freedom of assembly', lays down that 'all Germans have the right to assemble peacefully and unarmed without prior permission or registration'. A restriction is, however, introduced for assemblies 'in the open air', where the right of assembly can be 'limited by law or on the basis of a law'.[34] Probably since the student protests of the 1960s, there has been an on-going discussion about the limitations on open-air assemblies – and in particular that type of assembly commonly known as a 'demonstration'. Essentially, the authorities are not happy about demonstrations, and this for two reasons: firstly, they introduce a popular element into a polity which is predicated on a 'top-down' structure,[35] and secondly, there is always the risk of a demonstration getting 'out of hand'[36] and acts of violence being perpetrated. The 'counter-demonstration strategy' of the state *apparat* has had two strands to it: firstly there have been attempts to stigmatise 'demonstrations' and 'demonstrators', and secondly, on the legislative/administrative level a number of regulations have been enacted which are designed to impede or even criminalise the participation in demonstrations, for example the *Vermummungsverbot* (masking ban), which makes it an offence for participants in open-air assemblies to cover their faces with the intention of impeding identification (although there have been no signs of this regulation being applied to the many carnival processions which take place in Germany around Shrove Tuesday!).

Given the arms build-up at demonstrations (firearms, clubs, rubber truncheons, tear gas, water cannon), participants might be forgiven for taking sensible precautions to protect themselves from the threat of violence – for example by wearing protective headgear or waterproof clothing. Certain authorities have, however, regarded such measures as escalating a potential conflict and have attempted to ban the wearing or carrying of any items which might be designed to 'act as a defence against law enforcement measures conducted by a legally empowered servant of the state'.[37] It is here that we approach the linguistic nub of the question, because the authorities sought to classify such items as *Schutzwaffen* – 'protective weapons'.[38]

The concept of *Schutzwaffen* is one which goes back to the Middle Ages, when a distinction was made between *Schutzwaffen* and *Trutzwaffen* (offensive weapons); the former traditionally encompassed helmet, armour and shield, and the right to bear the latter was the right of a free man. Although the term *'Schutzwaffen'* persisted into the nineteenth century, it was clearly marked as an historical – i.e., archaic – term.[39]

In its resurrected form, the core meaning of *Schutzwaffen* as a 'means of passive defence' is maintained, and 'officially' it has two applications; it can refer either to objects which are designed, constructed or constituted specifically for the purpose of 'passive defence', or it can be applied to objects which, although not primarily designed for the purpose, can be used thus.[40]

Without wishing to propagate an extreme 'conspiracy theory', it could be suggested that the measures envisaged (the banning of *Schutzwaffen*) and the linguistic/semantic engineering in which state authorities have engaged, serve a number of functions.

The first could be intimidatory. The only 'law enforcement measures conducted by a legally empowered servant of the state' against which items such as protective helmets and waterproofs offer protection are acts of physical violence – e.g., truncheon blows aimed at the head; by seeking to deprive 'demonstrators' of protection against such summary measures, the authorities wish to ensure that the police maintain an armed superiority which will enable them to quell any possible disturbance.

The second function can be perceived as a further item in a series of measures designed to criminalise the participation in protest demonstrations in an attempt thus to reduce the incidence of such protest.

The third could be the most far-reaching. Should the authorities succeed in establishing the currency of a term *Schutzwaffen*, they would then legitimately be able to refer to the presence of 'armed demonstrators' ('(schutz-) bewaffnete Demonstranten'), which, apart from making it possible to stigmatise 'demonstrations' still further, would finally remove from those engaging in political protest any residual protection that they might still have had under Section 1 of Article 8 of the Constitution, which, as we saw above, only grants the right of assembly to 'Germans who assemble peacefully and *unarmed*'.

The contention, therefore, is that by seeking to regulate a very small segment of language use, authorities can 'create realities' which may have far-reaching consequences.

3—Making women visible

The third case study of politically relevant linguistic developments in post-war (West) Germany concerns the linguistic dimensions of the growth of a 'new' women's movement[41] from about the mid-1970s onwards. As Kolinsky establishes:

In the 1970s, perceived discrepancies between the motivations and self-perceptions of women and the place women could secure in society gave rise to the women's movement. Although the movement seemed to focus on abortion as a yardstick of self-determination, the underlying theme was that of equality and the mismatch between expectations and realities. The women's movement sensitised women and men of all age cohorts to the patterns of inequality and it generated in women the expectation if not the confidence that home or work, motherhood or career need no longer be dichotomies and restrict their choice.[42]

As Kolinsky points out, one of the indicators of the higher 'political profile' of women in West Germany is the increased level of participation in the formal political process from the beginning of the 1970s onwards; in addition, women have been particularly active in 'alternative' forms of political activity such as the peace movement and the 'green' movement. In the present study, it is neither possible nor necessary to enter into a long account of the various strands within what is known as the 'women's movement'; the basic analysis from which we shall be working is that women represent an 'oppressed majority'. The contradiction of gender is postulated as being more fundamental than other contraries – for example that of labour and capital; for some feminists at least, capitalism is seen as a consequence of patriarchalism rather than vice versa.

The issue presents a myriad of social, economic and political facets, and in its ramifications could have far-reaching consequences,[43] but the relevant aspects for our present purposes are the linguistic ones. Linguistic critique plays a major role in feminist political action, and feminist linguistic critique represents a powerful force for linguistic change, providing a good example of the type of intentional language change postulated by Mattheier to which we referred in Chapter 2.[44] In his study of language planning and social change,[45] Cooper acknowledges the importance of the feminist critique by using it as one of the four basic case studies on which he bases his analysis.

When looking at the effects of the feminist movement on language development, we can at one level simply record the way in which the re-emergence of feminist awareness has helped enrich the vocabulary, giving us for example new derogatory terms such as *Emanze* and *Chauvi* or new analytical concepts such as 'androcentricity', but the mechanical recording of such items can only be a preliminary to a consideration of the strategies for language change developed to counter the ways in which language is perceived as being an instrument of sexual discrimination and oppression – in other words, as a means of exercising domination and power. The concern for and with these aspects is well documented, and has given rise to an increasing number of publications, which provide further evidence of what can be called a body of 'politically committed linguistics' in West Germany, in which linguists deploy their academic skills and expertise in support of their political convictions.[46]

The feminist linguistic analysis rests on two theses: the first is that language – in this case the German language – is systemically discriminatory in its usage and suppresses the existence of women, and the second is that male conversational strategies towards women represent a form of violence. In the present study we shall concentrate on the specifically German manifestations of the first thesis; the second is of more general significance, as evidenced by the reception by German linguists of work produced in the Anglo-American tradition.[47]

The contention that the German language is constitutive of discrimination against women is derived at least in part from the gender system of the language and from the morphology of feminine nouns, and can be summed up in the claim that women are 'invisible' in the language and that often, when they do 'emerge', it is as an appendage of the male. A further aspect of discrimination, it is claimed, rests in the construction of names and modes of address. Let us therefore examine the analysis, and then consider a counter-analysis before proceeding to an account of some of the linguistic strategies developed to counter the discrimination.

German displays three grammatical genders, traditionally classified as 'masculine', 'feminine' and 'neuter', marked in the nominative singular by the definite articles *der*, *die* and *das*, and although there is some correspondence between natural and grammatical gender (*der Mann*, *die Frau*), the two do not coincide completely. The application of this aspect of German grammar gives rise to two bones of contention for feminists.

The first is that in some cases, female persons are referred by 'neuter' nouns (*das Mädchen*, *das Fräulein*), which comes about because diminutives (marked by the suffixes '-chen' and '-lein') are always neuter; the problem is aggravated by the fact that there are no corresponding 'male' diminutives *Knechtlein/Knäblein* and *Herrlein* used in the same manner. The particular bone of contention has been that the diminutive *Fräulein* was conventionally used as a mode of address for unmarried women – and we shall return to this point when we consider the wider question of modes of address.

The second, and greater, problem is that of the 'androcentric generic', i.e., the way in which the masculine form is deployed as the generic form and, connected with this, the status of the indefinite third-person singular pronoun 'man' (corresponding to the French *on* or the English 'one'). Instances of the androcentric generic are legion, including the nationality statement in the front of a German passport that 'Der Inhaber dieses Passes ist Deutscher', regardless of the gender of the bearer, and there is a consistent use of the generic masculine in the Constitution – including the titles of the offices of state and parliament – thus the Speaker of the *Bundestag* is *Der Bundestagspräsident*, a title which gave rise to some controversy when a woman was appointed to the office for the first time.   Another area in which the androcentric generic has consistently been observed is in job titles and the situations-vacant columns, and this brings us straight to the question of noun morphology and the formation of female denotations.

We shall restrict ourselves in the main to job titles and descriptions, as these seem central to the feminist concerns and therefore form the main data for this study. Morphologically, the items in question correspond to one of three main patterns:

1. derivates (root + affix(es)) – e.g., (a) *lehr-* (teach) + *er = Lehrer*
   (b) (inflected form) *delegier-* + *–t +e/er = Delegierte(r)*
2. compounds – e.g., *kauf-* + *mann = Kaufmann* (merchant)
3. 'monoliths' (often of foreign derivation), e.g., Arzt (doctor), Chirurg (surgeon).

In the cases 1 (a) and 3, a feminine form is typically derived by adding the suffix '-in', thus *Lehrer* → *Lehrerin, Arzt* → *Ärztin*; in case 2, if the compounding element '*mann*' is used, then the corresponding feminine designation is inserted, thus *Kaufmann* → *Kauffrau*, or the '*-in*' derivation applies if the defined element allows of this, thus *Hausmeister* (caretaker) → *Hausmeisterin*; finally, in case 1 (b), the resultant noun is declined according to gender, i.e., *ein Delegierter, eine Delegierte*, etc. There are gaps in the system, and certain mismatches: for example, in the case of nurses there is a form *Krankenschwester*, but no longer any corresponding *Krankenbruder* – instead, the form *Krankenpfleger* is used (which then permits the derived form *Krankenpflegerin!*), and although there is a morphological pair *Sekretär* – *Sekretärin*, there is now no semantic equivalence; in German, *Sekretär* is only found in compounds such as *Generalsekretär*[48], which denote a prestigious position, which is more than can be said of the lowly post of a *Sekretärin*.

Article 3 of the German Constitution lays down that men and women have equal rights[49] and outlaws sexual discrimination; supporting legislation in the field of employment is provided by Article 611 of the *Bürgerliches Gesetzbuch* (Civil Code), which was revised in 1980 in line with an EC Directive from 1978.[50] Although Article 611 BGB specifies that vacancies 'shall not' be advertised as only for men or only for women,[51] this is not consistently applied, particularly in the private sector. For this reason, situations-vacant advertisements in Germany provide a valuable corpus for gauging changes in job titles and descriptions. Even a cursory perusal of the situations-vacant columns of the German press will reveal a lack of uniformity in the treatment of job titles and descriptions in respect of masculine and feminine forms within the spectrum provided by the feminine form and the masculine form.

At each end of the spectrum, one finds titles which are clearly intended to signify that a woman or a man is 'required' for the post – e.g., a woman as a childminder – 'Kinderpflegerin/ Erzieherin für 4 Kinder in Dauerstellung gesucht', or a retired police*man* for some unspecified (security?) task abroad – 'Polizei-beamter a.D. für verantwortungsvolle Aufgabe im Ausland'.[52]

Then posts are advertised using only the masculine form for which – in principle – women could also be considered, for example as Export Manager in the machine-tool industry; in some advertisements of this type, the generic nature of the title is acknowledged in the details of the post by including women in the candidate pool – thus in an advertisement for a Section Head for Overheads Control, the post is classified as that of an *Abteilungsleiter*, but further on we read 'Als ideale/r Bewerber/in sind Sie ...',[53] i.e., an attempt has been made to include both forms and not to exclude women – although this concession is some-times made rather grudgingly, as in an advertisement for a Person-nel Manager (*Personalleiter*), where the consultant handling the appointment writes 'Der geeignete Bewerber zwischen 30 und 40 – auch Damen besitzen eine Chance – ...'[54] ('ladies *also* have a chance'). The attempt to include both genders, however, can lead to linguistic clumsiness – thus in the formulation 'Als ideale/r Bewerber/in', the masculine ending forms an appendage to the adjective, but the feminine ending forms an appendage to the

noun, which gives rise to a mis-match – a further exanple of which
will be noted later.

The formulation 'als ideale/r Bewerber/in' brings us to the third
variant, the use of both the feminine and the masculine forms in
the job heading – for example heading a service team for trade
fairs as a *Messebauleiter/in*,[55] and in advertisements for posts in the
public sector, the use of both forms is now mandatory. There
appear to be three main ways of handling this 'dual form': either
the '-in' suffix is separated by a stroke (/), or it is placed in brackets
(e.g., *Chemie-Ingenieur(in)*[56]), or both full forms are used (e.g.,
Diplomchemiker Diplomchemikerin[57]). In the latter case, the masculine form is usually placed first, although this then leads to
problems with the syntax, as can be seen from the formulation
'die Stelle einer/eines Diplom-Theologen/in',[58] in which the feminine form of the indefinite article appears first, but the feminine
noun ending appears as an appendage of the masculine; in the
case of the *Messebauleiter/in*, the attempt to handle the two forms
leads to some confusion in the phrase 'Von unsere(er)em
zukünftigen Leiter/in ...', where an extra 'e' has crept into the
possessive – which acquires a form no grammar would recognise.
The more elegant formulations often appear to be those where the
feminine form is accorded precedence, as in 'Die Wahren-
dorffschen Kliniken ... suchen ... eine/n Oberärztin/ Ober-arzt',
where it is possible to maintain a sequence feminine – masculine,
but to have the reverse sequence would require a repetition of the
whole indefinite article (*einen Oberarzt/eine Oberärztin*).

A fourth strategy which some advertisers deploy is to avoid the
use of gender-specific formulations, for example by using 'neutral'
job headings – e.g., 'Geschäftsleitungsaufgabe. Kaufmännische
und technische Verantwortung bei ...' and then addressing potential applicants in the second person – 'Sie verfügen über gute
betriebswirtschaftliche Kenntnisse ...'.[59] In advertisements such as
this one, however, and in some of those which use both masculine
and feminine forms, one finds certain stereotypes being perpetu-
ated in the 'small print'; at the risk of parodying, one could suggest
that if applicants are to be 'young, charming and adaptable', then
the advertiser is more likely to be thinking in terms of a female,
whereas if applicants are required to be 'independent, assertive,
with qualities of leadership', these are often regarded as 'male'
attributes.[60]

This confusion of forms is, it is suggested, typical of a time of linguistic change, in which concurrent forms co-exist until some measure of consensus has been established. So much is clear, however: with the large number of different forms existing, it is very difficult to maintain that the masculine form in job advertisements is still being used as a generic, because each advertisement where only the masculine form is used has to be seen in the context of other advertisements which specify both forms.

The counter-analysis rests on two main points. The first is that, with reference to the 'androcentric generic', the proponents of change are committing a basic error in confusing 'grammatical' and 'natural' gender, and that the 'problem' would not exist if genders were labelled with neutral terms such as 'one', 'two' and 'three'. The weaker form of this argument is that the generic really does include both male and female equally. Unfortunately, however, this interpretation takes insufficient account of both reference and usage. The first problem is that of the 'unmarked masculine'; the masculine form serves a dual function – as male and generic reference – while the feminine form only serves for female reference. That is, the masculine form can be used to exclude the female, but not to exclude the male; as Trömel-Plötz points out, a sentence such as 'Alle Schweizer haben das Wahlrecht' could have exclusively male reference at a time when the Swiss constitution did not allow for female suffrage, and a sentence such as 'Alle Schweizer außer den Frauen wurden eingeladen' (All the Swiss were invited except for the women) would be permissible, while one such as 'Alle Schweizer außer den Männern wurden eingeladen' (All the Swiss were invited except for the men) would be regarded as deviant.[61]

The second point on which the counter-analysis rests is that linguistic phenomena such as those discussed above simply refer existing discrimination without reinforcing it or contributing to it; this of course is another version of the position that language simply reflects or mediates a reality which exists independently of it, and that if one could find ways of eradicating discrimination, then language use would no longer be felt to be discriminatory either. With reference to job titles, a similar line of argument runs that most managing directors and other senior executives are male, so the use of a masculine form simply reflects an existing reality. What such arguments deny is that language is in any way constitutive of reality, and that language change can be an element in social change. That, however, is not the position which is being taken up here; we have already provided evidence to suggest that language plays a significant role in forming perceptions and that social change and language change are codeterminant, and we shall now argue that the types of linguistic change which feminist language strategies seek to effect are indeed a powerful factor in changing social attitudes.

The changes concern three main areas: modes of address, generic forms and the impersonal third person pronoun 'man'.

The principal controversy in the first area surrounds the title *Fräulein*; the objections are based firstly on its form (as a diminutive), and secondly on the fact that it traditionally implied unmarried status, whereas the address *Herr* for a male is neutral as regards marital status. The feminist objective was to establish *Frau* as a general form for all women, regardless of marital status, and one can state with some confidence that this objective has now been achieved. For some feminists, however, this is still not enough; there have been efforts before the courts to establish that the equivalent to *Herr* is in fact *Dame* not *Frau*, but (so far) they have been unsuccessful.

With generic forms, the objective appears to be to establish an equal status for the feminine form of nouns, and to cancel the status of the androcentric generic. The evidence of the situations-vacant columns – especially for posts in the public service – would suggest that this 'campaign' is also meeting with some success, and that it is becoming less possible to claim generic status for the masculine form. The problem that arises here, however, is whether this means that the generic form *per se* disappears, or whether a different generic is introduced. Using both forms in job advertisements or written documents generally is all well and good – although it does, as we have seen, lead to some syntactic confusion and infelicitous formulations – but the system becomes somewhat clumsy in the spoken mode. There is a school of thought which argues that the feminine form should be established as the generic, and morphologically there are arguments in favour of this, as the feminine form does in fact 'embrace' the male.[62] This, however, then gives rise to the converse problem of distinguishing the feminine form from the generic – in the same way that traditionally it was impossible to distinguish the generic from the masculine. One solution which has been proposed, and which can be observed in *die tageszeitung – taz* is the use of the feminine form with a capital on the suffix – e.g., 'Student*I*nnen' – as a generic, which again works perfectly well in writing, but causes problems in the spoken mode. Incidentally, the use of the '-In' form again seems to be functioning as one of those shibboleths by which one can establish one's 'progressive' credentials.

The use of the impersonal *man* is another aspect of the generic discussion which has been the subject of efforts at reform. Attempts have been made, for example, to replace it with *frau* or with *mensch*, but they do not appear to have led to the kind of change which can be observed in the case of gender-specific noun forms, and apparently there is a danger of 'frau' being used in a patronising way by at least some men.[63]

In the same way that the feminist linguistic critique is part of a wider campaign to counter perceived sexual discrimination, the specific linguistic reforms outlined above have to be seen as part of a wider scenario which has institutional implications. It is becoming increasingly common in public authorities to appoint *Frauenbeauftragte* (women's officers) to oversee the success of anti-discrimination measures, and part of their remit is often to monitor official documents for instances of discriminatory language use. Official guidelines are laid down for this purpose – for example, on 3 September 1985 the Bremen Senate issued a decree governing the equal treatment of women and men in official forms,[64] in which *inter alia* it is specifically laid down that both feminine and masculine forms are to be stated, and that the masculine form cannot be regarded as a generic.[65]

The fundamental questions of whether discrimination can be removed by legislation and whether the removal of perceivedly discriminatory forms from language will lead to the eradication of discrimination are ultimately not ones which are amenable to simple answers; in the interaction between 'language' and 'society' it is a mistake to expect monocausality or unidirectionality. What can be said, however, is that the type of intentional language change which a feminist linguistic critique is attempting to achieve will at least help to remove linguistic forms which some members of the speech community find offensive. It is to be hoped that it will go further and will influence attitudes and non-linguistic social behaviour, if only by raising the level of awareness of the speech community and drawing attention to tacit and implicit forms of discrimination; it should, however, do more, because it will affect the stereotypes which language incorporates and will thus influence linguistically constructed value-systems.

Conclusion

The above three case studies have been presented for a dual purpose. The first was to complete the chronological account of significant politico-linguistic issues in Germany up to the beginning of German unification in the autumn of 1989, and the second was to illustrate a further facet of the relationships between language, perception and 'reality' by providing evidence of how perceptions can be influenced and 'realities' constituted through intentional linguistic innovation and change in a process which in two instances we chose to call 'semantic engineering'.

All three represent a form of conscious language planning in the sense of Mattheier's category of 'intentional language change', and in all of them an attempt is being made to effect language change for political purposes in order to influence perceived realities.

In the first two of the cases presented, there was a clearly identifiable non-linguistic background – Europe was (and still is) bristling with thermonuclear weapons of mass destruction, and some 'demonstrators' at Wackersdorf were taking counter-measures to protect themselves against the risk of physical assault by superior-armed police forces. However, until the background was structured, linguistically constituted, it remained undefined, perceptually amorphous. By the process of linguistic constitution, it could be categorised and thus politically activated in such a way that further consequences could ensue (a weapons build-up in the one case, the prospect of further legislation and criminalisation in the other).

The third case was different, and in some ways more complex: the 'background' again was identifiable, for example in the form of certain power structures (and employment patterns), but the question was not solely one of how that was then to be linguistically constituted so that further action could then ensue. The proposition was rather that the background itself was at least in part linguistically constituted, so that a linguistic restructuring was an essential element in the initiation of non-linguistic change.

Notes

1 Longer-Range Intermediate Nuclear Forces

2 'Die SS-20-Rakete ist eine grundlegende Neuerung und keine Modernisierung im sowjetischen Raketenpotential' Der Bundesminister der Verteidigung (ed.), *Weißbuch 1979. Zur Sicherheit der Bundesrepublik Deutschland und zur Entwicklung der Bundeswehr*, Bonn, 1979. The present study is not the appropriate place to embark upon an extended critique of the NATO position, but the tenor of the argument should indicate a certain scepticism towards it

3 Some of which, for example, have been treated in A. Burkhardt, F.Hebel and R.Hoberg (eds), *Sprache zwischen Militär und Frieden: Aufrüstung der Begriffe?*, Tübingen, 1989

4 Cf. M. Townson, 'Anglizismen in der Sprache der Verteidigungspolitik', *Muttersprache*, Bd. 96, Heft 5–6, 1986

5 E.g., in section 7: 'Die Minister haben daher beschlossen, das LRNTF-Potential der NATO durch die Dislozierung von amerikanischen boden-gestützten Systemen in Europa zu modernisieren.' Quoted from *Weißbuch 1983*, p. 194

6 I.e., in sections 140, 147, 357, 358, 360

7 *Vorrüstung, vorrüsten* are words which go back beyond the nineteenth century (they are to be found, for example, in both Campe's and Grimms' dictionaries), but basically they were RÜST[1] words, virtually synonymous with *Vorbereitung, vorbereiten* (preparation, prepare).

8 For a discussion of the development of the term in this context, see M. Wengeler, 'Nachrüstung – Von der Legitimationsvokabel zum "vorbelasteten Begriff"', Burkhardt *et al.*, *Sprache zwischen Militär und Frieden*, pp. 233–45

9 For a fuller account of the history and function of the *Weißbücher*, see C. Conrad , 'Sprachliche Aspekte der Wende in der Sicherheitspolitik', Burkhardt *et al.*, *Sprache zwischen Militär und Frieden*, pp. 125–46 and M. Townson, 'Das *Weißbuch 1983* und das *Statement on the Defence Estimates 1986* – zwei Beispiele zur Abschreckung' , Burkhardt *et al.*, *Sprache zwischen Militär und Frieden*, pp. 147–63, esp. 150f

10 'Mit dem Doppelbeschluß wurde erstmals der Versuch unternommen, die Kette von Vorrüstung und Nachrüstung zu unterbrechen und statt dessen Abrüstung zu vereinbaren'. *Weißbuch 1983*, p. 222

11 As recorded in F. Duve (ed.), *Die Nachrüstungsdebatte im Deutschen Bundestag*, Reinbek bei Hamburg, 1984

12 'Der Deutsche Bundestag erinnert daran, daß das Bündnis trotz einer massiv betriebenen sowjetischen Vorrüstung mit modernen Mittelstrecken-raketen vier Jahre lang auf die Nachrüstung verzichtet und sich ernsthaft um Verhandlungen und ein für beide Seiten annehmbares Ergebnis bemüht hat'. *Antrag der Fraktionen der CDU/CSU und FDP*, Bundestagsdrucksache 10/620, quoted from *Die Nachrüstungsdebatte im Deutschen Bundestag*, p. 272

13 *Die Nachrüstungsdebatte im Deutschen Bundestag*, p. 147

14 *Die Nachrüstungsdebatte im Deutschen Bundestag*, p. 95

15 This is perhaps hardly surprising, given that Helmut Schmidt was one of the guiding spirits behind the 'dual-track decision'

16 *Die Nachrüstungsdebatte im Deutschen Bundestag*, p. 146

17 Graffiti often provide examples of a high level of creativity in political discourse

18 For a concise account of the change from the 'dynamic' peace concept of the SPD to security policy as a maintenance of the status quo under Kohl, see Conrad, 'Sprachliche Aspekte der Wende in der Sicherheitspolitik', esp. pp. 142-3

19 *Die Nachrüstungsdebatte im Deutschen Bundestag*, p. 58

20 *Die Nachrüstungsdebatte im Deutschen Bundestag*, pp. 36-8

21 *Die Nachrüstungsdebatte im Deutschen Bundestag*, p. 37

22 'Was soll eigentlich die Kreml-Herren bewegen, auf ihre kostspieligen Raketen, mit denen sie Europa beherrschen wollen, zu verzichten, solange sie hoffen können, mit Hilfe der Friedensbewegung und nun auch noch mit Ihrer (i.e., 'der SPD') Hilfe aus der Alternative "Abrüstung oder Nachrüstung" entlassen zu werden?' *Die Nachrüstungsdebatte im Deutschen Bundestag*, p. 50

23 *Die Nachrüstungsdebatte im Deutschen Bundestag*, p. 12

24 *Die Nachrüstungsdebatte im Deutschen Bundestag*, pp. 57f

25 'für mich (gehören) zur Friedensbewegung die jungen Polizeibeamten, die draußen gegenüber Gewalttätern augenblicklich die Freiheit der Entscheidung unseres deutschen Parlaments sichern. Zu der Friedensbewegung, die ich meine, gehören die Soldaten unserer Bundeswehr, die die Freiheit der Wahlentscheidung in diesem Lande sichern.' *Die Nachrüstungsdebatte im Deutschen Bundestag*, p. 58

26 'Ich möchte in diesem Zusammenhang auch den fünf Millionen Männern danken, die ihren Wehrdienst geleistet haben und sich damit an einer aktiven Friedenspolitik beteiligt haben. Sie sind eine Friedensbewegung unserer Demokratie.' *Die Nachrüstungsdebatte im Deutschen Bundestag*, p. 88

27 Burgmann (Grüne): '... Wenn im Bundestag heute über Frieden geredet wird, dann muß ich feststellen, daß draußen Krieg herrscht. Mit unheimlich brutalem Polizeieinsatz wird draußen demonstriert, was diese Regierung unter Frieden versteht.' *Die Nachrüstungsdebatte im Deutschen Bundestag*, p. 32

28 (Burgmann): 'Wer hier mit Raketen, mit Gewalt den Frieden will, der wird den Unfrieden in diesem Lande schaffen.' *Die Nachrüstungsdebatte im Deutschen Bundestag*, p. 34

29 Frau Beck-Oberdorf (Grüne): '... Sie halten Freiheit für wichtiger als Frieden, und das zeugt von einer falschen Rangordnung der Werte; denn angesichts der Möglichkeit eines Atomkrieges oder der unvorstellbaren Zerstörungen eines konventionellen Krieges kann Freiheit durch Krieg nicht mehr gesichert werden.' *Die Nachrüstungsdebatte im Deutschen Bundestag*, p. 226

30 For an account of the development of environmental awareness in the West German state, see for example U. Margedant, 'Entwicklung des Umweltbewußtseins in der Bundesrepublik Deutschland', *Aus Politik und Zeitgeschichte*, B.29/87, pp. 15-28

31 Probably only matched by the Germans' addiction to the motor car

32 A condition originally attached to a demonstration planned for 26 December 1986

33 'Demonstration' is in fact not a legally recognised term in German

34 Artikel 8 [Versammlungsfreiheit] (1) Alle Deutschen haben das Recht, sich ohne Anmeldung oder Erlaubnis friedlich und ohne Waffen zu versammeln. (2) Für Versammlungen unter freiem Himmel kann dieses Recht durch Gesetz oder auf Grund eines Gesetzes beschränkt werden. *Grundgesetz für die Bundesrepublik Deutschland*, Textausgabe. Stand: Oktober 1990, Bonn 1990

35 Cf. the comments p. 202 above: 'In the Federal Republic, politics is regarded as the monopoly of the political establishment, it is essentially mediated by the state'

36 The fear of violence has been vindicated on more than one occasion by fatal shootings at demonstrations; for example, on 2 June 1967 the student Benno Ohnesorg was shot dead in Berlin by a police officer during protests against a visit by the Shah of Iran, and two policemen were shot during protest demonstrations against the building of a new runway at Frankfurt Airport in 1985

37 'Vollstreckungsmaßnahmen eines Trägers von Hoheitsbefugnissen abzuwehren'. *Frankfurter Rundschau*, 2 December 1987

38 These are not to be confused with *Verteidigungswaffen* – 'defensive weapons'

39 Cf., for example, the relevant entry in the *Brockhaus* of 1895: 'Schutzwaffen: tragbare Deckungsmittel, die im Altertum und Mittelalter zum Schutz des Körpers gegen die Angriffswaffen dienten; sie zerfielen in Helm, Rüstung und Schild.' *Brockhaus Konversations-Lexikon*, Vol. 14, Leipzig 1895, p. 660

40 This definition is derived from a reply from the Bavarian Ministry of the Interior to a query from Dr Wolfgang Teubert from the Institut für Deutsche Sprache in Mannheim; I am very grateful to Dr Teubert for providing data on which this case study is based. His paper has been published as W. Teubert, 'Politische Vexierwörter' in Klein, *Politische Semantik*, pp. 51–68

41 'new', because back in Wilhelmine Germany there was a women's movement, which, for example, Ludwig Thoma was satirising in an article '"Amalie

Mettenleitner". Ein Beitrag zur Frauenbewegung' in: *Simplicissimus*, 4 March 1899, pp. 18f

42 E. Kolinsky, 'The SPD and the second "Fräuleinwunder"' in Kolinsky and Gaffney, *Political Culture*, pp. 221f

43 For example in the definition of 'work' and the way in which the product of economically relevant activity is computed

44 Cf. Chapter 2, pp. 42ff above

45 R. Cooper, *Language Planning and Social Change*, Cambridge, 1989

46 Similar developments from other disciplines can be seen, for example, in the emergence of the Union of Concerned Scientists in the USA and of the Medical Campaign against Nuclear Weapons and Scientists against Nuclear Arms in Britain

47 For example, of the seventeen contributions to S. Trömel-Plötz (ed.), *Gewalt durch Sprache. Die Vergewaltigung von Frauen in Gesprächen*, Frankfurt, 1984, ten are translations of papers originally produced in English

48 *Sekretär* is, however, used in Austria, but there it is used more in the sense of 'functionary' (e.g., in a trade union) and is thus still indicative of a different status

49 '2. Männer und Frauen sind gleichberechtigt 3. Niemand darf wegen seines Geschlechtes ... benachteiligt oder bevorzugt werden.' *Grundgesetz für die Bundesrepublik Deutschland*

50 'Gesetz über die Gleichbehandlung von Männern und Frauen am Arbeitsplatz und über die Erhaltung von Ansprüchen bei Betriebsübergang (Arbeitsrechtliches EG-Anpassungsgesetz) vom 13 August 1980', *Bundesgesetzblatt*, Teil 1, p. 1308

51 'Der Arbeitgeber soll einen Arbeitsplatz weder öffentlich noch innerhalb des Betriebes nur für Männer oder nur für Frauen ausschreiben', § 611b BGB – whereby the modal *soll* does not have the force of *darf*

52 Both examples from the *Frankfurter Allgemeine Zeitung (FAZ)*, 1 June 1991, p. V66

53 *FAZ*, p. V55

54 *FAZ*, p. V19

55 *FAZ*, p. V55

56 *FAZ*, p. V62

57 *Die Zeit*, 24 May 1991, p. 42

58 *Die Zeit*, 24 May 1991, p. 43

59 *FAZ*, 1 June 1991, p. V55

60 Cf. E. Brockhoff, 'Wie fragt Mann nach Frauen' , *Die Zeit*, 2 January 1987

61 Trömel-Plötz, *Gewalt durch Sprache*, pp. 55f

62 One is reminded here of the analysis of French adjectives which works from the feminine form as the base, from which the masculine form is derived by deletion, instead of trying to derive the feminine form from the masculine by addition. Cf. S.A. Schane, *French Phonology and Morphology*, Cambridge (Mass.), 1968, pp. 2–4

63 According to Gerhard Stickel, Director of the Institut für Deutsche Sprache, in a personal communication

64 *Runderlaß des Senats der Freien Hansestadt Bremen über die Gleichbehandlung von Frauen und Männern in Vordrucken vom 3. September 1985.* Similar regulations have been issued in the other federal states as well

65 '4. Die männliche Form einer Bezeichnung kann grundsätzlich *nicht* als ein Oberbegriff angesehen werden, der weibliche und männliche Personen einschließt'

Selective bibliography

H.-P. Althaus, H. Henne and H.-E. Wiegand, (eds) *Lexikon der Germanistischen Linguistik* (Studienausgabe), Tübingen, 1980, 2nd edn.

U. Ammon, *Probleme der Soziolinguistik*, Tübingen, 1971

S -G. Andersson, 'Deutsche Standardsprache – drei oder vier Varianten?', *Muttersprache* 93, 1983, pp. 259–83

R. Bachem, *Einführung in die Analyse politischer Texte*, Munich, 1979

R. Bachem, 'Rechtsradikale Sprechmuster der 80er Jahre. Eine Studie zum Sprachgebrauch der "harten NS-Gruppen" und ihnen nahestehender Rechtsextremisten,' *Muttersprache*, 93, 1983, pp. 59–81

W. Bahner and K-E. Heidolph, W. Neumann and J. Schildt (eds), *Jacob und Wilhelm Grimm als Sprachwissenschaftler. Geschichtlichkeit und Aktualität ihres Wirkens*, Berlin, 1985

W. Bahner/W. Neumann (eds), *Sprachwissenschaftliche Germanistik. Ihre Herausbildung und Begründung*, Berlin, 1985

G. Bauer, *Sprache und Sprachlosigkeit im 'Dritten Reich'*, Cologne, 1988

H. Bechtel, *Wirtschafts- und Sozialgeschichte Deutschlands*, Munich, 1967

G. Beck, *Sprechakte und Sprachfunktionen. Untersuchungen zur Handlungsstruktur der Sprache und ihren Grenzen*, Tübingen, 1980

O. Behagel, *Geschichte der deutschen Sprache*, Strasbourg, 1911, 3rd edn

M. Behland, 'Nationale u. nationalistische Tendenzen in Vorreden zu wissenschaftlichen Werken ', B. v. Wiese and R. Henß (eds), *Nationalismus in Germanistik und Dichtung*, Berlin, 1967, pp. 334–46

M. Behrens, W. Dieckmann and E. Kehl, 'Politik als Sprachkampf. Zur konservativen Sprachkritik und Sprachpolitik seit 1972', J. H. Heringer (ed.), *Holzfeuer im hölzernen Ofen. Aufsätze zur politischen Sprachkritik*, Tübingen, 1982, pp. 216–65

W. Bergsdorf (ed.), *Wörter als Waffen. Sprache als Mittel der Politik*, Stuttgart, 1979

C. Berning, *Vom 'Abstammungsnachweis' zum 'Zuchtwart'. Vokabular des Nationalsozialismus*, Bern, 1964

H. Bernsmeier, 'Der Deutsche Sprachverein im "Dritten Reich"',
   Muttersprache, xciii (1983), pp. 35–58
H. Berschin, *Deutschland – ein Name im Wandel*, Munich/Vienna,
   1979
W. Besch, O. Reichman and S. Sonderegger (eds), *Sprachgeschichte.
   Ein Handbuch zur Geschichte der deutschen Sprache und ihrer
   Erforschung*, 2 vols, Berlin/New York, 1984–5
E. Blackall, *The Emergence of German as a Literary Language*,
   Cambridge, 1959
K. Bochmann (ed.), *Eigenschaften und linguistische Analyse politischer
   Texte*, Berlin 1986
H. Böhme, *An Introduction to the Social and Economic History of
   Germany. Politics and Economic Change in the Nineteenth and
   Twentieth Centuries*, transl. by W. R. Lee, Oxford, 1978 (orig.
   *Prologomena zu einer Sozial- und Wirtschaftsgeschichte
   Deutschlands*, Frankfurt 1972)
S. Bork, *Mißbrauch der Sprache. Tendenzen nationalsozialistischer
   Sprachregelung*, Bern/Munich, 1970
K.-H. Brackmann and R. Birkenhauer, *NS-Deutsch.
   'Selbstverständliche' Begriffe und Schlagwörter aus der Zeit des
   Nationalsozialismus*, Straelen, 1988
H. Brekle and U. Maas (eds), *Sprachwissenschaft und Volkskunde.
   Perspektiven einer kulturanalytischen Sprachbetrachtung*, Opladen,
   1986
E. Brinkmann to Broxten, 'Der allgemeine Mensch ist immer
   männlich', *Der Sprachdienst*, 5/1990, pp. 141–48
P. Brückner, *Versuch, uns und anderen die Bundesrepublik zu erklären*,
   Berlin, 1978
O. Brunner, W. Conze and R. Koselleck (eds), *Geschichtliche
   Grundbegriffe. Historisches Lexikon zur politisch-sozialen Sprache in
   Deutschland*, Stuttgart, first published 1972
A. Burkhardt (ed.), *Hochschule und Rüstung. Ein Beitrag von
   Wissenschaftlern der Technischen Hochschule Darmstadt zur
   ("Nach"-) Rüstungsdebatte*, Darmstadt, 1984
A. Burkhardt, F. Hebel and R. Hoberg (eds), *Sprache zwischen Militär
   und Frieden: Aufrüstung der Begriffe?*, Tübingen, 1989
J. H. Campe, *Wörterbuch zur Erklärung und Verdeutschung der unserer
   Sprache aufgedrungenen fremden Ausdrücke. Ein Ergänzungsband zu
   Adelungs Wörterbuche*, Bd. 1, 2, Braunschweig, 1801. Neue stark
   vermehrte und durchgängig verbesserte Ausgabe, Braunschweig,
   1813
J. H. Campe, *Ueber die Reinigung und Bereicherung der Deutschen
   Sprache. Dritter Versuch welcher den von dem königl. Preuß*

Gelehrtenverein zu Berlin ausgesetzten Preis erhalten hat,
Braunschweig, 1794

F. Capra, *The Turning Point. Science, society and the rising culture,* New
York, 1983

M. Cattaneo, 'Sprachanalyse und Politologie', R. Schmidt (ed.),
Methoden der Politologie, Darmstadt, 1967, pp. 330–48

D. Cherubim, 'Sprachentwicklung und Sprachkritik im 19.
Jahrhundert. Beiträge zur Konstitution einer pragmatischen
Sprachgeschichte', Th. Cramer (ed.), *Literatur und Sprache im
historischen Prozeß* – Band 2 Sprache, Tübingen, 1983, pp. 170–
88

D. Cherubim, G. Objartel and I. Chikorsky, '"Geprägte Form, die
lebend sich entwickelt", Beobachtungen zu institutsbezogenen
Texten des 19. Jhdts.', *Wirkendes Wort* 2/87, pp. 144–76

D. Cherubim and K. Mattheier (eds), *Voraussetzungen und Grundlagen
der Gegenwartssprache. Sprach- und sozialgeschichtliche
Untersuchungen zum 19. Jahrhundert,* Berlin, 1989

P. Chilton, 'Orwell, Language and Linguistics', *Language and
Communication,* Vol. 4, No. 2, 1984, pp. 129–46

N. Chomsky, *Deterring Democracy,* Cambridge, 1990

H. Christmann (ed.), *Sprachwissenschaft des 19. Jahrhunderts,*
Darmstadt, 1977

M. Clyne, *Language and Society in the German-speaking countries,*
Cambridge, 1984

C. Conrad, 'Sprachliche Aspekte der Wende in der
Sicherheitspolitik', Burkhardt *et al., Sprache zwischen Militär und
Frieden,* Tübingen, 1989, pp. 125–46

K. Conrady, W. Killy, E. Lämmert and P. v. Polenz, *Germanistik – eine
deutsche Wissenschaft,* Frankfurt am Main, 1971

R. Cooper, *Language Planning and Social Change,* Cambridge, 1989

E. Coseriu, *Sprachtheorie und Allgemeine Sprachwissenschaft,* Munich,
1975

F. Coulmas, *Sprache und Staat. Studien zu Sprachplanung und
Sprachpolitik,* Berlin, 1985

Th. Cramer (ed.), *Literatur und Sprache im historischen Prozeß* – Band
1: Literatur, Band 2: Sprache, Tübingen, 1983

W. Dahle, *Der Einsatz einer Wissenschaft. Eine sprachinhaltliche
Analyse militärischer Terminologie in der Germanistik 1933-1945,*
Bonn, 1969

F. Debus, M. Hellmann and H. Schlosser, *Sprachliche Normen und
Normierungsfolgen in der DDR,* Hildesheim, 1985

W. Dieckmann, 'Kritische Bemerkungen zum sprachlichen Ost–West-
Problem', *Zeitschrift für deutsche Sprache,* 23, 1967, pp. 136–65

W. Dieckmann, *Sprache in der Politik. Einführung in die Pragmatik und Semantik der politischen Sprache*, Heidelberg, 1969

W. Dieckmann, *Politische Sprache, politische Kommunikation*, Heidelberg, 1981

W. Dieckmann and P. Held, *Sprache und Kommunikation in politischen Institutionen. Interdisziplinäre Bibliographie zur politischen Sprache in der Bundesrepublik Deutschland 1975-1984 (1986)*, Berlin, 1986

W. Dieckmann, 'Deutsch-deutsche Sprachentwicklung', *Zeitschrift für Germanistische Linguistik*, 17. 2, 1989, pp. 162–81

H. Dunger, 'Wider die Engländerei in der deutschen Sprache', in: *Zeitschrift des Allgemeinen Deutschen Sprachvereins*, XIV, 12 December 1899, cols, 241–51

F. Duve (ed.), *Die Nachrüstungsdebatte im Deutschen Bundestag*, Reinbek bei Hamburg, 1984

M. Edelmann, *Political Language. Words that Succeed and Politics that Fail*, New York, 1977

H. Eggers, *Deutsche Sprachgeschichte*, Hamburg, 1963-77

H. Eggers (ed.), *Der Volksname deutsch*, Darmstadt, 1970

J. Erben, 'Jacob Grimm als Redner in der Paulskirche. Bemerkungen über Veränderungen im Stil der Abgeordnetenrede', *Zeitschrift für deutsche Philologie* 105, 1986/1, pp. 100–13

F. H. v. Eemeren, *Speech Acts in Argumentative Discourse*, Dordrecht, 1984

J. Ernst, *The Structure of Political Communication in the United Kingdom, the United States and the Federal Republic of Germany*, Frankfurt, 1988

I. Fetscher and H. E. Richter (eds) *Worte machen keine Politik – Beiträge zu einem Kampf um politische Begriffe*, Reinbek, 1976

W. Fleischer, 'Die deutsche Sprache in der DDR. Grundsätzliche Überlegungen zur Sprachsituation', D. Nerius (ed.), *Entwicklungstendenzen der deutschen Sprache seit dem 18. Jahrhundert*, Berlin, 1983

W. Fleischer *et al.*, *Wortschatz der deutschen Sprache in der DDR. Fragen seines Aufbaus und seiner Verwendungsweise*, Leipzig, 1987

N. Frei and J. Schmitz, *Journalismus im Dritten Reich*, Munich, 1989

Friedrich-Ebert-Stiftung (ed.), *Politik und Sprachentwicklung in der DDR. Zu neuen Ufern*, Bonn, 1989

R. Glunk, 'Erfolg und Mißerfolg der nationalsozialistischen Sprachlenkung', in *Zeitschrift für Deutsche Sprache*, Vols. 22–7, 1966–71

M. Greiffenhagen (ed.), *Kampf um Wörter – Politische Begriffe im Meinungsstreit*, Munich/Vienna, 1980

F. Greß, *Germanistik und Politik. Kritische Beiträge zu einer nationalen*

Wissenschaft, Stuttgart, 1971

J. Grimm, *Geschichte der deutschen Sprache,* Leipzig, 1880 (Nachdruck der 4. Auflage – 2 Bde in 1 Band, Hildesheim: Olms, 1970)

J. Grimm and W. Grimm, *Deutsches Wörterbuch,* Bd 1, Leipzig, 1854; Bd 5, bearbeitet von Dr Rudolf Hildebrand, Leipzig, 1873

J. Grimm, 'Über den werth der ungenauen wissenschaften', *Kleinere Schriften,* Bd. VII, Hildesheim, 1966

R. Grosse and A. Neubert, *Soziolinguistische Aspekte der Theorie des Sprachwandels,* Berlin, 1982

H. Gründler, 'Kernenergiewerbung. Die sprachliche Verpackung der Atomenergie. Aus dem Wörterbuch des Zwiedenkens', *Literaturmagazin,* 8/1977, reprinted in K. Blanc, *Tatort Wort,* Munich, pp. 107–24

H. Grünert, *Politische Reden in Deutschland* Frankfurt, Berlin, 1976

H. Grünert, 'Politische Geschichte und Sprachgeschichte', in *Sprache und Literatur in Wissenschaft und Unterricht,* 14.2.1983, pp. 43–58

J. Habermas, *Strukturwandel der Öffentlichkeit. Untersuchungen zu einer Kategorie der bürgerlichen Gesellschaft,* Darmstadt/Neuwied, 1962 (transl. by T. Burger as *The Transformation of the Public Sphere,* Cambridge, 1989)

M. Halliday, *Language as social semiotics. The social interpretation of language and meaning,* London, 1978

M. Hartig, 'Sprachwandel und sozialer Wandel', Th. Cramer (ed.), *Literatur und Sprache im historischen Prozeß,* Tübingen, 1983, Vol. 2, pp. 189–201

U. Haß, 'Interessenabhängiger Umgang mit Wörtern in der Umweltdiskussion,' Klein, *Politische Semantik,* pp. 153–86

W. Haug, *Vom hilflosen Antifaschismus zur Gnade der späten Geburt,* Hamburg, Berlin 1987

M. Hausherr-Mälzer, *Die Sprache des Patriarchats,* Frankfurt, 1990

G. Helbig, *Geschichte der neueren Sprachwissenschaft,* Leipzig, 1986 (Nachdr. d. 1. Auflage)

M. Hellinger (ed.), *Sprachwandel und feministische Sprachpolitik: Internationale Perspektiven,* Opladen, 1985

M. Hellmann (ed.), *Öffentlicher Sprachgebrauch in der Bundesrepublik Deutschland und in der DDR,* Düsseldorf, 1973

M. Hellmann, 'Bemerkungen zur Entwicklung und zur gegenwärtigen Lage des Arbeitsgebietes "Ost–West-Sprachdifferenzierung"', *Mitteilungen des Instituts für Deutsche Sprache,* 11, 1985, pp. 76–92

M. Hellmann, 'Deutsche Sprache Ost und West', *Mitteilungen des Instituts für Deutsche Sprache,* 11, 1985, pp. 63–8

W. O. Henderson, *The State and the Industrial Revolution in Prussia*

1740–1870, Liverpool, 1967

H. Heringer (ed.), *Holzfeuer im hölzernen Ofen. Aufsätze zur politischen Sprachkritik*, Tübingen, 1982

H. Heringer, *"Ich gebe Ihnen mein Ehrenwort": Politik, Sprache, Moral*, Munich, 1990

F. Hermanns, 'Deontische Tautologien. Ein linguistischer Beitrag zur Interpretation des Godesberger Programms (1959) der Sozialdemokratischen Partei Deutschlands', Klein, *Politische Semantik*, pp. 69–149

E. Hobsbawm, *Nations and nationalism since 1780. Programme, myth, reality*, Cambridge, 1990

H. Jaeger, *Geschichte der Wirtschaftsordnung in Deutschland*, Frankfurt, 1988

J. Janota (ed.), *Eine Wissenschaft etabliert sich 1810-1870. Wissenschaftsgeschichte der Germanistik III*, Tübingen, 1980

F. Januschek (ed.), *Politische Sprachwissenschaft. Zur Analyse von Sprache als kultureller Praxis*, Opladen, 1985

C. Jochmann, *Über die Sprache*, Heidelberg, bei C. F. Winter, 1828

C. Jochmann, "Über die Öffentlichkeit", in *Allgemeine politische Annalen*. Neueste Folge, C. v. Rotteck (ed.) Erster Band, Zweites Heft, München/Stuttgart/Tübingen, in der J. G. Cotta'schen Buchhandlung. April 1830, pp. 105–43.

G.-K. Kaltenbrunner (ed.), *Sprache und Herrschaft*, Munich, 1975

G. Kettmann, 'Die Existenzformen der deutschen Sprache im 19. Jahrhundert', in Schildt *et al.*, *Die Auswirkungen*, 1981, pp. 35-97

M. Kinne and B. Strube-Edelmann, *Kleines Wörterbuch des DDR-Wortschatzes*, Düsseldorf, 1980, 2nd edn

A. Kirkness, 'Das Phänomen des Purismus in der Geschichte des Deutschen', W. Besch, O. Reichman and S. Sonderegger (eds) *Sprachgeschichte*, 290ff

M. Kitchen, *The Political Economy of Germany 1815-1914*, London, 1978

W. Klein (ed.), *Politische Semantik: bedeutungsanalytische und sprachkritische Beiträge zur politischen Sprachverwendung*, Opladen, 1989

V. Klemperer, *LTI. Notizbuch eines Philologen*. Leipzig, 1975

T. Kochs, 'Nationale Idee und nationalistisches Denken im Grimmschen Wörterbuch', B. v. Wiese and R. Henß (eds), *Nationalismus in Germanistik und Dichtung*, Berlin, 1967, pp. 273–84

E. Kolinsky, 'The SPD and the second "Fräuleinwunder" ' in Gaffney and Kolinsky, *Political Culture*, 1991, pp. 221f

E. Kolinsky and J. Gaffney (eds), *Political Culture in France and*

Germany: A Contemporary Perspective, London, 1991

K. Korn, *Sprache in der verwalteten Welt*, Freiburg i. B., 1959, Munich, 1962

O. Kronsteiner, 'Sind die *slovene* "die Redenden" und die *nemici* "die Stummen"? Zwei neue Etymologien zum Namen der Slawen und der Deutschen', in P. Weisinger (ed.), *Sprache und Name in Österreich*, Vienna, 1980, pp. 339ff.

G. Lakoff and M. Johnson, *Metaphors we live by*, Chicago, 1980

E. Lämmert, 'Germanistik – Eine deutsche Wissenschaft', B. v. Wiese and R. Henß (eds), *Nationalismus in Germanistik und Dichtung*, Berlin, 1967, pp. 15–36

G. Leech, *Semantics*, Harmondsworth, 1974

G. Leibniz, *Ermahnung an die Teutsche, ihren verstand und sprache besser zu üben, sammt beygefügten vorschlag einer Teutsch gesinten Gesellschaft* (*c.* 1630), reprinted in *Wissenschaftliche Beihefte zur Zeitschrift des Allgemeinen Deutschen Sprachvereins*, 4, 29, 1907

G. Leibniz, *Unvorgreiffliche Gedancken betreffend die Ausübung und Verbesserung der Teutschen Sprache*, reprinted in *Wissenschaftliche Beihefte zur Zeitschrift des Allgemeinen Deutschen Sprachvereins*, No. 30, April 1908, pp. 327ff

Th. Lewandowski, *Linguistisches Wörterbuch*, Heidelberg, Wiesbaden, 1985, 4th edn

P. Longerich (ed.), *'Was ist des Deutschen Vaterland?' Dokumente zur Frage der deutschen Einheit 1800-1990*, Munich, 1990

P. C. Ludz, *Mechanismen der Herrschaftssicherung. Eine sprachpolitische Analyse gesellschaftlichen Wandelns in der DDR*, Munich, Vienna, 1980

U. Maas, *"Als der Geist der Gemeinschaft eine Sprache fand." Sprache im Nationalsozialismus. Versuch einer historischen Argumentationsanalyse*, Opladen, 1984

U. Maas, 'Der kulturanalytische Zugang zur Sprachgeschichte', *Wirkendes Wort* 2/87, pp. 87-104

L. Mackensen, *Verführung durch Sprache*, Munich, 1973

H. Marcuse, *One Dimensional Man*, London, 1972

W. Maser, *Hitlers Mein Kampf. Entstehung, Aufbau, Stil, Änderungen, Quellen, Quellenwert, kommentierte Auszüge*, Rastatt, 1966, 1983

K. Mattheier, 'Allgemeine Aspekte einer Theorie des Sprachwandels', W. Besch, O. Reichman and S. Sonderegger (eds), *Sprachgeschichte. Ein Handbuch zur Geschichte der deutschen Sprache und ihrer Erforschung*, 1. Hbd 1984, 2. Hbd 1985, Berlin/ New York, pp. 720ff

K. Mattheier, 'Industrialisierung der Sprache. Historisch- soziologische Überlegungen zur Sprache im Industriebetrieb des

19. Jhdts', *Wirkendes Wort*, 2/87, pp. 130–44

Ministerium für Auswärtige Angelegenheiten der Deutschen Demokratischen Republik (ed.), *Beziehungen der Deutschen Demokratischen Republik zur Bundesrepublik Deutschland und zu Berlin (West)*, Berlin, 1990

H. Moser (ed.), *Das Aueler Protokoll. Deutsche Sprache im Spannungsfeld zwischen West und Ost*, Düsseldorf, 1964

C. Mueller, *The Politics of Communication*, New York, 1973

J. Müller, *Germanistik und deutsche Nation 1806–1848. Zur Konstitution bürgerlichen Bewußtseins*, Stuttgart, 1974

D. Nerius (ed.) *Entwicklungstendenzen der deutschen Sprache seit dem 18. Jahrhundert*, Berlin, 1983

E. Oksaar, 'Zum Prozeß des Sprachwandels: Dimensionen sozialer und linguistischer Variation', H. Moser *et al.* (eds), *Sprachwandel und Sprachgeschichtsschreibung. Jahrbuch 1976 des IDS.* Düsseldorf, 1987, pp. 98–117

M. Opitz, *Buch von der deutschen Poeterei*, Wilhelm Braune (ed.). Abdruck der ersten Ausgabe (1624), Tübingen

G. Orwell, *Nineteen Eighty-four*, Harmondsworth, 1983

F. Palmer, *Semantics. A new outline*, Cambridge, 1976

F. Pasierbsky, *Krieg und Frieden in der Sprache*, Frankfurt, 1983

W. Paterson, '*Vergangenheitsbewältigung* to the *Historikerstreit*', in Woods, R. (ed.) *Vergangenheitsbewältigung West und Ost*, Birmingham, 1989, pp. 27–37

P. v. Polenz, 'Sprachkritik und Sprachwissenschaft', *Neue Rundschau*, 74, 1963, pp. 381–403

P. v. Polenz, *Geschichte der deutschen Sprache*, Berlin, 1978

P. v. Polenz, 'Sozialgeschichtliche Aspekte der neueren deutschen Sprachgeschichte', Th. Cramer (ed.) (1983), *Literatur und Sprache im historischen Prozeß*, Tübingen, 1983, Bd. 2 pp. 3–24

P. v. Polenz, *Deutsche Satzsemantik. Grundbegriffe des Zwischen-den-Zeilen-Lesens*, Berlin, 1985

P. v. Polenz, 'Grundsätzliches zum Sprachwandel', *Der Deutschunterricht*, Jg. 38, 4, 1986, pp. 6ff

P. v. Polenz, '"Binnendeutsch" oder plurizentrische Sprachkultur? Ein Plädoyer für Normalisierung in der Frage der "nationalen" Varietäten', *Zeitschrift für Germanistische Linguistik*, 16, 1988, pp. 198–218

U. Pörksen, *Deutsche Naturwissenschaftssprachen. Historische und kritische Studien*, Tübingen, 1986

U. Pörksen, *Plastikwörter. Die Sprache einer internationalen Diktatur*, Stuttgart, 1988

L. Pusch, *Das Deutsche als Männersprache*, Frankfurt, 1984

L. Pusch, *Alle Menschen werden Schwestern*, Frankfurt, 1990

I. Reiffenstein, 'Bezeichnungen der deutschen Gesamtsprache', W.
Besch, O. Reichman and S. Sonderegger (eds), *Sprachgeschichte*,
pp. 1717ff

B. Rindermann and J. Schildt, *Politisch-sozialer Wortschatz im 19.
Jahrhundert. Studien zu seiner Herausbildung und Verwendung*, 2
Bde, Berlin, 1986

R. Robins, *A Short History of Linguistics*, London, 1967

R. Römer, *Die Sprache der Anzeigenwerbung*, Düsseldorf, 1971 2nd edn

H. Roth, *'Deutsch' Prolegomena zur neueren Wortgeschichte*, Munich,
1978

S. L. Rubinstein, *Sein und Bewußtsein*, s'Gravenhage, 1971

C. Schäffner and A. Neubert (eds), *Politischer Wortschatz in textueller
Sicht*, Berlin, 1986

W. Scherer, *Zur Geschichte der deutschen Sprache*, Berlin, 1868

J. Schiewe, *Sprache und Öffentlichkeit. Carl Gustav Jochmann und die
politische Sprachkritik der Spätaufklärung*, Berlin, 1989

J. Schildt (ed.), *Erbe – Vermächtnis und Verpflichtung. Zur
sprachwissenschaftlichen Forschung in der Geschichte der AdW der
DDR*, Berlin, 1977. Includes: Suchsland, Peter: 'Gottfried
Wilhelm Leibniz (1646-1716). Über sein theoretisches und sein
politisches Verhältnis zur deutschen Sprache'; Löther, Burkhard:
'Kritische Aneignung des Erbes und bürgerliche Jacob-Grimm-
Rezeption'

J. Schildt, *Abriß der Geschichte der deutschen Sprache. Zum Verhältnis
von Gesellschafts- und Sprachgeschichte*, Berlin, 1981

J. Schildt (ed.), *Die Auswirkungen der industriellen Revolution auf die
deutsche Sprachentwicklung im 19. Jhdt.* Berlin, 1981

J. Schildt, 'Die Bedeutung von Textsorten für eine Theorie des
Sprachwandels', *Zeitschrift für Germanistik*, 2. 87, pp 187–98

J. Schildt, 'Sprache und Sozialgeschichte', Cherubim and Mattheier,
*Voraussetzungen und Grundlagen der Gegenwartssprache. Sprach-
und sozialgeschichtliche Untersuchungen zum 19. Jahrhundert*,
Berlin, 1989, pp. 31ff

T. Schippan,'Das "Deutsche Wörterbuch" im historischen Kontext',
Bahner *et al.*, (eds), *Jacob und Wilhelm Grimm als
Sprachwissenschaftler. Geschichtlichkeit und Aktualität ihres
Wirkens*, Berlin, 1985 pp. 243–58

H. Schlaffer, 'Beiträge zur Naturgeschichte der bürgerlichen
Gesellschaft. Physiologie und Roman im 19. Jahrhundert' , Th.
Cramer (ed.), *Literatur und Sprache im historischen Prozeß*, Vol 1.
Literatur, Tübingen, 1983, pp. 303–13

H. D. Schlosser, 'Die Verwechslung der deutschen Nationalsprache mit einer lexikalischen Teilmenge', *Muttersprache*, xci, 1981, pp. 145–56

H. D. Schlosser, 'Überlegungen und Beobachtungen zur Alltagssprache in der DDR', *Deutsche Studien*, 97, xxv Jg. 1987, pp. 31–42

G. D. Schmidt, 'Die deutschen Varianten des Deutschen. Zum Einfluß der Politik auf Interpretation, Bewertung und Verlauf der Sprachentwicklung in der DDR', *Muttersprache*, xciii, 1983, pp. 284–89

W. Schmidt, 'Charakter und gesellschaftliche Bedeutung der Fachsprache', in *Sprachpflege* 18, 1969, pp. 10–21

F. Schneider, *Pressefreiheit und politische Öffentlichkeit*, Neuwied/Berlin, 1966

M. Shapiro, *Language and Political Understanding*, New Haven and London, 1981

E. Seidel and I. Seidel-Slotty, *Sprachwandel im Dritten Reich. Eine kritische Untersuchung faschistischer Einflüsse*, Halle, 1961

G. Simon, *Sprachwissenschaft und politisches Engagement. Zur Problem- und Sozialgeschichte einiger sprachtheoretischer, sprachdidaktischer und sprachpflegerischer Ansätze in der Germanistik des 19. und 20. Jahrhunderts*. Wenheim, Basel, 1979

G. Simon, 'Sprachwissenschaft im III Reich. Ein erster Überblick', Januschek (ed.), *Politische Sprachwissenschaft.* , pp. 97–141

A. Stedje (ed.), *Die Brüder Grimm – Erbe und Rezeption. Stockholmer Symposium 1984*, Stockholm, 1985

H. Steger, 'Sprache im Wandel', *Sprache und Literatur in Wissenschaft und Unterricht* 63, 1989

G. Steiner, *Language and Silence*, London, 1985

J. P. Stern, *Hitler. The Führer and the People*, Glasgow, 1975

D. Sternberger, G. Storz and W. Süskind, *Aus dem Wörterbuch des Unmenschen*, Hamburg, Düsseldorf 1968, 3rd edn

G. Stötzel, 'Nazi-Verbrechen und öffentliche Sprachsensibilität' in *Sprache und Literatur in Wissenschaft und Unterricht*, 63, 1989

E. Straßner, *Ideologie – SPRACHE – Politik. Grundfragen ihres Zusammenhangs*, Tübingen, 1987

G. Strauß, *Der politische Wortschatz*, Tübingen, 1986

G. Strauß, U. Haß and G. Harras, *Brisante Wörter von Agitation bis Zeitgeist*, Berlin/New York, 1989

W. Teubert, 'Politische Vexierwörter', in: Klein, *Politische Semantik*, 1989, pp. 51–68

S. Trömel-Plötz, *Frauensprache – Sprache der Veränderung*, Frankfurt, 1982

S. Trömel-Plötz (ed.), *Gewalt durch Sprache. Die Vergewaltigung von*

Frauen in Gesprächen, Frankfurt am Main, 1984

R. Vespignani, *Nach den zwanziger Jahren: Faschismus*, Berlin/ Hamburg, 1976

R. Vogt, 'Demonstranten und Chaoten. Zum Zusammenhang von Bezeichnungskonventionen und ideologischen Einstellungen in Presseberichten', *OBST*, 29, December 1984, pp. 118–44

H. Weinrich, *Linguistik der Lüge*, Heidelberg, 1966

L. Weisgerber, 'Der Mensch im Akkusativ', *Wirkendes Wort*, viii, 4, 1958

B. v. Wiese and R. Henß (eds), *Nationalismus in Germanistik und Dichtung*, Berlin, 1967 (Dokumentation des Germanistentages, Munich, 17–22 October, 1966)

J. Wilson, *Politically Speaking. The Pragmatic Analysis of Political Language*, Oxford 1990

R. Wimmer, 'Neue Ziele und Aufgaben der Sprachkritik' in *Kontroversen, alte und neue. Akten des VII Internationalen Germanisten-Kongresses Göttingen 1985*, Vol. 4, Tübingen, 1986, pp. 146–58

L. Winckler, *Studie zur gesellschaftlichen Funktion faschistischer Sprache*, Frankfurt, 1970

R. Wittemöller, *Weibliche Berufsbezeichnungen im gegenwärtigen Deutsch*, Frankfurt am Main, 1990

J. Wulf, *Aus dem Lexikon der Mörder. "Sonderbehandlung" und verwandte Wörter in nationalsozialistischen Dokumenten*, Gütersloh, 1963

W. Wülfing, *Schlagworte des Jungen Deutschland. Mit einer Einführung in die Schlagwortforschung*, Berlin, 1982

Index